# South Bend/Elkhart
## Michiana

### *StreetFinder*®

D1591424

## page    Contents

PageFinder™ Map U.S. Patent No. 5,419,586.
Canadian Patent No. 2,116,425.
Patente Mexicana No. 188186

Information included in this publication has been checked for accuracy prior to publication. Since changes do occur, the publisher cannot be responsible for any variations from the information printed.

One inch equals 0.5 mile
0   0.25   0.5 mile

NORTH BOUNDARY

N

1   2   3   4   5   6   7   8   9

Madron Lake

Madron Lake Rd

Camp Madron Rd    CAMP MADRON

Coveney Rd

1000

13900

A

13000

14000

Wolkins Rd

N Main St

41°52'00"

2300

Miller Rd   2600

Miller Rd

14200

14400

B

Wagner Rd

WEAVER PARK

14000

14400

Madron Lake Rd

N Main St

14400

41°51'30"

41°51'00"

Lake Drain

15200

Wagner Rd

14400

14600

Fedore Rd

BUCHANAN TOWNSHIP

Madron Lake Rd

Reed Rd

14600

Broceus School Rd

Moon Lake

OLD INDIAN TREATY BOUNDARY

Moccasin Tr

C

WEST BOUNDARY

D

W Clear Lake Rd

2300

14800

14800

3500

Andrews Rd

900

41°50'30"

E Warren Woods Rd

2400

E

15500

Bailey Ln

Round Lake

Lakeview Dr

2000

Columbian Rd

Weaver Lake

15800

Hickory Ln

Buchanan

Chippewa St

BUCHANAN MIDDLE SCHOOL

Fourth St

Towline Rd

W 4th St

500

41°50'00"

Pearl
Pleasant
Lake

Clear Lake

OTTAWA ELEMENTARY SCHOOL

Ottawa Ct

Miller St

Mc Cumber St

N Cayuga St

49107

Elm

Maple

Beech St

Oak St

Pine St

Roe St

Walnut St

E Clear Lake Rd

2100

Elm Valley Rd

800 Ottawa

700

S Cayuga St

F

Mud Lake

Elm Valley Rd

W Front St

OAK RIDGE CEMETERY

Colonial Ct

Willow

Roe St

700

Glazer St

Roe St

Smith St

Hilliview Av

Hill St

BUCHANAN HIGH SCHOOL

41°49'30"

Polis St

Terre Coupe St

1500

Post Rd

G

Wells Rd

W Clear Lake Rd

Runyon Rd

Burrus Lake

OLD INDIAN TREATY BOUNDARY

Post Rd

McCoy Creek

Bakertown Rd

41°49'00"

16400

16800

Dayton Rd

1400

Branch Creek

Galien-Buchanan Rd

High Bridge Rd

CEMETERY

Hass Rd

4100

Chamberlain Rd

Franklin Rd

H

1600

1   2   3   4   5   6   7   8   9

JOINS PAGE 12

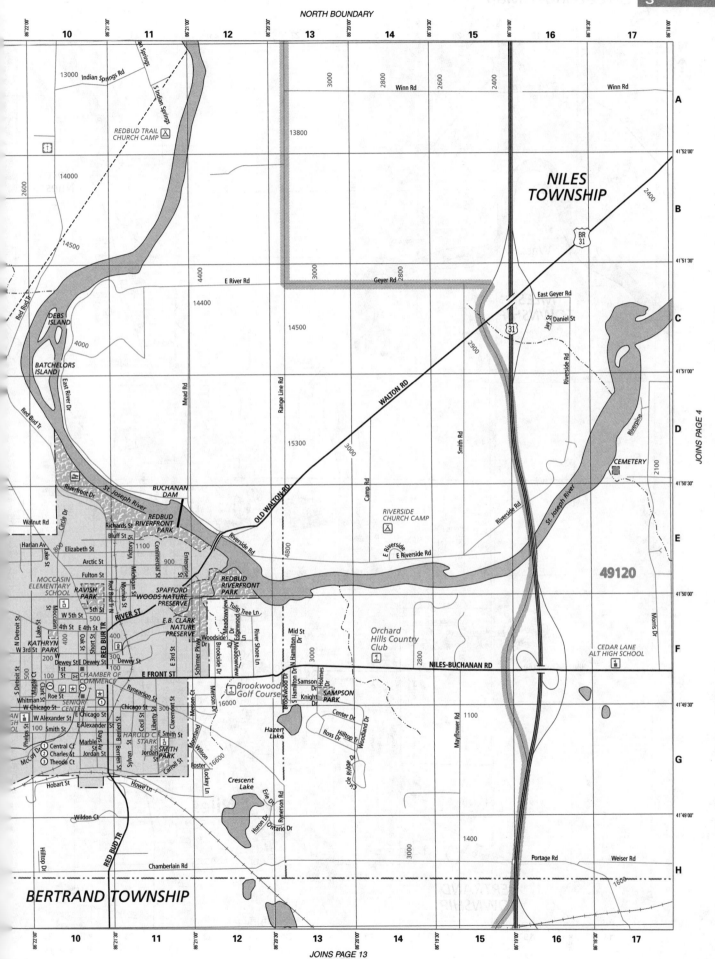

One inch equals 0.5 mile

0   0.25   0.5 mile

NORTH BOUNDARY

N

18  19  20  21  22  23  24  25

JOINS PAGE 3

Warsaw

**NILES TOWNSHIP**

North Niles

Winn Rd
WALTON RD
Joan Dr  Carol Av
Geiger Rd  Jenny Ln
E Winn Rd
BR 31
E WINN RD
Kruger Dr  Irma Av
Derm St
BR 31

Creek Rd
Pucker St
Meade Rd
N FIFTH ST
51
Dowagiac River

Ullery Rd
Pritchard Dr
Scenicview Dr

Frances St  Rex Ct
Bluff St  Thomas Dr
Bruce Av
Monroe St  Monroe St
Clark St  Jackson St
Harger Av
Gene  James St  Jackson St  Clare
Arnold Ct

Valley View Dr  Echo Valley Dr
Westview Dr
Southworth Dr
Morris Dr  Eastview Dr
River-Bluff Rd

NORTHSIDE CHILD DEVELOPMENT CENTER
Third St  Fourth  Wurz St
Hill St  Burns St  Walker
Dulin St
Plym Park Golf Course

Phillip Rd
Harrah Rd
Morris Dr

N 5TH ST

Lake St
Clarendon Av
Eastlake Ct  Sheridan Av
Poplar St  Vine St
Sheffield Av  Sheffield Av
Merrifield Av  Merrifield Av
Louis St  NILES HIGH SCHOOL
Wayne St  Eagle St  Eagle St

49120

Powers St
Howard St

Hance St
Winchester Ct
Kensington Dr
Brown St
Rolling Hills Dr
Beechwood Dr  Skyline Dr
Christiana Cres
Platt Rd
Platt St
Bryant St

Marmont St
River St  Desaix St
St Joseph River
FRONT ST
Plym Park Dr
PLYM PARK
Pokagon St
Canal St  Dey St
Central St
Eagle St

Cass St  EAST SIDE ELEMENTARY SCHOOL
Ferry St
Sycamore St  Cedar St
Regent St

Lykins Ln
Christiana Dr
Isaac Mc Coy Dr
Dublin Rd  Shamrock Dr
Erin Dr  Shillelagh Ln
Blarney  Kilarney Ln
Dunehaven Dr
Carey Mission Rd
Parkside Ln
GRANT ST
NILES-BUCHANAN RD

Howard St  Howard St
First Ct
W Main St  YMCA
N Fairview Av
N Barrett St  Arbor St
Washington  Union St  Union St
LAKELAND MEDICAL CENTER
BR 12  Grant
Park Central School

Cedar St
Regent St
Cedar St  Stowe Ct
Broadway
OAK ST

Park Ln
Grand Av  Fairview Av
Emmons St  Clay St
Emmons St
Nieb St  Market
CALVARY CEMETERY
WESTSIDE SCHOOL
Brookfield
Pine St  Elm St
Madison St  Birch St
Meadow

Hickory St  Hickory St
Maple St  Maple St
CLEVENGER PARK
Cherry St  Cherry St
SILVER BROOK CEMETERY
Michigan St
Huron St

S 11TH ST
E MAIN ST
Cable St
Tyler
Edeb Ct

Kings West Dr
Kings East Dr
Evergreen Rd  King Rd
Sioux Tr
Old Sauk Tr
Ottawa Tr
BALLARD ELEMENTARY SCHOOL
CHICAGO RD
Woodruff Rd
Topinabee Rd
Nieb St
S State St  S Lincoln
Parkway
ISLAND PARK
Michigan St
Huron St  Huron St
Luth Ln
Forest Av
Superior St

French St
Springfield Cir
Gettysburg Dr
Riverview Dr
Silverbrook Av
Silverbrook Av
THOMAS MEMORIAL STADIUM
Lambert St  Beaver St
Taft St
Inner Dr  Silverbrook Av

Weiser Rd
Orchard Ln
Mayflower Dr
Miami Dr  Tomanee Ln
Sassafras Dr  Wesaw Rd
Hawthorne Ln  Laurel Dr
Maplewood Dr
Otis Dr
Plym Rd
FORT ST. JOSEPH MONUMENT
Bond St
FORT ST. JOSEPH PARK
ALLOUEZ PARK
Vernon St
Decker St
Fort St
Jerome St
Bybee Ct
Marion St
Thirteenth St
Fourteenth St

**Niles**

Signal Point Golf Club
Purdy St
Brandywine
Brandywine Creek
North St
Pinehurst
Gleneagle
Leaton

**BERTRAND TOWNSHIP**
BR 12

ODD FELLOWS PARK

NORTH BOUNDARY

26 27 28 29 30 31 32 33

**A**

Burton Rd

Burton Rd
2400
Korn St
Korn St
1600
McKinzie Creek

**B**

41°52'00"

Barron Lake Rd
Grille Av
Hoyt St
2800

**HOWARD TOWNSHIP**

41°51'30"

Alane Av
Aiman Av
Center Av
Van Lue Dr
Huntly Rd
Smith St
Eleanor St
Wilson Ln
Harrison St
Barron Lake Rd

Thomson Rd
2500
Thomson Rd
2400
Terminal St
2300
Terminal St
Zilke St
Rose Bush Cir
2500
1300

**C**

41°51'00"

DICK CEMETERY

BARRON LAKE CEMETERY
Dick St
Dover St
Cedarhurst St
Norwood St
Amherst St
Huntly Rd
Mars Dr
Oriole St
Sunset Ln
Mary St
Rose Dr
Genes Cir
Breezy Beach
Horton Ct
Mannix St
2700
2800
Ma St

**D**

41°51'00"

Industrial Dr
Renaissance Dr
BERRIEN COUNTY
CASS COUNTY
Airport Rd
Terminal Rd
E Jeanine Ct
Jeanine Ct

Eddie Dr
Bartak St
Kennedy St
Williams St
Little St
Holley St
Wild St
Huntly Rd
Brook St
Prospect Pt
Barron Lake
Starr Av
Arbor St
Mulberry St
Huff Rd
Huff Av
Huff Ct
JAMES ELLIS ELEMENTARY SCHOOL
HOWARD ELEMENTARY SCHOOL

JOINS PAGE 6

**E**

41°50'30"

Lake St
2300
Thompson Rd
1200
1200
Huntly Rd
Heath Dr
Centerfield Av
Greenfield Av
Reese Dr
Lynn Dr
Reese Dr
1100
Shady Shores Dr
Lakeshore Dr
Elder Ct
2600

Jerry Tyler Memorial Airport
G LARDNER IOR HIGH OOL
N 18th St
S 19th St
Kristine Dr
Marshlyn Dr
Janellen Dr

Lakeshore Dr
Fisk Av
Pearson Av
Hyme Av
Rivers Ct
Coquillard Dr
Lone Elm St
HOWARD TWP PARK
Leet Rd
1100

**F**

41°50'00"

Ivy Ct
Carberry Rd
1000
Almaugus Dr
1000
Blanchard Dr
2400
Bame Av
Bailey Av
Lilac Av
Juniper Av
2600
Juniper Av
Gilbert Av
Gilbert Av
Wolf Rd
Kish Rd
1000
Yankee St

Cedar St
S 18th St
2200
BUS 60
20th Pl
Alice Ct
Sandy Ln
Randall Av
Ruth Ct
YANKEE ST

**G**

41°49'30"

OAK MANOR ELEMENTARY SCHOOL
Baldwin Dr
Tyler St
Kathryn St
Lewis Dr
Spanish Dr
2400
Rebecca Layne
Ruth Ln
Kathryn St
Honeysuckle St
Mobil Blvd
Evergreen St
60
Jeremy Ln
Yankee St
Runkle St
Rd

Miller Dr
George St
Rodgers St
Spencer St
Lawton St
900
North Park Dr
Cross St
Hatcher Av
Mulder St
Woodard St
Lizzi St
COGIC St
Caruthers St

**H**

41°49'00"

Edward St
Margaret St
Herbert St
Morris St
BR 12
US 12
Walnut St
West Park Dr
Beckman Ln
Duggan Dr
East Park
Reum St
2200
SOUTHWESTERN MICHIGAN COLLEGE
2300

Peterson Rd
700
**MILTON TOWNSHIP**

41°48'30"

26 27 28 29 30 31 32 33

0    0.25    0.5 mile
One inch equals 0.5 mile

NORTH BOUNDARY

N
↑

34    35    36    37    38    39    40    41    42

49031

60

A

Anderson Rd    63200

Dodd Rd

ek

41°52'00"

B

Hoyt Dr    3000    2900    1500

3200

McKinzie Creek

Anderson Rd

41°51'30"

C

1400    3100    CEMETERY    28000    Coulter St

Mudd Lake Ext Drain

41°51'00"

2800    Mannix St    Burn Lynd St    1200

D

Carrage Ln    3000    67000    Conrad Rd

Mudd Lake    27000

41°50'30"

60    Pine Lake St    PINE LAKE ST    6600    Pine Lake

JOINS PAGE 5

Ford St

E

1100    Giles Rd    *HOWARD TOWNSHIP*    Anderson Rd    1000

Leet Rd

41°50'00"

F

Leet Rd    Yankee St

41°49'30"    3200

G

49120    Leet Rd    66000

Runkle St    Yankee Ln    67500

Beebe Rd

41°49'00"    Tiara Tr

H    Leet Rd    Dibble Lake    800

700

Beebe Rd    Runkle St    *MILTON TOWNSHIP*    RODGERS CEMETERY

41°48'30"

34    35    36    37    38    39    40    41    42

JOINS PAGE 16

NORTH BOUNDARY

| 42 | 43 | 44 | 45 | 46 | 47 | 48 | 49 | 50 |

Mullien Lake

Goose Lake

A

41°52'00"

64000

**49031**

B

Library Rd

Dailey Rd

Evan St

Mullen Rd

41°51'30"

Jefferson Center St

Jefferson Center St

C

62
Oil City Rd

64600

27000

Slab Lake

Gray Lake

41°51'00"

65000

D

**JEFFERSON TOWNSHIP**

Crooked Lake

Dailey Rd

Hess Rd

Mullen Rd

George Lake

25000

65100

Long Lake

41°50'30"

TOWNSHIP HALL

66000

E

Indigan Ln

White Oak St

41°50'00"

CRAWFORD CEMETERY

**49112**

Ashton Rd

F

62

Oil City Rd

Harris St

41°49'30"

67000

Deerfield Ln

Ashton Rd

G

Yankee St

Davis Lake St

Davis Lake St

41°49'00"

68000

Lane Rd

67500

Dailey Rd

Hess Rd

KAMP KOZY ST

H

Baker Dr
Cedar St
Wade Dr
Rema Dr
Brandon Dr

Long Lake

**ONTWA TOWNSHIP**

Elsie Ln
Oak St
Suzanne Dr
Cherry Ln
Lansdale St
Sassafrass St

41°48'30"

Curtis Dr

Spring

| 42 | 43 | 44 | 45 | 46 | 47 | 48 | 49 | 50 |

JOINS PAGE 17

JOINS PAGE 8

0    0.25    0.5 mile

One inch equals 0.5 mile

N

NORTH BOUNDARY

| 50 | 51 | 52 | 53 | 54 | 55 | 56 | 57 | 58 |

A

REAMS-NORTON
CEMETERY

Cemetery St

63000

62

41°52'00"

Puterbaugh
Lake

Cooks
Lake

Crooked Creek Rd

Cassopolis Rd

ROBINSON RD

B

Evan St

Leninger
Lake

Robinson
Lake

41°51'30"

Oil City Rd

64600

C

Jefferson Center St

41°51'00"

Mount Zion St

Mount Zion St

Brick Church Rd

D

ROBINSON RD

Christiana Lake

Cassopolis Rd

41°50'30"

MONETTE ST

23000

MONETTE ST

22000

Turpin Rd

21100

E

JEFFERSON
TOWNSHIP

CALVIN HILL ST

41°50'00"

Redfield
Hall

Kaminski
Lake

F

Oil City Rd

Bulhand St

41°49'30"

SHORE DR N

Davis
Lake

Tamarack Rd

G

Ponderosa Rd

49112

Cardevaant Dr
Painter St
Channel
Juno Ln
St  Jamie Ln

Painter
Lake

Prairie St

Bulhand St

Davis Lake St

41°49'00"

Thatcher Rd

SHORE DR N

Phillips St

Juno
Lake

H

SHORE DR N

Lost Rd

Wade Dr
Rena Dr
Dr

Old Rd

Lakeview Dr

N Park Dr

Lisa Ter

Eagle
Lake

ONTWA
TOWNSHIP

Pearl St
Harding St
Island Park Rd

Christiana Dr

Hwy N

41°48'30"

Park

| 50 | 51 | 52 | 53 | 54 | 55 | 56 | 57 | 58 |

JOINS PAGE 7

JOINS PAGE 18

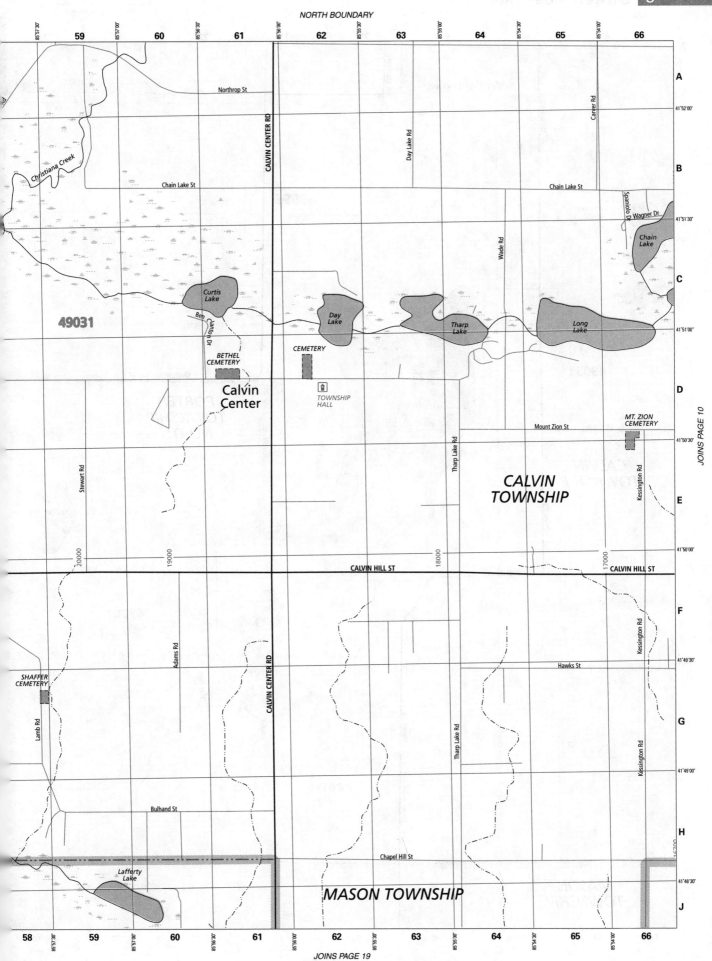

59    60    61    62    63    64    65    66

A

B

C

D

E

F

G

H

J

85°57'30"  85°57'00"  85°56'30"  85°56'00"  85°55'30"  85°55'00"  85°54'30"  85°54'00"

41°52'00"
41°51'30"
41°51'00"
41°50'30"
41°50'00"
41°50'00"
41°49'30"
41°49'00"
41°48'30"

Northrop St

Christiana Creek

Chain Lake St

CALVIN CENTER RD

Day Lake Rd

Chain Lake St

Carver Rd

Spaniolo Dr

Wagner Dr

Chain Lake

Wade Rd

Curtis Lake

Day Lake

Tharp Lake

Long Lake

49031

Ben Clanto Dr

BETHEL CEMETERY

CEMETERY

Calvin Center

TOWNSHIP HALL

MT. ZION CEMETERY

Mount Zion St

Kessington Rd

Tharp Lake Rd

CALVIN TOWNSHIP

Stewart Rd

20000

19000

18000

17000

CALVIN HILL ST

CALVIN HILL ST

Adams Rd

CALVIN CENTER RD

Tharp Lake Rd

Kessington Rd

Hawks St

Kessington Rd

SHAFFER CEMETERY

Lamb Rd

Bulhand St

Chapel Hill St

Lafferty Lake

MASON TOWNSHIP

JOINS PAGE 10

58    59    60    61    62    63    64    65    66

85°57'30"  85°57'00"  85°56'30"  85°56'00"  85°55'30"  85°55'00"  85°54'30"  85°54'00"

0    0.25    0.5 mile
One inch equals 0.5 mile

N
A

NORTH BOUNDARY

67    68    69    70    71    72    73    74

Williamsville St

63100

Williamsville

WALNUT RD
Timber Rd

63800
15000
East St

South St

41°52'00"

B

64000

16700
UNION RD

17000

BIRCH RD

Merritt Cemetery

**49095**

64500

Stage Lake

Chain Lake St

CHAIN LAKE CEMETERY

41°51'30"

Chain Lake

65000

Stage Lake St

14000
14400

C

Round Lake

N Peninsula Dr

Water Cress Wy

14200

14300

Cannaday St

41°51'00"

WEST HARMON PARK

EAST HARMON PARK

Irby Rd

65900

Shavehead Lake

Harmon Dr

**49031**

D

Center Dr N

Pennsula Dr W
Pennsula Dr E

Shavehead Lake

Rutherford Ct

Lakeview Dr

SHAVEHEAD LAKE ST

65800

**PORTER TOWNSHIP NORTH**

66000

16500

South St

Mt. Zion St

Center St

Center Dr S

Lakeshore Dr

Glendon Rd

Birch Rd

Rainbow Dr

41°50'30"

JOINS PAGE 9

RY

**CALVIN TOWNSHIP**

E

UNION RD

Emma Ln

Joseph Rd

66000

Teasdale Lake

41°50'00"

16300

14000

UNION RD

Dolan Rd

Teasdale Lake St

F

17800

66500

Rainbow Rd

Carter Lake

67200

**49061**

41°49'30"

Hawks St

67000

67000

16500

Steele Rd

Carter Lake St

G

UNION RD

15300

68600

41°49'00"

**49130**

67400

13600

Birch Rd

Mud Creek

H

16700

15700

Chapel Hill St

67800

14500

Chapel Hill St

41°48'30"

J

**MASON TOWNSHIP**

68900

66    67    68    69    70    71    72    73    74

| 75 | 76 | 77 | 78 | 79 | 80 | 81 | 82 |

Spatterdock Lake

(40)

Withers St
62300
63500
4100

**49061**

Withers St

THREE RIVERS STATE GAME AREA

CAMP TAMARACK

Mill Creek

64100

Spatterdock Lake St

12000

Little Wood Lake

Wood Lake

**PORTER TOWNSHIP NORTH**

Norton Rd

Robbins Lake Rd

65000

13000
65400
12000
11000
10000

SHAVEHEAD LAKE ST

**49042**

Hebron Rd

SHAVEHEAD CEMETERY

12000
11000

Teasdale Lake St

66000
67200

TOWN HALL

68700

CASS COUNTY
ST. JOSEPH COUNTY

Robbins Lake

LONG CEMETERY

**49099**

(40)

Valley Rd

Malcalm St

Hebron Rd

Carter Lake St

Hillcrest Dr

Robbins Lake Rd
67500
67500

**PORTER TOWNSHIP SOUTH**

(12) Old 112

OAKGROVE CEMETERY

1500

| 75 | 76 | 77 | 78 | 79 | 80 | 81 | 82 |

EAST BOUNDARY

0    0.25    0.5 mile

One inch equals 0.5 mile

JOINS PAGE 2

N

| 1 | 2 | 3 | 4 | 5 | 6 | 7 | 8 | 9 |

86°26'00"  86°25'30"  86°25'00"  86°24'30"  86°24'00"  86°23'30"  86°23'00"  86°22'30"

J

Branch Creek

Bakertown

Hass Rd  1600

1800

Dayton Rd

High Bridge Rd

Franklin Rd

Franklin Rd

2200

41°48'00"

K

OLD INDIAN TREATY BOUNDARY

Dayton Lake

1500

PULASKI HWY

5800

1900

12

Pike Lake

1600

Bakertown Rd

1900

Dayton Dells Rd

**49107**

41°47'30"

L

2300

41°47'00"  Buffalo Rd

WEST BOUNDARY

2600

M

Dayton Rd

2500

Bakertown Drain

4600

41°46'30"  2200

4800

3100

Curran Rd

N

Spirea Rd

Sage Rd

Oak Forest Rd  2800

41°46'00"

4400

P

2700

Bertrawd Rd

South Clear Lake

BERRIEN COUNTY

ST. JOSEPH COUNTY

41°45'30"

29100

Chicago Tr

Brush Tr

Chicago Tr

**WARREN
TOWNSHIP**

Q

Temarac Rd

**46552**

Rosewood

Deer Lake

Mud Lake

41°45'00"

Alden Rd

2700

Redwood Tr

80  90  INDIANA EAST WEST TOLL RD

R

Sycamore Rd

Elbel Park
Golf Course

26000  Auten Rd

26400

7th

Pinehurst Dr

Watch Ct

Ridge Ct

| 1 | 2 | 3 | 4 | 5 | 6 | 7 | 8 | 9 |

86°26'00"  86°25'30"  86°25'00"  86°24'00"  86°23'30"  86°23'00"  86°22'30"

JOINS PAGE 22

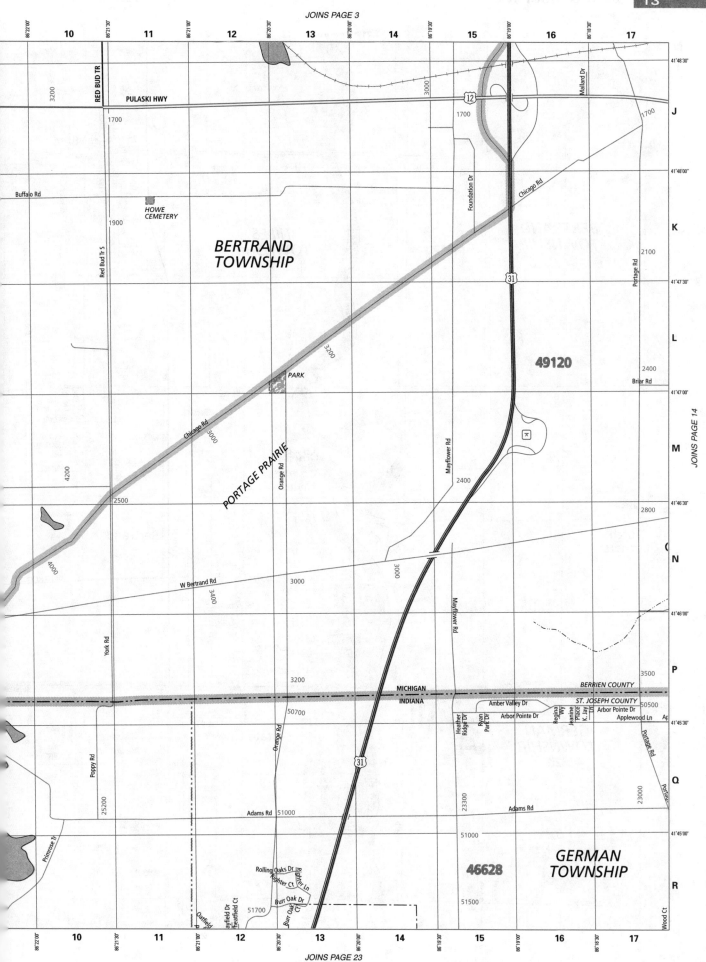

JOINS PAGE 3

| 10 | 11 | 12 | 13 | 14 | 15 | 16 | 17 |

RED BUD TR

PULASKI HWY

3200

1700

J

Mallard Dr

12

Foundation Dr

Chicago Rd

Buffalo Rd

HOWE CEMETERY

1900

K

Red Bud Tr S

2100

Portage Rd

**BERTRAND TOWNSHIP**

31

L

49120

3200

2400

Briar Rd

PARK

Chicago Rd

3000

M

Mayflower Rd

*x*

4200

*PORTAGE PRAIRIE*

Orange Rd

2400

2500

2800

4000

N

3000

3000

Mayflower Rd

O

W Bertrand Rd

3400

41°46'00"

York Rd

P

3500

3200

**BERRIEN COUNTY**

MICHIGAN

INDIANA

**ST. JOSEPH COUNTY**

50500

Amber Valley Dr

50700

Regina Wy

Arbor Pointe Dr

Arbor Pointe Dr

Applewood Ln

Heather Ridge Dr

Ryan Park Dr

Jeanine Place

K. Jay Dr

Portage Rd

Orange Rd

Poppy Rd

31

Q

23000

25200

23300

Adams Rd

51000

Adams Rd

Primrose Tr

51000

41°45'00"

46628

**GERMAN TOWNSHIP**

Rolling Oaks Dr

Righter Ln

Righter Ct

R

Burr Oak Dr

Mayfield Dr

Wheatfield Ct

Oatfield

51700

Burr Oak Ct

51500

Wood Ct

| 10 | 11 | 12 | 13 | 14 | 15 | 16 | 17 |

JOINS PAGE 23

JOINS PAGE 14

One inch equals 0.5 mile

| 0 | 0.25 | 0.5 mile |

JOINS PAGE 4

N

18 19 20 21 22 23 24 25

**BERTRAND TOWNSHIP**

49120

**NILES TOWNSHIP**

ODD FELLOWS PARK

CEMETERY

NEW BELL SCHOOL

NILES TOWNSHIP HALL

PARK

BELL EDUCATION CENTER

CHICAGO RD

BR 12

Ellison Dr

Joliet Dr

Marquette Dr

Allouez Dr

Champlain Dr

Cedar Point Dr

Beeson Rd

Symonds Rd

Bell Rd

Ferndale Blvd

Country Club Dr

Crescent Ln

South St

Oakdale Av

PULASKI HWY

Greendale Av

Lawndale Av

Basswood Dr

Linden Ln

Dogwood

Ash

Burr Oak

Chestnut

Cypress

Almond

Juniper

Peachtree

Aspen

Willow

S 14th St

S 15th St

S 14th St

North St

Pinehurst

Gleneagle

Balmoral

Boca Raton

BRANDYWINE JUNIOR HIGH

Cherry Ln

Weaver Rd

West River Rd

St Joseph River

Bond St

Briar Rd

Hartman Rd

Davis St

Higgins St

ST JOSEPHS CEMETERY

Hawthorne

Thornapple Dr

Washington Ct

Madeline

Bertram

Bertrand Rd

Garnsey St

Silsbee St

Congress St

Madison St

Berris St

Mason St

Brick St

Adams St

Wrenhaven Dr

Shoreland Dr

N Fair Oaks Dr

S Fair Oaks Dr

Fair Oaks Dr

Calvert Ln

Emerald Dr

Nightman

Scott St

Bicknell Av

Mc Kee St

Fulkerson Rd

Park View

Pletcher Av

De Witt Av

12th St

14th St

16th St

Halliday Dr

Armstrong Ct

E Bertrand Rd

Fairfield Dr

Woodside

Floral Ct

Northfield Dr

Eatfield Dr

Florence Av

La Salle Av

Mould Av

MERRIT PRIMARY SCHOOL

Allegan St

S 17th St

BRANDYWINE ELEMENTARY SCHOOL

**Bertrand**

West St

East St

ONTARIO RD

S 11TH ST

Owen St

Owen Ct

Green Gables St

Brooks St

Sorin St

Marks St

Roberts St

Belton Ct

Gary Ln

Apple Ln

Dewberry Av

Linda Gale Dr

14th St

15th St

Church St

Woodlawn St

**Dutch Corners**

Chevy Chase Av

Chaplegate Av

Woodland Av

Holstein St

Miller St

MADELINE BERTRAND PARK

**GERMAN TOWNSHIP**

46628

MICHIGAN

INDIANA

BERRIEN COUNTY

ST. JOSEPH COUNTY

State Line Rd

**State Line**

Applewood Ln

Portage Rd

Sandridge Ln

Pine Hollow

Sandybrook Dr

Shady Hollow Ln

Oak Hollow Ln

Clear Water Ln

Tee Ct

Kolo Ct

Gee Ct

Bee Ct

Silver Spring Dr

Whitewater Ln

Sean Ct

Elkton Dr

Nottingham Ct

Burrowood Dr

Forest Glen Dr

Fernwood Ct

Armwood Ct

Wakerobin Dr

Teton Ct

Ravenna Dr

Chateau Ct

Anjou Dr

Copp Rd

N Linden Rd

ST. PATRICKS COUNTY PARK

Old Walnut

Winfield Ct

Green Hill Ct

Kroft Dr

Moyer Dr

Green Hill Dr

Wallen Dr

Mansfield Ct

Outer Dr

Burnette Ct

Auten Rd

Stonemill Dr

Manion Rd

Laurel Rd

Oakland St

Wedgewood Dr

Layden St

Elizabeth St

Claffey St

Constance St

Palisade Av

Beechwood St

Wentland Dr

Kelley St

Adams Rd

Michigan St

Orchard St

Lily Rd

Prescott Av

Barnes St

Walker St

Auten Rd

Croswell St

Jane St

Eaton St

Oakdale Av

Lindenwood Ct

Lindenwood Dr W

Laurelwood

Sprucewood

Hammerschmidt

Kenilworth Rd

Pond St

Schmidt St

Wedgewood

Dreamwood

Staffordshire Dr

Parian Ct

Marian Dr

Haviland Av

Lenox Av

Greenacre St

Greenacre St

Delft Dr

Hollyhock Rd

Notre Dame Av

Wendron Dr

Layden St

Dresden Av

Wembleton

Stone Ridge Ct

Constance St

Adams Rd

Forestbrook Av

Barnes St

Walker St

Helman Av

Myrtle Dr W

Myrtle Dr E

Helen Av

EDWARD EGGLESTON ELEMENTARY SCHOOL

JOINS PAGE 24
JOINS PAGE 13

26   27   28   29   30   31   32   33

86°14'00"  86°13'30"  86°13'00"  86°12'30"  86°12'00"  86°11'30"  86°11'00"  86°10'30"  86°10'00"

PULASKI HWY

Frantz Dr

Brandywine Creek

Surges Rd

Leet Rd

J

41°48'00"

BRANDYWINE JUNIOR AND SENIOR HIGH SCHOOL

Worrell St   2400   2500   600   2700   600

K   41°47'30"

Bell Rd   2200   Bell St   49120

2400

L

21st St

Ironwood Rd   400

41°47'00"   2600   12   400

Osborn Ct   2300   300

MILTON TOWNSHIP

TRUITT CEMETERY

M

E Bertrand Rd   MILTON TOWNSHIP COMMUNITY CENTER

SCHOOL   2200

41°46'30"

Inez St   Reynolds St   2700   Paul St   Earl St   Ironwood Rd   Roosevelt   Edison   Lafollette St   Elizabeth St   Dennis Dr   Midway Dr   Batchelor Dr   Carter Av   Gumwood Rd   300   2600

Washington

Winkler St

Jones Dr   Shirley   200   2300   2500   N

REDFIELD ST

41°46'00"

BERRIEN COUNTY   CASS COUNTY

IRONWOOD RD   100

Song Sparrow Tr   Killdeer Ct   Kestrel Hills Dr   Gumwood Rd   Maple Leaf Tr

P

State Line Rd   41°45'30"

ST. JOSEPH COUNTY   Viola   Green Oaks Ct   Broderick Hill   Barryknoll Wy   Rockridge Ln   Barryknoll Wy   Marlowe Wy   16300   50500   N Wagon Wheel   Victorian

Allegheny Ct   Crocus   Polaris   Bending Oaks Ct   Ashdale Ct   Stonegate Ct   Crestview   Cedar   Linden Grove   Smokey   Don Wheel W   Jamie Dr

46637   Mallow   Buckland Dr   Geranium   Sonera   Mercury Dr   Turnbury Ct   Shandwick Ln   Crest Ct   Regency Park   Homestead   Summerlyn Dr   Partridge Tr

CLAY   Atlas Ln   Galaxy Dr   Trail North   Ridgefield   Woodshire Ct   Barrington   Old Lantern Tr   Heather Hill Ln   Canyon Ln   Windfield   Sunrise Tr

TOWNSHIP   Sundrop   Bush Ln   50900   Meadow   Old Dover Ln   Wheatridge Ct   17000   Summit Hill Ct   Brockton   St. Andrews   Murfield   Birddale   Pine Tree   50900

50800   Juno Ln   50800   Redstone   Killarney Ct   Hampton Dr   Baywood Ln   Lincolnshire Ct   Woodhaven   Amston   Canyon Ridge   Ridgewood   Country Knolls Ct

Asford Ln   Harbour Town   Pencross Dr   Woodstream   Beywood Dr   50000   Pointe Ct   Pembroke

Candlelight Dr   Candlewood   Fairway   Shamrock   Knollwood Golf Course

Augusta   ADAMS RD   ADAMS RD   Q

Drury Ln   Briarwood Ct   Shamrock Hills Dr   46530   HARRIS   Quail Ridge   50600   Windridge   Durham Wy   E

Williamsburg Dr   Prince   Stonehedge Dr   Dannybrook   Shannonbrook   TOWNSHIP   Candlewycke Ct   Woodbourne   Brenshire   Spring Meadow Ln   41°45'00"

Highmeadow Dr   Albert Ct   Erin Glen Dr   ① Bent Tree Dr   Huntington   Oak Hill Ct   Oak Hill Blvd   Midlothian   Signal Hill Ct

Fox Den Dr   ② Cinnamon Teral Ct   Harwich Ct   Durham Wy   Golfview Ct

Deer Path Dr   Village Green Dr   Pheasant Run Ct   ③ Highland Shore Ct   Cedar Ridge Ct   Preswick Ln   Fieldcrest Ct

St. Patricks Ct   Dublin Ln   ④ Kings Crossing   Hidden Pines Ct   Grape Rd   Windsor   Chadwick Ct   Ashville Ln   Huntington Ridge Tr   Bennington

⑤ Wallington Ct   Old   Buckmore   Wellington   Wellington   Billington   Wicklow

Colleen   ⑥ Wetherington Ct   Norwich Dr   Grand Oaks Ct   Northill Ct   Pembridge Dr   Manor Ct   Cambridge   Waterside   Tabor Hill Ct   Bluffside Ct

18200   Simmons Dr   ⑦ Woodcliff Ct   Linfield Ct   Autumn Ridge Dr   Harrington   Stapleford   Cold Spring   Countryview Ct

Auten Rd   Hickory Rd   Orchard Ridge Ct   Woodland Hills Dr   Stratton Ct   Hall   Buckingham   Gumwood Rd   Pebble Beach Ct   Saddle

51500   Waterford Ln   Stock Bridge Ln   Hazel Rd   Canterbury Ln   Wild Cherry Dr   Dartmore   Fox Run   Fox Pointe Ct   Cold Spring Ct   Regis

51600   Meadow Pond Dr   R   Waterbury Pond   41°44'00"

26   27   28   29   30   31   32   33

86°14'00"  86°13'30"  86°13'00"  86°12'30"  86°12'00"  86°11'30"  86°11'00"  86°10'30"  86°10'00"

JOINS PAGE 16

0   0.25   0.5 mile
One inch equals 0.5 mile

JOINS PAGE 6

| 34 | 35 | 36 | 37 | 38 | 39 | 40 | 41 | 42 |

N

J

Runkle St

Beebe Rd

3000

700

3200

500

Follmer St

K

49120

Brush Tr

MILTON TOWNSHIP

Groose Lake

Anderson Rd

500

3300

400

12

L

Red Oak Tr

400

3000

Brizandine Rd

May St

M

TRUITT CEMETERY

Rieder Ct

Rieder Dr

200

Brush Rd

JOINS PAGE 15

Conrad Rd

200

Fir Rd

Edwards Wy

N

SMITH CHAPEL CEMETERY

Brush Rd

REDFIELD RD

REDFIELD RD

Maple Leaf Tr

Redfield Inn

P

Fir Rd

Brush Rd

100

Kline Rd

100

100

CASS COUNTY

ST. JOSEPH COUNTY

MICHIGAN

INDIANA

Heatwood Dr

Stonington Dr

Northampton Dr

Northampton Dr

Hedgewood Ct

Greylock

Glenshire Ct

Ironwood Ct

Rocky Ridge Tr

Cactus Ct

Tombstone Tr

Tumbleweed

Pacific Dr

Dr

Chestnut Rd

Fox Tr

Cherry Rd

Bittersweet Tr

Silver Spur Ct

Buffalo Tr

Chestnut Ridge

Pickett Ridge Ct

Bridle Wood

Holly Brook Ct

Fox Chase Dr

Heathside Dr

Shafer Tr

50700

Fountain Ct

Saddle Horn Ct

Painted

Painted Ridge Tr

Lions Gate Dr

Clover Ridge Dr

Post Rd

Old Farm Rd

West Abbey Dr

Worthington Dr

Stonebridge Dr

Bromley Ct

Lexington Glen Cir S

Lexington Glen Cir N

Shafer Tr

50000

Sturdy Oaks Ln

Sorrel Ct

Cherry Dr

Golden Harvest

NORTHPOINT ELEMENTARY SCHOOL

McCombs Landing Field

Princess Wy

St. Thomas

Beckley St

Prairie St

Winchester

11600

Q

Safari Dr

Clover Dr

Derbyshire Dr

Taddington Dr

Red Fox Dr

Rothbury Dr

Tenbury

Elm Rd

14000

Lexington Glen Dr

13800

Kingsfield Ct

Herbert St

Alke Av

Mall St

EDWARDSBURG HWY

Granger

Quail Hollow Ct

E Durham Wy

Placid Pointe Ct

N Brandychase

Harris Prairie Cemetery

Mill Valley Ln

Northfield Dr

Sussex Point Dr

Lexingham Dr

EDWARDSBURG HWY

51500

Industrial Dr N

Industrial Dr

51200

Brions Wy

Streamwood

51100

Lake Pointe

W Brandychase

Ellington Dr

HARRIS TOWNSHIP

46530

Elm Rd

51400

23

Cherry Rd

51400

Ashland St

Avon St

Arch St

Bittersweet Rd

Alexander Dr

Timberline Trace W

Duxbury Ct

51600

Fieldstone Ct

Timberline Trace E

R

Pebble Beach Ct

Field Pointe

S Hunting Ridge Tr

N Hunting Ridge Tr

Prairie Ct

Tulip Ct

Pioneer Ct

S Country Side Dr

Steeple Chase Dr

Harvester Dr

Woodfield Dr

James Lawrence Pkwy

Willow Bend

Chestnut Rd

Currant Rd

Anchor Ln

Timberline Foxhollow

Bittern Ct

Bowood

Shaker Ln

Trailwood Ct

Timberline Trace

Roswell

Longford Dr

Wexford Dr

Sage Crest Dr

Cliften Dr

Fir Rd

Country Side Dr

Cooperpenny Dr

Tranquil Ct

Skybreeze Dr

Patton

Long Bridge Dr

Rodeo Ct

Bluebonnet Ln

Mark Ct

| 34 | 35 | 36 | 37 | 38 | 39 | 40 | 41 |

JOINS PAGE 26

JOINS PAGE 7

JOINS PAGE 18

JOINS PAGE 27

0   0.25   0.5 mile
One inch equals 0.5 mile

JOINS PAGE 8

50   51   52   53   54   55   56   57   58

N

J

Eagle Lake

Park Shore Dr

Christiana Lake

Spanish Terrace Rd

Wagon Wheel Ln

Rodway Dr

McClain Ln

Channel Pkwy N

George F Smith St

Cassopolis Rd

Brady St
A Av
B Av
South Shore Dr
West St
South Shore Dr
South St

8th St   6th St   3rd St   Brady Rd
C Av

Twilight St
Twilight St
Dawn St
Sunset St
Christiana St
Christiana Lake Rd

MASON ST

K

Eagle Lake Elementary School

Country Trace

41°47'30"

Four Lakes Golf & Country Club

Creek Haven Rd
Christiana Creek Rd

Grange St

L

ONTWA TOWNSHIP

Eagle Lake Rd

12

Adamsville

Franklin
Perry
Manroe
Monroe St

49112

Reservoir Dam

Cemetery

Starbrick St

May St

Putterbaugh Lake

M

Deer Run

Pullman Corners

41°46'30"

Martin Rd

Adamsville

Adamsville Rd

Sunrise Rd

N

23000

Redfield Rd

21400

205

41°46'00"

Gods Half Acre Cemetery
71400

Maple Glen

Allenton

Cassopolis St

Ebersole Rd

Christiana Creek

Maple Glen

Maple Glen

P

CASS COUNTY
ELKHART COUNTY

MICHIGAN
INDIANA

41°45'30"

CLEVELAND TOWNSHIP

Adamsville Rd

Northcrest Dr

Corry Ln
Heather Ln
Killian Av
Shady Ln
Jonathan Dr
Shellgyne Ct
Hampton Woods Dr
51100
Turtle Ct
Ridge Dr
N Shore Dr

29300

Woodhaven Dr

50700

Fern Ct
Glick
Sturdy
Oak Dr
Hill Dr
George Dr
Coventry Ct
Sigerfoos Dr
Roberts Ct
23400
Bell Av

Q

7

Simonton Lake

Cottage Av
Douglas Av
Thompson Av
Sigerfoos Av
N Shore Dr
51200

Simonton Lake

Stratford Ct
Carriage Ct
Creekhaven Dr
Aspenwood
Springcrest Dr
Ray Dr
Ray Ct

BOOT LAKE NATURE PRESERVE

Boot Lake

Stratford Dr
Dowling Ct
Courtyard Ct

20100

Waleko Dr

3   Gerr-Inn Blvd

Deer Creek Ln
Dumbartan Ct
Field Farm Fields
Bridgewater Fields
23900

Roseland Rd

26400
A St   B St   C St   D St
Lakewood Dr

Lakeland Rd

R

Carpenters Dr
Carpenters Dr
51800

46514

Winding Waters Ln
Silver Water Wy
Spring Tr
Spring Tr

Lakeview Av

Sweetwater Wy
Northfield Dr
Stoney Creek
51700
19
Leland Rd
9

Christ
Meado

Parkview Av

MARY FEESER ELEMENTARY

200

41°44'30"

50   51   52   53   54   55   56   57   58

JOINS PAGE 28

JOINS PAGE 17

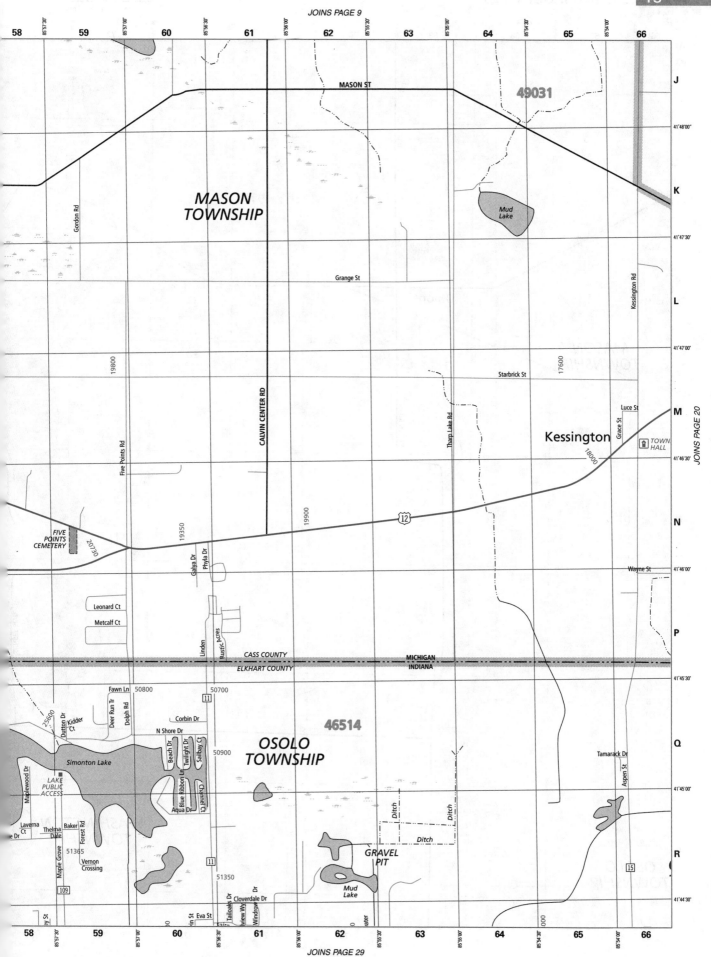

JOINS PAGE 9

**58** | **59** | **60** | **61** | **62** | **63** | **64** | **65** | **66**

MASON ST

49031

J

*MASON
TOWNSHIP*

Gordon Rd

Mud
Lake

K

Grange St

Kessington Rd

L

19800

17600

Starbrick St

Luce St

CALVIN CENTER RD

Tharp Lake Rd

Grace St

Kessington

TOWN
HALL

M

JOINS PAGE 20

Five Points Rd

18000

19900

19350

12

N

FIVE
POINTS
CEMETERY

20730

Galya Dr

Phyla Dr

Wayne St

Leonard Ct

Metcalf Ct

P

Linden

Rustic Acres

CASS COUNTY

MICHIGAN

ELKHART COUNTY

INDIANA

Fawn Ln  50800

50700

11

46514

25600

Dutton Dr

Kidder
Ct

Deer Run Tr

Dolph Rd

Corbin Dr

N Shore Dr

*OSOLO
TOWNSHIP*

Tamarack Dr

Q

Beach Dr

Twilight Dr

Sailbay Ct

50900

Maplewood Dr

Simonton Lake

LAKE
PUBLIC
ACCESS

Blue Ribbon Ln

Chandel Ct

Aqua Dr

Ditch

Ditch

Aspen St

Laverna
Ct

Thelma
Dale

Baker

Forest Rd

Ditch

Maple Grove

51365

Vernon
Crossing

11

*GRAVEL
PIT*

15

R

109

51350

Mud
Lake

**58** | **59** | **60** | **61** | **62** | **63** | **64** | **65** | **66**

Eva St

Tailoaks Dr

Windrow Wy

Cloverdale Dr

0    0.25    0.5 mile
One inch equals 0.5 mile

JOINS PAGE 10

N

66   67   68   69   70   71   72   73   74

85°53'30"   85°53'00"   85°52'30"   85°52'00"   85°51'30"   85°51'00"   85°50'30"   85°50'00"

J

Guyer St   16000

Bellows Lake

Birch Rd

41°48'00"

Baldwin Prairie Rd

CAMP BELLWOOD

K

49130

12

17000

MASON ST

Birch Rd

41°47'30"

16000

PLUM GROVE CEMETERY

68300

15000

TOWNSHIP HALL

14000

Lake Front Dr

CAMP SUN-CHI-WIN

L

Union

15000

RINEHART CEMETERY

BALDWIN PRAIRIE SCHOOL

Vera Dr

Johnson St

Oak St

Pleasant Rd

Hazel Rd

41°47'00"

MASON TOWNSHIP

Trout Rd

70000

Baldwin Lake

70000

M

17000

49112

UNION RD

70000

Hilltop Dr

41°46'30"

TOWNSHIP HALL

JOINS PAGE 19

N

70000

Baldwin Prairie Rd

Terrie Shore Rd

71000

15000

14000

Hollywood Shores Rd

S Baldwin Lake Dr

41°46'00"

Wayne St

16000

Spencer Rd

Wayne St

50000

Indiana Lake Rd

P

21400

Indiana Lake

SUNSET BLVD

Lake

State Line Rd

State Line Rd

41°45'30"

Johnny Ct

51000

3000

East Indiana Lake Rd

Church

23

Oaktree Ln

20700

21

Teal Rd

Cornwall Rd

Q

2

WAYNE ST

20000

51000

Rou Lak

41°45'00"

19

46507

Rebecca Ln

WASHINGTON TOWNSHIP

R

46514

Washington Township Ditch

OSOLO TOWNSHIP

21000

4

17

52000

21

51900

Glen

66   67   68   69   70   71   72   73   74

85°53'00"   85°52'30"   85°52'00"   85°51'30"   85°51'00"   85°50'30"   85°50'00"

41°44'30"

JOINS PAGE 11

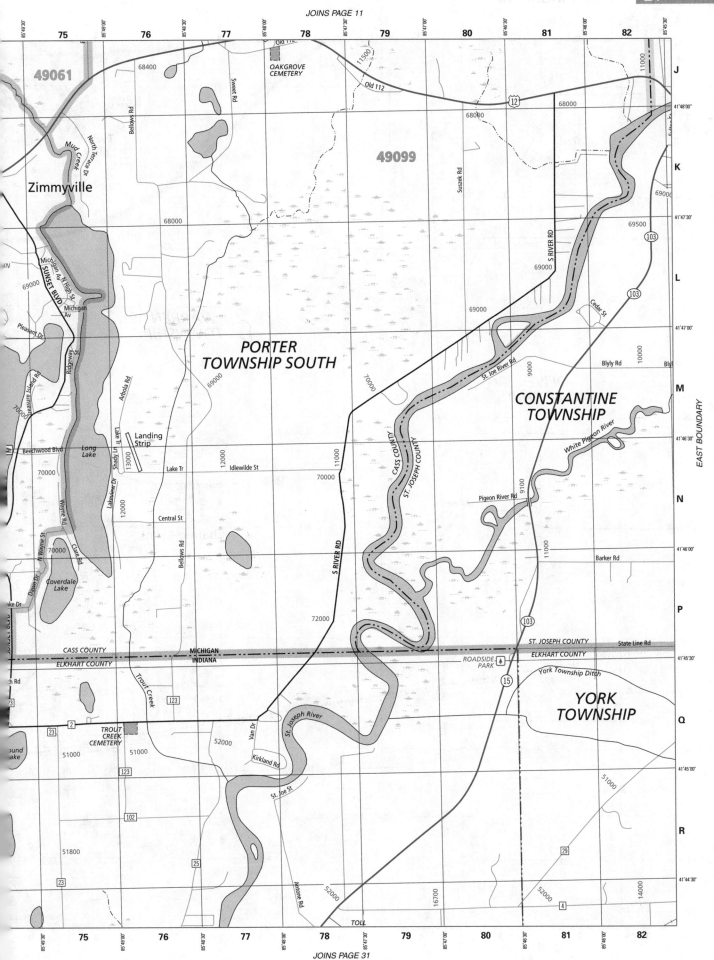

0    0.25    0.5 mile
One inch equals 0.5 mile

N

1  2  3  4  5  6  7  8  9

INDIANA EAST WEST TOLL ROAD

Auten Rd
Pinehurst Ct
Clubhouse Ct
Olympic Dr
St. Ann's Inverness Dr  Westwind Dr
Clubhouse Ct
Water Watch Ct
Northridge Ct
Windy Ridge Ct
Wes Hills
Windy Ridge Dr
Wood Song Dr
Vance Vista
Twinlake Ct

WESTWOOD SHORES AT ELBEL

Waters Edge Ct

Twin Lakes

80  90

WESTWOOD HILLS AT ELBEL

Northridge Dr

Primrose Rd

S

51900

Tamarack Rd

52000

41°44'30"

41°44'00"

Rose Rd

Sycamore Rd

27900

Darden Rd
Darden Rd

T

29700

26500

Fox

Hound Tr

46552

WARREN TOWNSHIP

53000

Tamarack Rd

U

Rosewood Rd

53200

Quince Rd

OLIVE TOWNSHIP

41°43'30"

41°43'00"

53300

V

27900

26500

LINCOLNWAY WEST

Ridgedale Rd

West Pointe Dr  Westmoreland Ct
Marshall Dr N
Bradley Ct
McArthur Ct
Marshall Sr S

Avalon Dr
Lakewood-Norwood Dr
Longwood Dr

Kenmore Dr

Hillside Dr
South Bend Dr
Mc Waade St
Eastwood Dr

20

29900

54100

Central

Fairview Dr

Chain-o-Lakes

Rose St

Lyndale Dr
Lawndale Av
Whitesell Dr

Greenview Dr
Oakside Dr
Lakewood Dr

54000

Evans Dr

Grant Ct
Prospect Dr

Longwood Ct

W

Sage Rd

54700

Augustine Dr
Avalon Dr

Kenwood Dr

Bell St

27000

26900

Dunn Rd

Southport Dr
Edgewater

Stroup Av

Bass Lake

41°42'30"

SOUTH SHORE LINE (METRA)

Pear Rd

SOUTH BEND

Lake Park

Edgewater Dr

Chain O Lakes Dr
Indiana Av

Clay St
Lynn St

29700

X

54500

Mina St
Avalon St

26400

Ln Salle St  South

Devonport St

41°42'00"

41°41'30"

27000

26500

WARREN ELEMENTARY SCHOOL

Szman Lake

Y

Tulip Rd

Early Rd

Early Rd

Fresno St

Humingbird Dr

55800

27900

Sandpiper Ct
Clyde Ct
Cardinal Ct
Cardinal Dr

Swallow Ct
Mallard Dr
Bluejay Dr
Lovers Ln

28800

Eaton Rd

Whippoorwill Dr

41°41'00"

Z

Rice Rd
56400

Lake Ln

Tyris Av

1  2  3  4  5  6  7  8  9

WEST BOUNDARY

JOINS PAGE 13

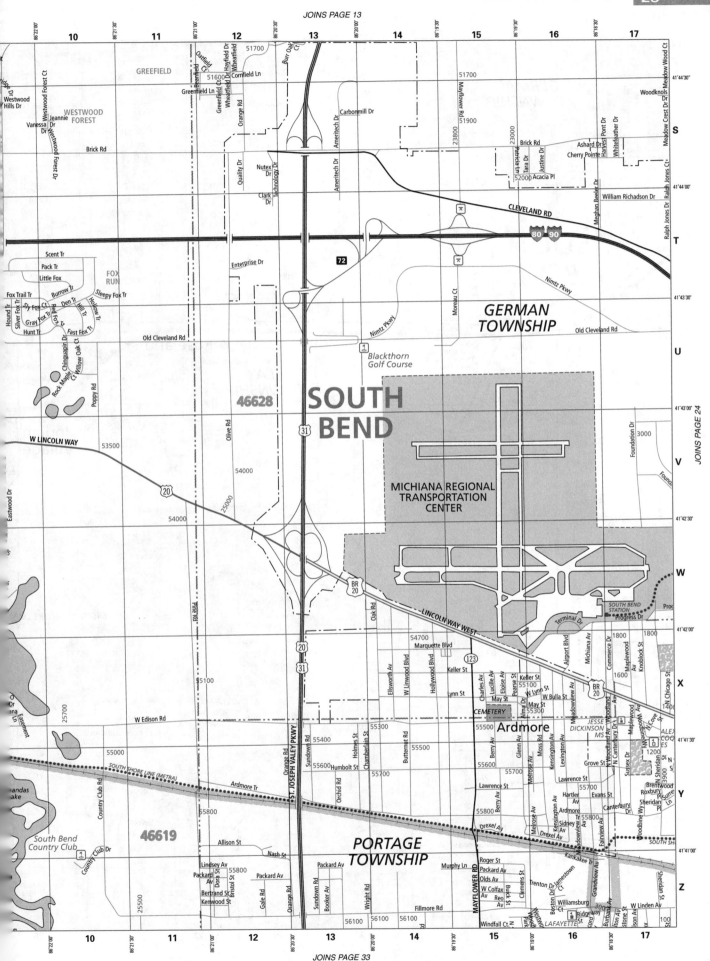

**GREEFIELD**

**WESTWOOD FOREST**

Westwood Hills Dr
Westwood Forest Ct
Jeannie Dr
Vanessa Dr
Westwood Forest Dr

Brick Rd

Oatfield Ct
Bramfield Ct
Greenfield Ln
Hayfield Dr
Wheatfield
Cornfield Ln

51700
51600

Burr Oak Ct

Carbonmill Dr

Mayflower Rd
51700
51900

Woodknols

Meadow Crest Dr
Meadow Wood Ct

**S**

Brick Rd

Orange Rd
Quality Dr
Nutex Dr
Technology Dr
Clark Dr

Ameritech Dr
Ameritech Dr

23800
23000
23000

Brick Rd
Justine Dr
Tara Dr
Patricia Ln

52000 Acacia Pl

Ashard Harvest Pont Dr
Cherry Pointe
Whitefeather Dr

Meghan Beeler Dr

William Richardson Dr

Ralph Jones Dr
Ralph Jones Ct

41°44'30"

41°44'00"

**CLEVELAND RD**

80 90

**T**

Scent Tr
Pack Tr
Little Fox
Fox Trail Tr
Sly Fox Ct
Silver Fox Tr
Gray Fox Tr
Hound Tr
Den Tr
Burrow Tr
Hill Tr
Fast Fox Tr
Hunt Tr
Fox Tr Pl
Hollow Tr
Sleepy Fox Tr

**FOX RUN**

72

Enterprise Dr

Nimtz Pkwy

Moreau Ct

Nimtz Pkwy

**GERMAN TOWNSHIP**

41°43'30"

Rock Maple Ct
Chinquapin Dr
Willow Oak Ct

Poppy Rd

Old Cleveland Rd

Nimtz Pkwy

Blackthorn Golf Course

Old Cleveland Rd

**U**

**46628**

Olive Rd

# SOUTH BEND

41°43'00"

**W LINCOLN WAY**
53500

20

54000

25000

54000

31

**MICHIANA REGIONAL TRANSPORTATION CENTER**

Foundation Dr
3000

Foundation

**V**

41°42'30"

Eastwood Dr

BR 20

Oak Rd

**LINCOLN WAY WEST**

Terminal Dr

SOUTH BEND STATION
Progress Dr
Prog

**W**

41°42'00"

Pine Rd

55100

54700
Marquette Blvd

123
Keller St

Ellsworth St
W Linwood Blvd
Hollywood Blvd
Lynn St

Charles St
Lucille Av
Pearse St
Eloise St
Keller St
Airport Blvd
Michiana Av
Commerce Dr
Maplewood Av
Knoblock St
Chicago St

1800
1800
1600

BR 20

**X**

May St
Ina Dr
W Lynn St
W Bulla St
55100
Meadowview Av
Woodland

25700

W Edison Rd

55300

May St
55300

CEMETERY

55500

**Ardmore**

JESSE DICKINSON MS

N Canterbury Dr
Newburgo Dr
Maplewood
Cove St
Sheridan Dr
Sussex Dr

ALEX COOK ES
1200

41°41'30"

55000

**SOUTH SHORE LINE (METRA)**

Ardmore Tr

St Joseph Valley Pkwy
Orange Rd
Sundown Rd
Holmes St
Chamberlain Rd
Buttermat Rd

55400
55600
Humbolt St
55300
55500
55700

Charles Av
Berry Av
Glenn Av
Moss Av
Melrose Av
Kensington Av
Lexington Av

55600
55700

Grove St
W Woodland Av
Brentwood
Roxbury Pl
Surrey Ln
Woodbine Way
Sheridan Pl
Canterbury Pl

55700
N Sheridan Dr

55800

Lawrence St
Lawrence St

Hartler Av
Evans St
Ardmore Tr
Sidney St
Fairview Av
55800

**PORTAGE TOWNSHIP**

**46619**

South Bend Country Club

Country Club Rd

55800

Country Club Dr

Allison St

Lindsey Av
Packard Av
Dora St
Bristol St
Bertrand St
Kenwood St

Nash St
Packard Av

25500

Gale Rd

Orange Rd
Sundown Rd
Booker Av

Packard Av
Wright Rd

Fillmore Rd

Murphy Ln

Mayflower Rd

Drexel Av

Roger St
Packard Av
Olds Av
W Colfax Av
Reo Av

Clemens St
Trenton Dr

Kankakee Tr

Boston Dr
Jamestown Ct
Williamsburg Dr

SOUTH SH

Grandview Dr
Woodbine Way
Burbank Dr
Hamilton Av
Sheridan St
W Linden Av

Ridgeway
200

Westmoor Park

**LAFAYETTE**

Windfall Ct N

41°41'00"

**Z**

56100
56100
56100

JOINS PAGE 24

JOINS PAGE 14

0    0.25    0.5 mile
One inch equals 0.5 mile

N

**GERMAN TOWNSHIP**

**SOUTH BEND**

Toll Road Industrial Park

1 Cross Creek Ct
2 Flat Creek Rd
3 Greenglade Ct
4 Hidden Oaks Ct
5 River Cove Ct

CROSS CREEK

HEALTHWIN HOSPITAL

46637

CLAY HIGH SCHOOL

CLAY MIDDLE SCHOOL

WHEELOCK PARK

CLEVELAND RD
E CLEVELAND RD
INDIANA EAST WEST TOLL ROAD

1 N Maple Hill Ct
2 N Mountain Maple Ct
3 N Norway Maple Ct
4 Powderhorn Cir
5 Stripped Maple Ct
6 White Maple Ct

Roseland

**CLAY TOWNSHIP**

TOLLGATE

**Indian Village**

BOLAND PARK

CORPUS CHRISTI SCHOOL

LASALLE PARK RECREATION CTR

PINHOOK PARK

Pinhook Lake

HIGHLAND CEMETERY

RIVERVIEW CEMETERY

ST. MARYS COLLEGE

COMMUNITY CEMETERY

St. Joseph's Lake

St. Marys Lake

46556

WOOLAWN PARK

CEMETERY

46628

HOLY CROSS JR COLLEGE

**UNIVERSITY OF NOTRE DAME**

SOUTH SHORE LINE (METRA)

MARQUETTE ES

KELLER PARK

BROWN CENTRALIZED KINDERGARDEN

University Golf Course

VOORDE PARK

FREMONT PARK

46616

ST. JOSEPHS HIGH SCHOOL

RYE MINI PARK

MUESSEL GROVE PARK

BROWNFIELD PARK

PARKOVASH PARK

CEDAR GROVE CEMETERY

NORTHERN INDIANA HOSPITAL & DEVELOPMENTAAL DISABILITIES CTR

ALEXIS COQUILLARD

LINCOLN WAY WEST

SHETTERLY PARK

NAKOMIS PARK

KELLY PLAYGROUND
St. Vincent

MUESSEL ES

VASSAR PARK

LEEPER PARK
JAMES ADISON

46617

KENNEDY PARK

CITY CEMETERY

MLK JR REC CNT

46601

ST. JOSEPH MEMORIAL HOSPITAL

SOUTH BEND REGIONAL MUS OF ART

CHAMBER OF COMERCE

ST. JOSEPH REGIONAL MED CTR

46619

City Hall

EAST RACE

JOINS PAGE 23

JOINS PAGE 34

# HARRIS TOWNSHIP

# CLAY TOWNSHIP

# Mishawaka

46635

46530

46545

46615

INDIANA EAST WEST TOLL ROAD

EDWARDSBURG HWY

ST. JOSEPH VALLEY MEMORIAL PARK

UNIVERSITY PARK MALL

WALMART/ SAM'S CLUB

DARDEN ELEMENTARY SCHOOL

NATIONAL CENTER FOR SENIOR LIVING

INDIAN VILLAGE

MAPLELANE PARK

BOOTH TARKINGTON PARK

BOEHM PARK

EDISON PARK

HELMAN PARK

THOMAS A. EDISON MIDDLE SCHOOL

COQUILLARD PARK

Morris Park Country Club

MC KINLEY ES

HENRY FRANK PARK

IMUS PARK

LIBERTY

NORMAIN HEIGHTS PARK

BETHEL COLLEGE

0   0.25   0.5 mile
One inch equals 0.5 mile

JOINS PAGE 16

N ↑

34   35   36   37   38   39   40   41

FAIRFIELD

DAWN MANOR

ZOOK'S

Grande Vista Dr

Montecito Dr
Monterosa Dr
Montevista Dr

Santa Monica Dr
Montezuma Dr
Kerlin Dr

Roscommon Ln
Strasbury
Brick Rd

Longford Dr
Wexford Dr
Westport
Valentia Dr
Tramore Ln
Clifden
Deer Trail Ln
Ridgecomb Dr
Coopertown Dr
Tranquil
Skybreeze Dr
Sulley
Paddock
Old Trace

W Bonanza
E Bonanza
Fairfield Dr
Eagle
Thelma
Falcon Ln
Lawrence Dr
James Dr
Evergreen Rd
Clover Tr

MALLARD POINTE

Teal Ct
Chase Dr
Drake
Watersedge Ct
Eagle
Robin Brook Dr

EDWARDSBURG HWY

Elm Rd
Ches

WOODS EDGE

Woodhaven Dr
Woodsedge Dr
Bush
Blue Spurce
Evard Dr
Mallard Pointe Dr
Pointers Wy
Barrington Pl
Woods Trail

WINDERMERE

BARRINGTON WOODS

52000

46530

HINTON'S BITTERSWEET

Kay Ln
Darlene Ct
Hinton Loop
Miller Dr
Shadow Ct
Vicki Ln
Mark Ct
Cheryl Ct
Pat Ln
Linda Ln
Ray Ln
Brick Rd
Frontier
N Wayne Ct
N Wayne
E Glen
W Pine
Oak Ln
W Glen
Golden Arrow
Campfire
Campfire Dr
Covered Wagon Ct

Rodeo Ct
Bluebonnet Ln
Cavalry Ct
Settlers
Cv Ct
Conestoga Ct
Saddle
Lariat
Lupine Ln

Peacock
Columbine Dr
Columbine Ct
Bellflower Ln
Pennyroyal Ln
Bellflowel Ln
Balsam Cir
Bergamot
Larkspur Ct
Gentian Ct
Chicory
Buttercup Ln

Stagecoach Ct

23

83

41°44'00"

Currant Rd
Capital Av

Judy Creek

HARRIS TOWNSHIP

Cleveland Rd
53000   53000   6   53000   53000

41°43'30"

County Murray Dr
Chalie Ln
St Mathews Ct
Judy Creek Dr
Lehner Ct
County Ct
Kerry Dr
Lindy Dr

JUDAY CREEK ESTATES

Bittersweet Rd

80 90

Juday Creek Golf Course

41°43'00"

41°42'30"

54000   54000   54000

Douglas Rd

JOINS PAGE 25

Heather Wood
Elm Brook Dr
Maitland Dr

46545

Fox Trail Ct
Fox Trail
Lake Ct
Dr
Meadows Ct

Willow Creek

PENN MEADOWS

FELICITY GARDENS

SAGEWOOD

Phoenia
Bamboo Ct
Old Pine Ln
Flamingo
Mystique Dr
Sagewood Dr
Deer Ct
Whitetail Dr
Oak Leaf Dr
Seaguilla
Lotus Ct
Pheasant
Clover Dr
Panda
Sage Ct
Deer Crossing Ct
Oak Leaf Ct
Mildon Ct
Elm Rd

WINDING BROOK PARK

Whispering Oak Dr
Carriage Ln
Timber Tr
Old Bedford
Branford Dr
Fox Run Tr
Merrifield Dr

Loyola Dr
Cranbrook Dr
N Gilliman Dr
Gillman Dr
Punn Rd
Cornell Dr
Colby Ct
Bethany Dr
Carlton Dr
Brimmer St
Day Tr

41°42'00"

Mishawaka

Day Rd

HARMONY PARK

STEEPLECHASE

Belmont Stakes Dr
Preakness Ln
Kentucky Derby Dr

WATSON PARK

Pine Top Trace
Cedar Springs Ct
Bridge Water Wy
Woodland
Lake Stream
George Lake
Rockwood

4200   4200
4000   4000
3800   3800
3600   3600

Willow Creek Rd
Ehman Rd
Currant Rd
Pokagon St
55000   55000   55000
Pokagon St
Willow Creek Dr

Jeffery Dr
Lori

41°41'30"

Port Ditch

3400   3400
3200   3200

Fir Rd
Stone Ct
Clover Rd
N Home St

Early Rd

PENN TOWNSHIP

Weber Dr
Timber Ln
E Weber Dr
Ritchie St
Margaret Av
Nursey Av
Penn Rd

41°41'00"

3000   3000
2800   2800
2600   2600

Minor St

Mick Ct

AM GENERAL CORP HOME OF THE HUMMER

Pogwood Rd
Erie Tr
Coyle Av
East Av
Chippewa Blvd
Filmore St
Candace
Van Buren St
Jackson St

BITTERSWEET ELEMENTARY SCHOOL

PENN HIGH SCHOOL

SCHMUCKER MIDDLE SCHOOL

LOCUST ADDITION

Andrea Ct
Cedar St

CEDAR CROSSINGS 2400

2200   2200   2200   2200
2000   2000   2000

Maplehurst Av
Lynn St
N 4th St
N 3rd St
N 2nd St
N 1st St
Cove Pl
McKnight St
E Ln Salle Av
Minor Rd

MC KINLEY AV
BR 20

Willow Creek
Old Creek Ct

ELSIE ROGERS ELEMENTARY SCHOOL

Judie Av
Miller Rd
Esther Av

Monroe St
Madison St
Pershing St
Kissinger
Harman Rd
Betscott Ct

JEFFERSON BLVD

Esther Av

34   35   36   37   38   39   40   41

JOINS PAGE 21

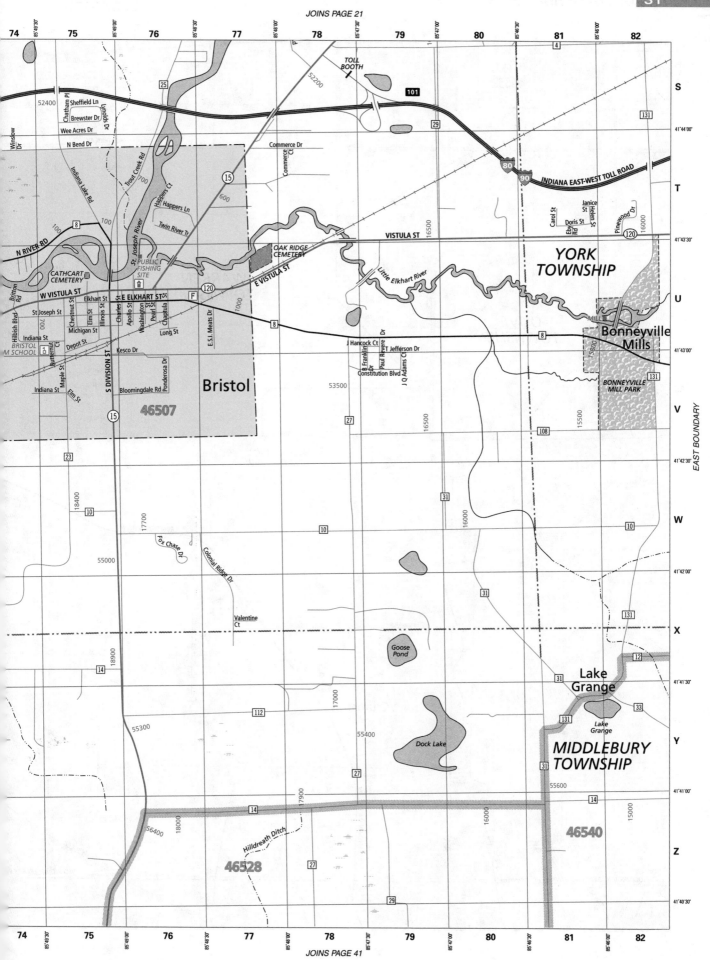

0    0.25    0.5 mile
One inch equals 0.5 mile

JOINS PAGE 22

N

**46552**

Lake Ln

Tyris Av

Lakeview Dr

Byron Av

Quince Av    Westfield Rd    Sonora    Riviera Blvd

Dolores St

Ritschard St

Riviera Blvd

29300    56000    28500    27900    27800    26700    **WESTERN AV**    26600

56800    56700

57000    Windsor Av    Huron St    Lombardy Av    Chelsea Av    Westfield Av    Oriole Av    Sonora Av    Auburn Av

Ford St

Grant Rd    30000    57000    26200

Spirea Rd    57000    **WARREN TOWNSHIP**    57000    Lone Oak    Pine View Dr    Klem

PINE VIEW STATES

57300    Rush Rd    ① Fallen Timber C
② Fireside Ct
③ Sandy Pine Tr
④ Scotch Pine Tr

Nature Tr    Mary Beth

**OLIVE TOWNSHIP**

Tulip Rd    Traders Post Ln    Blacksmith Ln

Trappers Pass    FIELDSTONE TRAILS

Paddlers Cove Ct    Old Settlers Trace    Ridge Tr    Vernon Rd    26200

57700    27900    Harrison Rd    27000    Pecan Rd    26300

WEST BOUNDARY

Harrison Rd    Caralou Dr    Wayne Ln    Wayne Ct

Hurd Rd    Pear Tr    Windsor Av

Ramblewoo Ln

Micha

58000    **CRUMSTOWN HWY**    58000

Henry Rd    58000

223

Spirea Rd

**46552**    30000    28600    27500    Inwood Rd    Quince Rd    59000

Gever Ditch

**46554**

Sycamore Rd    Daniel    Joy Dr    59000

Sherry Dr    Rose Ct    Dr

James Ct

Tamarack Rd    59000    **Crumston**

North St

Holler St

Crum St    Railroad St    27000    26300

CRUMSTOWN HWY

AG    Jackson Rd

60000    60000

OLD INDIAN TREATY BOUNDARY    Johnson Rd    OLD INDIAN TREATY B

Crumstown Tr

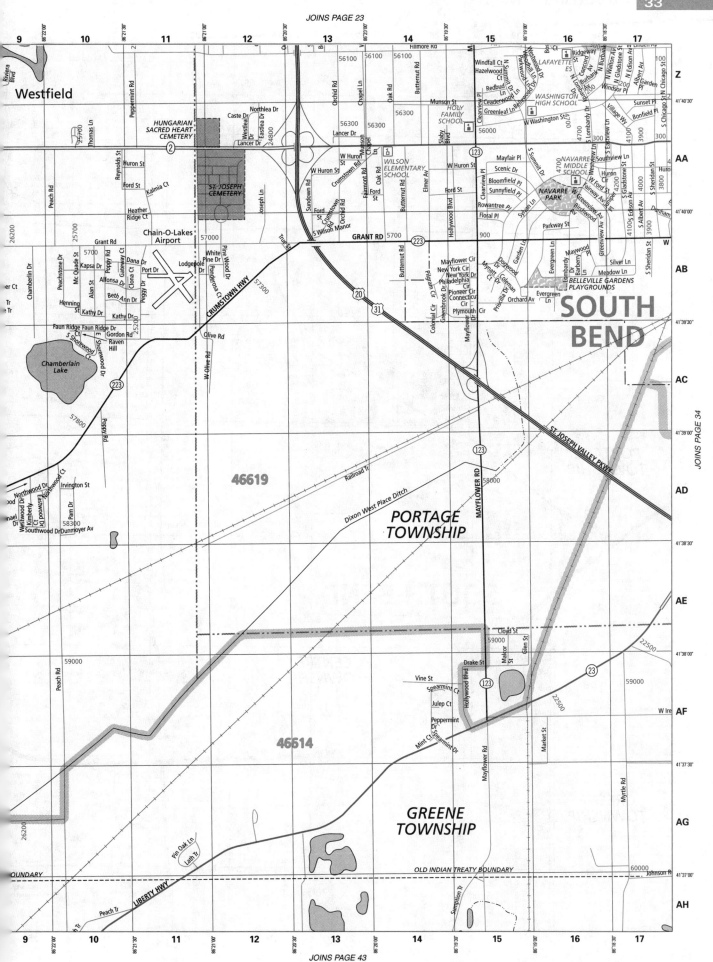

JOINS PAGE 23

Westfield

HUNGARIAN
SACRED HEART
CEMETERY

ST. JOSEPH
CEMETERY

Chain-O-Lakes
Airport

Chamberlain
Lake

CRUMSTOWN HWY

Olive Rd

W Olive Rd

Poppy Rd

46619

Railroad Tr

Dixon West Place Ditch

PORTAGE
TOWNSHIP

46514

GREENE
TOWNSHIP

OLD INDIAN TREATY BOUNDARY

LIBERTY HWY

Peach Tr

WILSON
ELEMENTARY
SCHOOL

GRANT RD

HOLY FAMILY
SCHOOL

WASHINGTON
HIGH SCHOOL

W Washington St

LAFAYETTE
ES

NAVARRE
MIDDLE
SCHOOL

NAVARRE
PARK

BELLEVILLE GARDENS
PLAYGROUNDS

SOUTH
BEND

ST. JOSEPH VALLEY PKWY

Mayflower Rd

Hollywood Blvd

JOINS PAGE 34

JOINS PAGE 43

Z

AA

AB

AC

AD

AE

AF

AG

AH

0    0.25    0.5 mile
One inch equals 0.5 mile

N
Z

17  18  19  20  21  22  23  24  25

**SOUTH BEND**

**PORTAGE TOWNSHIP**

**CENTRE TOWNSHIP**

**GREENE TOWNSHIP**

JOINS PAGE 33

LaSalle Park Recreation Center
Benjamin Harrison Elementary School
Harrison Park
Indiana Vocational Technical School
Pulaski Park
Oliver Park
Copshaholm House Museum / Northern Indiana Center for History
Stanley Coveleski Regional Stadium
Studebaker National Museum
City County Building
College Football Hall of Fame
Century Center
East Race Waterway / Seitz Park
Howard Park
Newman Recreation Center
St. Joseph Regional Med Ctr
Ravina Park
Studebaker Park
Henry Studebaker ES
Studebaker Municipal Golf Course
J. Whitcomb Riley High School
James Monroe Elementary School
O'Brien Park
Erskine Municipal Golf Course
Broadmoor Shop C
Andrew Middle
Forest G. Hay
Walker Field
Rum Village Park
Rum Village Annex
High Pointe Estates
Baneberry Hills
Whispering Hills
Greenridge

46619  46613  46614  46620  46616  46601

W Colfax Av
W Western Av
Western Av
W Sample St
W Sample St
Jefferson Blvd
W Jefferson Blvd
W Washington St
W Poland St
W Dunham St
W Fisher St
Davis Dr
W Indiana Av
W Dubail Av
W Calvert St
W Ewing Av
E Ewing Av
W Victoria St
W Fairview Av
Irvington St
Donmoyer Av
Assumption Dr
W Chippewa Av
W Ireland Rd
Jackson Rd
Johnson Rd
Sample St
Ohio St
E Broadway
E Indiana Av
E Dubail Av
S Michigan St
Main St
St. Joseph St
Prairie Av
Maple Rd
Magnolia Rd
Lafayette St
S Bend Byp
US 20 / 31
933
23
Linden Av

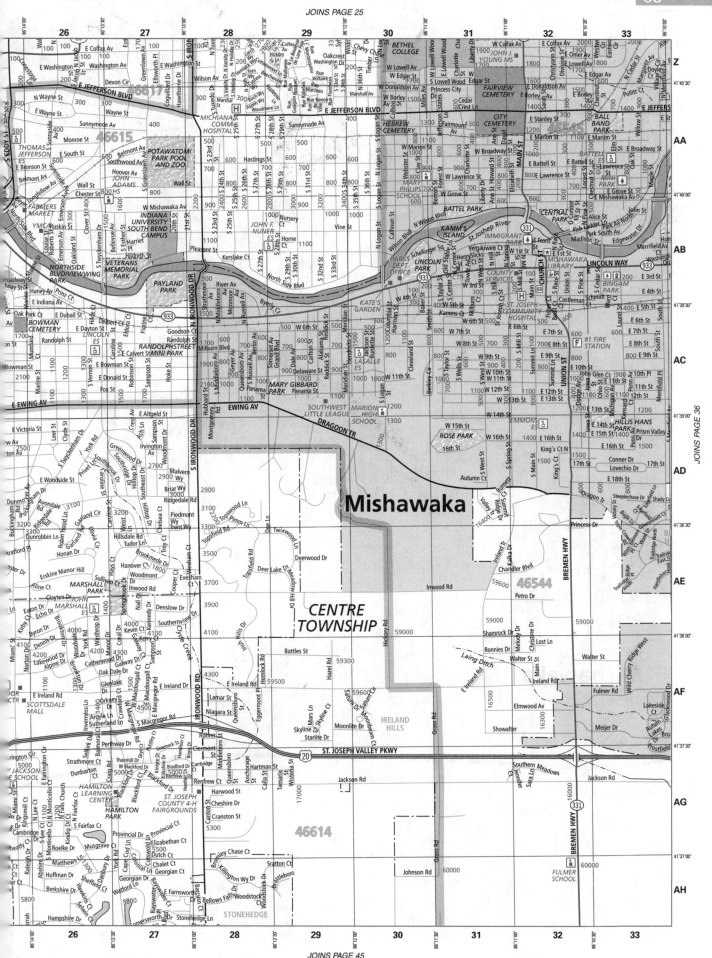

Mishawaka

CENTRE
TOWNSHIP

46544

46614

STONEHEDGE

JOINS PAGE 36

One inch equals 0.5 mile

0   0.25   0.5 mile

JOINS PAGE 26

34   35   36   37   38   39   40   41

N

**PENN TOWNSHIP**

46545

JEFFERSON BLVD

St. Joseph River

RIVERPOINT ESTATES

STICKLER PARK

PRICKETT MARINA PARK

TWIN BRANCH ENERGY PARK

BARRINGTON ESTATES

Eberhart Municipal Golf Course

MIAMI "MONKEY" ISLAND PARK

PETRO PARK

MERRIFIELD PARK

BORLEY PARK

POOL RINK

LINCOLNWAY EAST

TWIN BRANCH PARK

STEELE FIELD

BENDIX PARK

Bendix Pond

WARD BAKER PARK

BYRKIT HS

FRED J. HUMS PARK

Woodward Ditch

Harrison Rd

REVERWOOD

SOUTHAMPTON EAST

SOUTHAMPTON

Harrison Creek Ct

REVERWOOD

TRADES PARK

BLAIR HILLS

AUTUMN TRAILS

GEORGE WILSON PARK

ROSEWOOD

Eller Ditch

Blackberry Rd

**Mishawaka**

Eutzler (Laing) Ditch

EUTZLER CEMETERY

ELM ROAD ELEMENTARY SCHOOL

CRESTON HILLS

ST. JOSEPH VALLEY PKWY

E Dragoon Tr

E Jackson Rd

60000   60000   60000

46544

Fir Rd

AA   AB   AC   AD   AE   AF   AG   AH

JOINS PAGE 35

34   35   36   37   38   39   40   41

**Map**

**WARREN TOWNSHIP**

**41**

JOINS PAGE 32

CRUMSTOWN HWY

CEMETERY

74  75  76

US 20

57900

DIVISION ST

15

Cobblestone Dr
Monticello Dr
Olde Town Rd

19000

Victoria Av
Andrew Dr
Dennis Av
Liesa Dr
Debra Dr

Jefferson View Park

Benedict Dr
Thomas Ln
Aaron Dr

JEFFERSON ELEMENTARY SCHOOL

58200
58400

20

82

AA

AK

AL

WEST BOUNDARY

Iderness Dr
Lower Ct
Franklin

Jefferson Ln

Pine Creek

North Fork

29

59600

20

AE

22

60000

24

18500

18300

59900

CORNELL CEMETERY

South Fork

AF

31

Wolf Lake

27

26

26

AG

**46540**

Woodstock Ln

Hoover Ditch

41°37'00"

126

17800
60500

60800

127

22

28

AH

Maplecrest Country Club

18000

MORRIS CEMETERY

Institution Dr

74  75  76  77  78  79  80  81  82

JOINS PAGE 51

One inch equals 0.5 mile

0    0.25    0.5 mile

6    7    8    9

Dixon West Place Ditch

26000

27000    Kline Tr    Kline Tr

Sunnyside Av    Roosevelt Rd    26000

223    23    27000

CRUMSTOWN HWY    LIBERTY HWY    Redwood Rd

28000    Layton Rd    27000

29000    Aldrich Ditch

Lath Tr    63000    26000

AM    Madison Rd    Kale Lake    Madison Rd    63000

63000    Pecan Rd

41°34'30"    Sousley Lake

AN    Thorn Rd    Rosewood Tr

41°34'00"

28000    27000

NEW RD    29000    NEW RD

AP    64000    64000    64000

41°33'30"

46554

LIBERTY
TOWNSHIP

AQ    Thorn Rd    LIBERTY HWY    Redwood Rd    Pear Rd

23    Liberty Tr    Sycamore Rd    Potato Creek

41°33'00"    Osborne Rd    29000    Osborne Rd    27000    Osborne Rd

1    2    3    4    5    6    7    8    9

86°26'00"    86°25'30"    86°25'00"    86°24'30"    86°24'00"    86°23'30"    86°23'00"    86°22'30"

SOUTH BOUNDARY

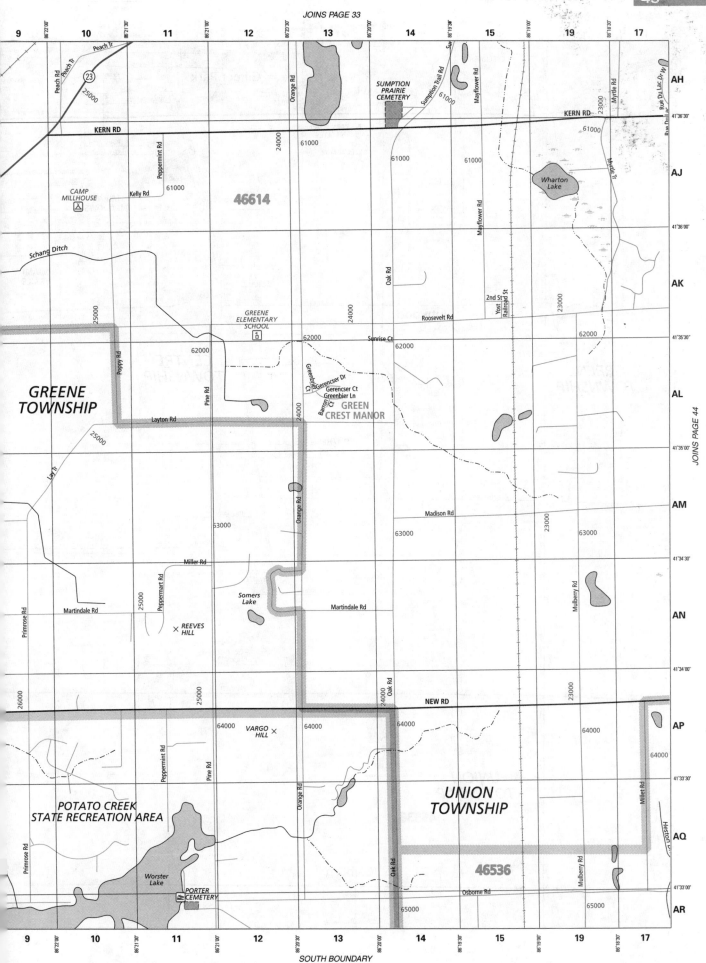

JOINS PAGE 33

JOINS PAGE 44

SOUTH BOUNDARY

0    0.25    0.5 mile
One inch equals 0.5 mile

JOINS PAGE 34

N
↑
AH

17   18   19   20   21   22   23   24   25

Rue Du Lac Dr W
Rue Du Lac Dr
Sans Souci
Lamplighter Ct
Candle Ct
Coachman Dr
Greenridge Dr
Carriage Dr
Phaeton Ct

GREENRIDGE FARMS

Lila
Chestwick
Whispering Creek Ct
Scott Wind
Quite Ride Ct
Clover Hill Ct
London Plane
Dunwoody Ct
Wyngate Ct
Wind Rush Ct
Walnut Farms Ct
Chelsen
Crown Ridge Ct

Gilmer Park

WHISPERING HILLS

Scott St
Pulling St
Gilmer St
Pasadena Av
Carroll St
Fellows St
Clave St
Garway Co

Detroit Av
Lucinda St
St. Joseph St
Carroll St
Lucinda

60000

Whispering Hills Dr
KERN RD

KERN RD
KERN RD

Auten Ditch
22000
61000

Old Spanish Tr
De Luna Wy

KERN ROAD ESTATES

Southland Av
Shirley Av
Rolling Acres
Oldridge St
Fellows St

SOUTHLAWN CEMETERY

Orchard
Edinburgh Dr
Strawberry Hill Rd

MIAMI MEADOWS

Heights Dr
Farmington Ln

AJ

41°36'00"

46614

Eberly Ditch

CAMP WAKINDA

Locust Rd

CENTRE ELEMENTARY SCHOOL

61000

31

Phillips Ditch
Miami Meadows Ct
Fellows St

Oriole Ct
Druid
Sunnyslope Tr
Sundale Dr
Greentree Dr
Brightwood Ln
Elderberry Ln
Meadowlark Ln

MIAMI TRAILS

AK

21000

Catfish Lake

Nutwood
62000

Roosevelt Rd
Ozone St
Douglas St
Weller Av
Roosevelt Rd

GREENE TOWNSHIP

41°35'30"

Whitner St
20000

DIXIE HWY

CENTRE TOWNSHIP

AL

41°35'00"

Auten Ditch
62000
Turkey Tr
62000

SOUTHERN ACRES

Roycroft Dr
Louise Ln
Southern Acres Dr
Dennison St

AM

22000
63000
Madison Rd
21000

Baughman Ct
63000
Miller Rd
19000

41°34'30"

MOUNT CALVARY CEMETERY

AN

Maple Rd
20000
Martindale Rd

Robin Hood Golf Course

Kingsway Ct
Wingsway Ct

41°34'00"

21000
NEW RD

AP

64000
64000
64000
64000

UNION TOWNSHIP

41°33'30"

46536

Heston Ditch

Maple Rd

AQ

Shidler-Hoffman Ditch
Kenilworth Rd
20000

Colburn
65000
Osborne Rd
31
Osborne Rd

AR

65000
65000
21000
Grant St
Cabot Av
Harlan Av
Newton Av

DIXIE HWY

17   18   19   20   21   22   23   24   25

JOINS PAGE 43

SOUTH BOUNDARY

| 26 | 27 | 28 | 29 | 30 | 31 | 32 | 33 |

STONEHEDGE

AH

Hampshire Dr
Norwich
Common
St
Harrah
5900
Oldham
Gotham
Stanmore Ct
Northouth
Ct
Somersworth Dr
5900
Bridgeton
Darby
Lansdown Ct
Old English Ct
Stonehedge Ln
Aberdeen Ct
Somersworth La
Tamer
Ct
Sunbury
Exeter
Croydon Ct
Ct
Riding Mall
Dr
Crown
Regent
Winslow
Chaucer Rd
Ladbrooke Ln
Tanerlane Dr
York Rd

KERN RD

FERRISVILLE
CEMETERY

KERN RD

331

AH

① Deerfield Tr
② Southfield Ct
③ Stone Ct

Stone Tr
Meadow
Ridge Tr
Southfield
Cir
Forest View Tr
Deerfield
Ct

Hickory Rd
17000

60000
61000

16000
61000

AJ

Grimes Ditch

Kelly Rd

41°36'00"

AJ

SOUTH
BEND

DIAMOND
POINTE
Diamond Pointe Ct

Paddington Paddington
Ct
Kingston
Ct
Brompton
Rd
Braewick
Ln
Pudding
Ln

KINGSWOOD
ESTATES

Haverford
Carrington
Ct
Miami Hwy

S IRONWOOD DR

Hawthorne Tr

PENN
TOWNSHIP

Roosevelt Rd
16500

BREMEN HWY

46544

AK

17000

AK

Roosevelt Rd

VAN BUSKIRK
CEMETERY

62000

46614

18000

41°35'30"

AL

CENTRE
TOWNSHIP

Buckheit Ditch

Layton Rd

17000

Layton Rd

AL

41°35'00"

JOINS PAGE 46

Miami Hwy

18000

Madison Rd
63000

16000

Madison Rd
63000
15000

Madison Tr

AM

41°34'30"

AM

MADISON
TOWNSHIP

331

Ladig Ditch

BREMEN HWY

46544

AN

S IRONWOOD DR

18000

ST. JOHNS
CEMETERY

41°34'00"

AN

NEW RD

NEW RD

19000

18000

17000

64000

64000

Woodland

AP

41°33'30"

AP

UNION
CEMETERY

Hickory Rd

Nicar Rd

16000

BREMEN HWY

AQ

Bunch Ditch

Miami Hwy

46506

17000

Gumwood Rd

AQ

UNION
TOWNSHIP

19000

Juniper Rd

65000

Osborne Rd

16000

41°33'00"

331

65000

AR

| 26 | 27 | 28 | 29 | 30 | 31 | 32 | 33 |

0   0.25   0.5 mile

One inch equals 0.5 mile

JOINS PAGE 36

N

34   35   36   37   38   39   40   41

86°10'00"   86°09'30"   86°09'00"   86°08'30"   86°08'00"   86°07'30"   86°07'00"   86°06'30"   86°06'00"

Rogers Ditch

GRISSOM MIDDLE SCHOOL

41°36'30"   KERN RD

61000

Elm Rd

AJ   Fir Rd   Dogwood Rd

Rogers Ditch

15000

41°36'00"

Kelly Rd

**PENN TOWNSHIP**

Fern Rd

AK   Kline Rd

14000   Roosevelt Rd   13000   12000

Roosevelt Rd   Roosevelt Rd

41°35'30"

**46544**

AL   Grimes Ditch   Fulline Ditch   Layton Rd   Dogwood Rd

62000

41°35'00"

Ladig Ditch   **46614**

AM   Madison Rd   Madison Rd

63000

41°34'30"

Marker Ditch

AN   Elm Rd   **MADISON TOWNSHIP**

JOINS PAGE 45

Madison Tr

41°34'00"   15000   14000   NEW RD   13000   12000

64000   Dogwood Rd

AP

41°33'30"

**46506**

AQ   Fir Rd   Dogwood Rd

Osborne Rd   Osborne Rd

41°33'00"   Elm Rd   65000

AR

34   35   36   37   38   39   40   41

86°10'00"   86°09'30"   86°09'00"   86°08'30"   86°08'00"   86°07'30"   86°07'00"   86°06'30"   86°06'00"

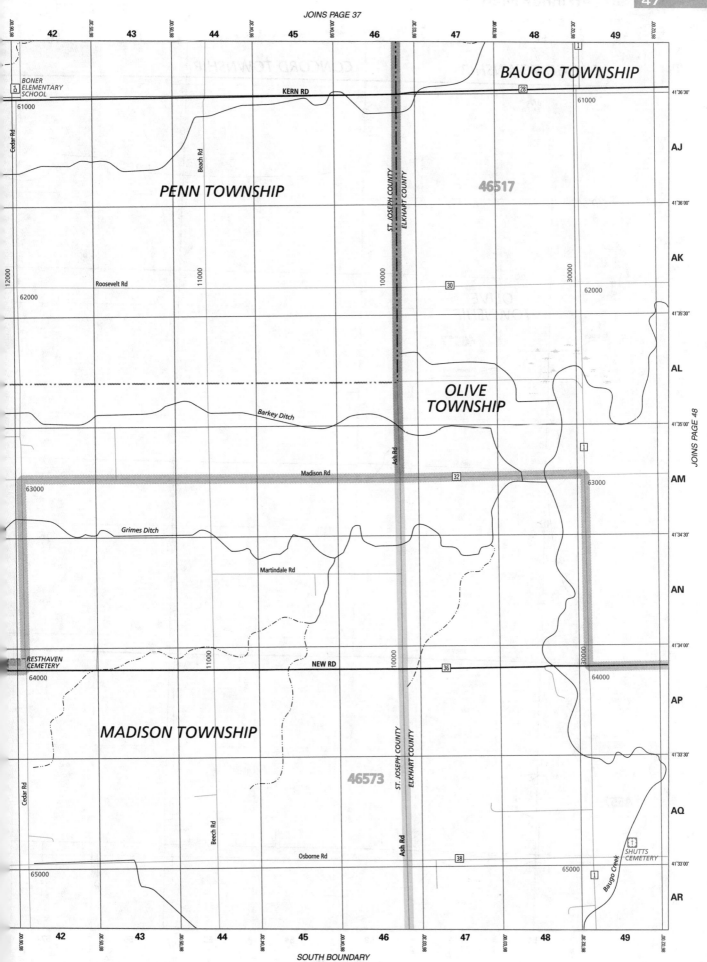

JOINS PAGE 37

BAUGO TOWNSHIP

BONER ELEMENTARY SCHOOL

KERN RD

PENN TOWNSHIP

46517

OLIVE TOWNSHIP

JOINS PAGE 48

Barkey Ditch

Madison Rd

Grimes Ditch

Martindale Rd

RESTHAVEN CEMETERY

NEW RD

MADISON TOWNSHIP

46573

Osborne Rd

SHUTTS CEMETERY

0    0.25    0.5 mile

One inch equals 0.5 mile

JOINS PAGE 38

50    51    52    53    54    55    56    57

N
↑

**BAUGO TOWNSHIP**    **CONCORD TOWNSHIP**    7    28

41°36'30"    61000

OLIVE CEMETERY

19

AJ    3    Hoke Ditch

41°36'00"

Baugo Creek

AK    29000    28000    62000    27000    30

**OLIVE TOWNSHIP**

41°35'30"

Township Ditch

**46517**

AL    Nunemaker Ditch

41°35'00"

JOINS PAGE 47

AM    Madison Rd    32    63000

41°34'30"    3

AN    Township Ditch

41°34'00"    29000    NEW RD    28000    36    27000
64000

AP    Nunemaker Ditch

41°33'30"

AQ    **46573**

38

41°33'00"    ERY    Township Ditch    65000

19    7

AR    3

50    51    52    53    54    55    56    57

JOINS PAGE 39

| 58 | | 59 | | 60 | | 61 | | 62 | | 63 | | 64 | | 65 | | 66 |

61000

Fulmer Ditch

61000

**AJ**

Marguerite Wy

Shaffer Ditch

Yellow Creek

STUTSMAN
CEMETERY

**AK**

26000

25000

24000

23000

62000

62000

BASHOR
CHILDRENS
HOME

Owl Creek

**46526**

Little Yellow Creek

**AL**

WENGER
CEMETERY

ST. JOHNS
CEMETERY

**HARRISON TOWNSHIP**

63000

63000

**AM**

Fetters Martin Ditch

**AN**

NEW RD

26000

25000

24000

23000

64000

64000

Leedy Ditch

**AP**

Yellow Creek

MILLER
CEMETERY

**AQ**

YELLOW
CREEK
CEMETERY

HARRISON
CHRISTIAN
SCHOOL

HOKE
CEMETERY

65000

65000

**AR**

| 58 | | 59 | | 60 | | 61 | | 62 | | 63 | | 64 | | 65 |

JOINS PAGE 50

0    0.25    0.5 mile
One inch equals 0.5 mile

JOINS PAGE 40

# JEFFERSON TOWNSHIP

N

66  67  68  69  70  71  72  73  74

Meadow Ln

Senecca Dr
Miami Pl
Deerfield Dr
Peddlers Village Rd
Redwood Av
Boulder Av
Willow Wy
Breezy Ln
Shady Ln
Cottonwood Dr

River Blvd
W Wilden Av
Elkhart River

Crabapple Dr
Goldstein Av
Ashwood Ct
Briarwood Blvd
Kundered Rd
Russel Sweet Briar Dr
Bodmere Ln

Hemlock Ct
Weaver Ln
Georgia St

**AJ**

Beachnut Ln
Boxwood Dr
Cat Tail Ct
Elmwood Ct
Fern Ln
Hummingbird Ct
Orchid Av
Pear Ln
Ripple Rock Rd
Spruce Ct
Stoneybrook Ct
Strawberry Ln

Pebblebrook
Poplar
Birch Ln
Oakwood Dr
Pinewood Dr
Cedarwood Ct
Edward Dr

60000
61000
23000

N Indiana Av
N 21

Skyview Dr
60000
61000

STUDEBAKE CEMETERY

Lakeview Dr

Sandy Dr
1000

Fescue Ct
Rye Grass Ct
Blue Grass Ct
Van Gilst Dr
Johnston St

N Main St
Hilltop Ct
Walnut Av
N 5th 6th

Shirley Dr
Colonial Manor Dr
William St
Liberty Ct
Westwood St
Cedar Ln
N Greene Rd
Linwood Dr
Cheryl St
Beckner St
Donald St
Homeacres St
Bashor Rd
Elizabeth St
Taylor St

Chicago Av
Bashor Rd
Virginia St
Michigan

WASTEWATER TREATMENT PLANT

OAKRIDGE PARK
OAKRIDGE CEMETERY

W 1st 2nd
W Oakridge Av
Queen
N 3rd St
E Oakridge Av
W Citizens Av
Garden Ct

**AK**

Bashor Rd
Springfield Dr
Post Rd
Northchurch
Winchester Dr
West Plains Dr
Mayfield Dr
Pringle St
River Av

Prospect
Mill St
CHAMBERLIN

NORTH PARK

Merlin Ct
Patterson Ct
Post Rd
Richmond Ct
Springfield Ct
Springfield Dr SW

Reliance Rd
Mossberg Ln
Remington Ln
Enfield Ln
Manchester Ln
Spencer Dr
Tanglewood Dr
Dahbury Dr
Sheridan Dr
Hawthorne Dr
Grant Dr
Edgewood Dr
Lexington Dr
Lee Dr
Revere Dr N
Mt. Vernon Dr
Park West Dr
Longwood Dr
Parkwood Dr
Sunset Blvd
Kansas St
Nebraska St
Cosmo St
N Riverside
Division St
Wilkinson St
High St

Pike St
Summer St
Huron St
Denver St
Oakland St
Chicago

W Pike St
E Pike St

RIVERDALE ES
Wilkinson St
WATER TREATMENT PLANT

Clinton St
Constitution Av
Revere Rd
Independence Dr
N Greenway Dr
W Lincoln Av
LINCOLN AV FIRE STATION

Clinton Woods
W Clinton St
W Clinton St

ROGERS PARK
COUNTY BLDG
JAIL

W Clinton St
E Clinton St

**AL**

# HARRISON TOWNSHIP

Kimberly Dr
Jennifer St
Michelle Dr
Stephanie St
Angela Dr
Thatchwood Dr
Sterling Ct
Redspire Blvd
Kousa Ct
N Greenway Dr
Fairfield Dr
Meadow Westpark
Westfield Ln
Greenway Dr E
Greenway Dr S
S Greene Rd

Tiffany Ct
Howard
Ashley Dr
Silverwood Ln
Graceland
Rye Ln
Hickory Pl
Glenwood Dr
Maple Ln
James Pl

PRINGLE PARK

WEST GOSHEN ELEM SCHOOL

West Av
Riverside Blvd
Hickory
Baker Av
S Winter St
Prairie Av

Linway Lake
NEW PARK

SHANKLIN PARK

W Washington St
W Jefferson St
W Madison St
W Monroe St

Berkey Av
Waneta
S Greene Rd
Berkey Av
Barley Ln

MODEL ELEMENTARY SCHOOL

Amberwood Dr

WEST GOSHEN PARK
WEST GOSHEN CEMETERY

W Purl St

**AM**

Leedy Ditch
63000
22800
32
63000

Greenwood Dr
Bainbridge Pl

Black Squirrel Golf Course

S Indiana Av

Copley Dr
Larimy Dr
Trenton Pl
Oxford Ct
Foxbriar Ln
Brixworth Ln

W Douglas St
W Garfield Av
Emerson Dr

S Main St

**AN**

46526

# ELKHART TOWNSHIP

17
22000
21000
21000

W Plymouth Av
119

GOSHEN MIDDLE SCHOOL

Twinflower Dr
Red Blossom Dr
Sweet Clover Dr
Sedgefield Dr
Glen Ct
Harvest Dr
Clover Trails Blvd

900
64000

**AP**

NEW RD
64000
64000

119
23000

Shadow Ridge Dr
Edgewater Dr
Meadowland Dr
Canyon Cv
Pleasant Dr
Bluff Dr

Elkhart River
SHOUP PARSONS WOODS
MILLRACE TRAILHEAD
DAM
PUBLIC ACCESS

Limber Lost Ct
River Vista Dr
Riverview Dr
Bluff Rd

Gra Roy Dr
Marilyn Av
Mayflower Pl
170
High

HESS CEMETERY

Peach Ridge Rd
Peach Tree Ln
Cherry Ln
Ravine Rd
Mc Intosh Ln
Apple Ln
Apple Blossom
Orchard Dr
Golden Rio Verde
Raintree Pl
Salem Dr

Goshen Dam Pond

**AQ**

INBODY CEMETERY
23000
65000
38
22000
65000
21000
W Kercher Rd

Martin Ma
VIOLETT CEMETERY

**AR**

17
19
21

66  67  68  69  70  71  72  73

JOINS PAGE 49

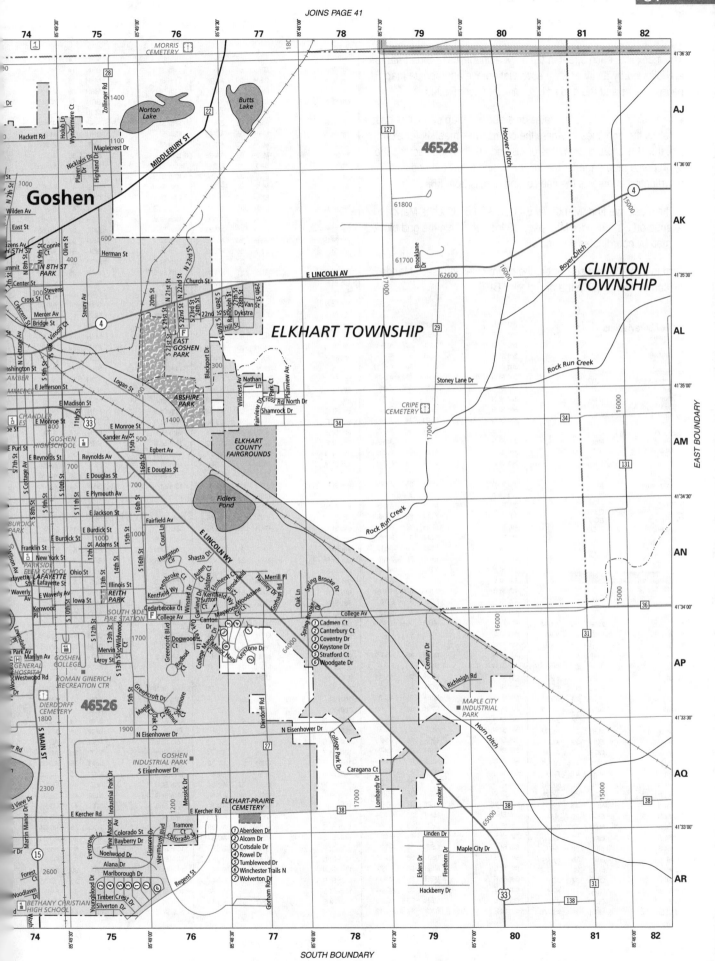

JOINS PAGE 41

74    75    76    77    78    79    80    81    82

MORRIS CEMETERY

AJ

Norton Lake

Butts Lake

46528

Hoover Ditch

Zollinger Rd

1400

Middlebury St

Hackett Rd

Maplecrest Dr

1100

Nicklaus Dr

Player Ln

Highland Dr

Wyndemere Ct

Holub Ln

Dr

Goshen

AK

4

15000

61800

Wilden Av

East St

Connie Ct

Olive St

600

Herman St

N 23rd St

61700

Brooklane Dr

62600

Boyer Ditch

CLINTON TOWNSHIP

E Lincoln Av

17000

16000

N 9th St

H 5TH ST

IN 8TH ST PARK

Summit Av

400

Center St

Stevens Ct

300

Cross St

Mercer Av

Bridge St

Steury Av

Vinson St

4

Church St

20th St

N 21st St

N 22nd St

S 23rd St

24th St

S 22nd

Randolph St

29th St

49th S

Hill St

Van St

Dykstra

ELKHART TOWNSHIP

29

AL

Rock Run Creek

E Jefferson St

E Madison St

Logan St

500

Blackport Dr

S 21st St

S 22nd St

EAST GOSHEN PARK

F

300

Nathan Ln

Park Ct

Plainview Av

Willcrest Av

Fairview Av

Cross Rd

North Dr

Shamrock Dr

Stoney Lane Dr

16000

AMBER
MMERCE

CHANDLER ES

E Monroe St

ABSHIRE PARK

1400

CRIPE CEMETERY

34

34

AM

E Monroe St

33

Sander Av

500

15th St

Egbert Av

ELKHART COUNTY FAIRGROUNDS

17000

131

GOSHEN HIGH SCHOOL

S 7th St

E Purl St

E Reynolds St

Reynolds Av

E Douglas St

E Douglas St

700

S Cottage Av

S 9th St

S 10th St

16th St

E Plymouth Av

700

Fidlers Pond

Rock Run Creek

BURDICK PARK

S 11th St

E Jackson St

E Burdick St

Fairfield Av

AN

S 8th St

Franklin St

E Burdick St

1000

Adams St

Court Ln

15th St

16th St

Hampton Cir

Shasta Dr

15000

36

New York St

12th St

S 16th St

Pembroke Ct

Auten

Ashton Ct

Merrill Pl

Spring Brooke Dr

PARKSIDE ELEM SCHOOL

Lafayette

E Lafayette St

13th St

Ohio St

Illinois St

Kentfield Wy

Winsted Dr

Garland Dr

Einhart Ct

Kentfield Wy

Brookfield

Parmley Ct

Gorham Rd

Oak Ln

Spring Brooke Dr

Waverly Av

Iowa St

REITH PARK

Cedarbrooke Ct

Maywood

Woodstone

College Av

41°34'00"

SOUTH SIDE FIRE STATION

F

College Av

16000

Kenwood Pl

S 12th St

1700

Dogwood Ct

Canton

Sutton

① Cadmen Ct

31

Park Av

Marilyn Av

GOSHEN COLLEGE

13th St

Wildwood Ct

Greencroft Blvd

Mervin St

College Manor Dr

Manor Haus

Keystone Dr

② Canterbury Ct

③ Coventry Dr

④ Keystone Dr

Westwood Rd

GENERAL HOSPITAL

H

ROMAN GINERICH RECREATION CTR

Leroy St

Redbud

⑤ Stratford Ct

⑥ Woodgate Dr

AP

Century Dr

Richleigh Rd

DIERDORFF CEMETERY

46526

15th St

Greencroft Dr

Maple

Oak

Walnut Ct

Sycamore

Dierdorff Rd

MAPLE CITY INDUSTRIAL PARK

1800

S MAIN ST

1900

N Eisenhower Dr

College Park Dr

Horn Ditch

41°33'30"

27

Caragana Ct

View Dr

GOSHEN INDUSTRIAL PARK

S Eisenhower Dr

Industrial Park Dr

Messick Dr

1200

17000

Lombardy Dr

Smoker Ln

15000

AQ

38

2300

E Kercher Rd

E Kercher Rd

ELKHART-PRAIRIE CEMETERY

38

65000

38

Martin Manor Dr

Colorado St

Bayberry Dr

Tramore Ct

Colorado

① Aberdeen Dr

Linden Dr

Maple City Dr

41°33'00"

15

Evergreen Ln

Pine Manor

Noelwood Dr

Weymouth Blvd

Lismore Rd

② Alcorn Dr

③ Cotsdale Dr

④ Rowel Dr

Elders Dr

Firethorn Dr

Forest

Dr

2600

Alana Dr

Marlborough Dr

Regent Dr

Gorham Rd

⑤ Tumbleweed Dr

⑥ Winchester Trails N

⑦ Wolverton Dr

33

31

AR

Woodlawn Dr

BETHANY CHRISTIAN HIGH SCHOOL

Youngblood Dr

Timber Crest Dr

Silverton Dr

Hackberry Dr

138

74    75    76    77    78    79    80    81    82

EAST BOUNDARY

The index lists each street in the book alphabetically. Street names are followed by a city or town abbreviation, the appropriate map page number and the grid or letter-number coordinates.

When using the grid coordinates on a specific map page, it is best to follow the grid lines to where the coordinates meet. If, for example, the street has coordinates of AB and 56, then look across the appropriate map page for the letter AB, and follow the grid line down until it intersects the line coming across from 56.

In the index, we find "Markle Av EKT 38 AB-56" which is Markle Avenue on StreetFinder Map page 38 located within the grid block formed by coordinates AB and 56.

Turn to page 38 and see where the coordinates intersect. Markle Av can be found within the grid block AB-56.

## Index Abbreviations

| City Name | Abr |
|---|---|
| Barron Lake | BLK |
| Bristol | BTL |
| Buchanan | BCH |
| Edwardsburg | EDW |
| Elkhart | EKT |
| Goshen | GSH |
| Indian Village | IVG |
| Mishawaka | MSH |
| Niles | NLS |
| Osceola | OCS |
| Roseland | RSL |
| South Bend | STB |
| Wyatt | WYT |

| County Name | Abr |
|---|---|
| Berrien | BRN |
| Cass | CSS |
| Elkhart | ECO |
| St. Joseph | SJO |

## STREET NAMES

| Name | City | Pg | Grid |
|---|---|---|---|
| 1st | MSH | 36 | AA-34 |
| 1st Av | ECO | 29 | X-65 |
| 1st St | OCS | 37 | AA-46 |
| 1st St | GHS | 50 | AK-73 |
| 1st St | BCH | 3 | F-10 |
| 1st St | EDW | 17 | K-43 |
| 1st St | ECO | 29 | S-64 |
| 1st St E | MSH | 35 | AB-32 |
| 1st St N | GHS | 50 | AK-73 |
| 1st St N | MSH | 26 | Z-35 |
| 1st St W | MSH | 35 | AB-32 |
| 2nd Av | ECO | 29 | X-65 |
| 2nd St | OCS | 37 | AA-46 |
| 2nd St | SJO | 43 | AK-15 |
| 2nd St | NLS | 4 | F-23 |
| 2nd St N | GHS | 50 | AK-73 |
| 2nd St N | GSH | 50 | AL-73 |
| 2nd St N | NLS | 4 | F-23 |
| 2nd St N | EKT | 28 | Y-56 |
| 2nd St N | MSH | 36 | Z-34 |
| 2nd St S | EKT | 28 | Y-57 |
| 2nd St S | EKT | 28 | Z-57 |
| 2th St | MSH | 36 | AA-34 |
| 3rd Av | ECO | 29 | X-65 |
| 3rd St | OCS | 37 | AB-43 |
| 3rd St | CSS | 18 | K-50 |
| 3rd St | EKT | 28 | Z-57 |
| 3rd St E | MSH | 35 | AB-33 |

| Name | City | Pg | Grid |
|---|---|---|---|
| 3rd St E | MSH | 36 | AB-34 |
| 3rd St E | MSH | 36 | AB-39 |
| 3rd St E | SJO | 37 | AB-42 |
| 3rd St E | BCH | 3 | F-11 |
| 3rd St N | GHS | 50 | AK-73 |
| 3rd St N | GSH | 50 | AL-73 |
| 3rd St N | NLS | 4 | E-23 |
| 3rd St N | NLS | 4 | F-23 |
| 3rd St N | EKT | 28 | Y-56 |
| 3rd St N | MSH | 36 | Z-34 |
| 3rd St S | GSH | 50 | AL-73 |
| 3rd St S | GSH | 50 | AM-73 |
| 3rd St S | NLS | 4 | F-23 |
| 3rd St S | BRN | 14 | L-23 |
| 3rd St S | EKT | 28 | Y-56 |
| 3rd St W | MSH | 35 | AB-31 |
| 3rd St W | BCH | 3 | F-9 |
| 3th St | MSH | 36 | AA-34 |
| 4th Av | ECO | 29 | X-65 |
| 4th St | MSH | 36 | AA-34 |
| 4th St | BCH | 3 | F-10 |
| 4th St | ECO | 29 | T-64 |
| 4th St | EKT | 28 | Z-56 |
| 4th St E | MSH | 35 | AB-33 |
| 4th St E | MSH | 36 | AB-34 |
| 4th St E | SJO | 37 | AB-42 |
| 4th St E | BCH | 3 | F-10 |
| 4th St N | NLS | 4 | E-23 |
| 4th St N | MSH | 36 | Z-34 |
| 4th St S | NLS | 4 | F-23 |
| 4th St S | EKT | 28 | Z-56 |
| 4th St W | MSH | 35 | AC-30 |
| 4th St W | BCH | 2 | F-9 |
| 5th St | MSH | 36 | AA-34 |
| 5th St | BCH | 3 | F-10 |
| 5th St E | MSH | 35 | AC-33 |
| 5th St E | MSH | 36 | AC-36 |
| 5th St N | GHS | 50 | AK-74 |
| 5th St N | NLS | 4 | D-23 |
| 5th St N | EKT | 28 | Y-56 |
| 5th St S | GSH | 50 | AM-74 |
| 5th St S | NLS | 4 | F-23 |
| 5th St S | NLS | 4 | G-23 |
| 5th St S | EKT | 28 | Z-56 |
| 5th St W | MSH | 35 | AC-31 |
| 5th St W | BCH | 3 | F-10 |
| 6th St | MSH | 36 | AA-34 |
| 6th St | EKT | 38 | AA-56 |
| 6th St | NLS | 4 | E-23 |
| 6th St | CSS | 18 | K-50 |
| 6th St E | MSH | 36 | AB-38 |
| 6th St E | MSH | 35 | AC-32 |
| 6th St E | MSH | 35 | AC-33 |
| 6th St E | MSH | 36 | AC-34 |
| 6th St E | MSH | 36 | AC-35 |
| 6th St E | SJO | 37 | AC-42 |

| Name | City | Pg | Grid |
|---|---|---|---|
| 6th St N | GHS | 50 | AK-74 |
| 6th St N | GSH | 50 | AL-74 |
| 6th St N | NLS | 4 | F-23 |
| 6th St N | EKT | 28 | Y-56 |
| 6th St S | GSH | 50 | AM-74 |
| 6th St S | EKT | 28 | Z-56 |
| 6th St W | MSH | 35 | AC-29 |
| 6th St W | MSH | 35 | AC-31 |
| 7h St | MSH | 36 | AA-35 |
| 7th | SJO | 12 | R-8 |
| 7th St | EKT | 38 | AA-56 |
| 7th St | NLS | 4 | E-23 |
| 7th St | ECO | 28 | W-54 |
| 7th St E | MSH | 35 | AC-32 |
| 7th St E | MSH | 35 | AC-33 |
| 7th St E | MSH | 36 | AC-34 |
| 7th St E | MSH | 36 | AC-35 |
| 7th St E | SJO | 36 | AC-38 |
| 7th St E | SJO | 37 | AC-42 |
| 7th St N | GHS | 51 | AK-74 |
| 7th St N | GSH | 50 | AK-74 |
| 7th St N | GSH | 51 | AL-74 |
| 7th St N | NLS | 4 | E-23 |
| 7th St S | ECO | 38 | AC-56 |
| 7th St S | GSH | 51 | AM-74 |
| 7th St S | NLS | 4 | F-23 |
| 7th St W | MSH | 35 | AC-31 |
| 8th St | EKT | 38 | AA-56 |
| 8th St | NLS | 4 | E-24 |
| 8th St | CSS | 17 | K-50 |
| 8th St | EKT | 28 | Z-56 |
| 8th St E | MSH | 35 | AC-32 |
| 8th St E | MSH | 35 | AC-33 |
| 8th St E | MSH | 36 | AC-36 |
| 8th St E | SJO | 36 | AC-38 |
| 8th St E | SJO | 37 | AC-42 |
| 8th St N | GHS | 51 | AK-74 |
| 8th St N | NLS | 4 | E-24 |
| 8th St N | NLS | 4 | F-23 |
| 8th St S | ECO | 38 | AC-56 |
| 8th St S | GSH | 51 | AN-74 |
| 8th St W | MSH | 35 | AC-31 |
| 9th St | EKT | 38 | AA-56 |
| 9th St | GSH | 51 | AL-74 |
| 9th St | NLS | 4 | F-24 |
| 9th St | EKT | 28 | Z-56 |
| 9th St E | MSH | 35 | AC-32 |
| 9th St E | MSH | 35 | AC-33 |
| 9th St E | MSH | 36 | AC-36 |
| 9th St N | GHS | 51 | AK-74 |
| 9th St N | NLS | 4 | E-24 |
| 9th St S | ECO | 38 | AC-56 |
| 9th St S | GSH | 51 | AL-74 |
| 9th St S | GSH | 51 | AN-74 |
| 9th St S | NLS | 4 | H-23 |
| 9th St S | NLS | 4 | H-24 |
| 9th St W | MSH | 35 | AC-31 |
| 10th Pl | MSH | 35 | AC-33 |
| 10th St | EKT | 38 | AB-56 |
| 10th St | EKT | 28 | Z-55 |
| 10th St E | MSH | 35 | AC-32 |
| 10th St N | NLS | 4 | E-24 |
| 10th St N | NLS | 4 | F-24 |
| 10th St S | ECO | 38 | AC-56 |
| 10th St S | GSH | 51 | AM-74 |
| 10th St S | GSH | 51 | AP-75 |
| 10th St S | NLS | 4 | F-24 |
| 10th St W | MSH | 35 | AC-31 |
| 11th St | EKT | 38 | AA-55 |
| 11th St | MSH | 35 | AC-33 |
| 11th St | GSH | 51 | AM-75 |
| 11th St E | MSH | 35 | AC-33 |
| 11th St E | MSH | 36 | AC-34 |
| 11th St E | EKT | 28 | Z-55 |
| 11th St N | NLS | 4 | D-24 |
| 11th St N | NLS | 4 | E-24 |
| 11th St N | NLS | 4 | F-24 |
| 11th St S | ECO | 38 | AC-56 |
| 11th St S | GSH | 51 | AN-75 |
| 11th St S | NLS | 4 | G-24 |

| Name | City | Pg | Grid |
|---|---|---|---|
| 11th St S | BRN | 14 | N-23 |
| 11th St W | MSH | 35 | AC-30 |
| 11th St W | MSH | 35 | AC-31 |
| 12th | BRN | 14 | K-24 |
| 12th St | MSH | 35 | AC-33 |
| 12th St | GSH | 51 | AN-75 |
| 12th St | BRN | 14 | M-24 |
| 12th St | EKT | 28 | Z-55 |
| 12th St E | MSH | 35 | AC-32 |
| 12th St E | MSH | 36 | AC-35 |
| 12th St N | NLS | 4 | D-24 |
| 12th St N | NLS | 4 | F-24 |
| 12th St S | GSH | 51 | AP-75 |
| 12th St S | NLS | 4 | F-24 |
| 12th St W | MSH | 35 | AC-31 |
| 13th St | EKT | 38 | AB-55 |
| 13th St | GSH | 51 | AN-75 |
| 13th St | GSH | 51 | AP-75 |
| 13th St E | MSH | 35 | AC-32 |
| 13th St E | MSH | 35 | AC-32 |
| 13th St N | NLS | 4 | F-24 |
| 13th St Rd S | BRN | 14 | L-24 |
| 13th St S | GSH | 51 | AP-75 |
| 13th St S | NLS | 4 | G-24 |
| 13th St S | NLS | 4 | H-24 |
| 13th St W | MSH | 35 | AC-31 |
| 14th St | EKT | 38 | AA-55 |
| 14th St | GSH | 51 | AN-75 |
| 14th St | BRN | 14 | P-24 |
| 14th St E | MSH | 35 | AD-33 |
| 14th St N | NLS | 4 | E-25 |
| 14th St N | NLS | 4 | F-25 |
| 14th St S | BRN | 14 | J-24 |
| 14th St S | BRN | 14 | K-24 |
| 14th St S | BRN | 14 | K-24 |
| 14th St S | BRN | 14 | M-24 |
| 14th St W | MSH | 35 | AD-31 |
| 15th St | EKT | 38 | AB-55 |
| 15th St | ECO | 38 | AC-55 |
| 15th St | GSH | 51 | AM-75 |
| 15th St | GSH | 51 | AN-75 |
| 15th St | GSH | 51 | AP-75 |
| 15th St | NLS | 4 | E-25 |
| 15th St | BRN | 14 | P-25 |
| 15th St E | MSH | 35 | AD-33 |
| 15th St N | NLS | 4 | F-25 |
| 15th St Rd S | BRN | 14 | J-25 |
| 15th St S | NLS | 4 | F-25 |
| 15th St S | NLS | 4 | H-25 |
| 15th St S | BRN | 14 | K-25 |
| 15th St W | MSH | 35 | AD-31 |
| 16th St | ECO | 38 | AC-54 |
| 16th St | MSH | 35 | AD-31 |
| 16th St | GSH | 51 | AM-75 |
| 16th St | GSH | 51 | AN-75 |
| 16th St E | MSH | 35 | AD-32 |
| 16th St E | MSH | 35 | AD-33 |
| 16th St N | NLS | 4 | E-25 |
| 16th St N | NLS | 4 | F-25 |
| 16th St S | GSH | 51 | AN-75 |
| 16th St S | NLS | 4 | G-25 |
| 16th St S | BRN | 14 | L-25 |
| 16th St S | BRN | 14 | M-25 |
| 16th St W | MSH | 35 | AD-31 |
| 17th St | EKT | 38 | AB-54 |
| 17th St | MSH | 35 | AD-32 |
| 17th St | MSH | 35 | AD-33 |
| 17th St N | NLS | 4 | E-25 |
| 17th St S | NLS | 4 | G-25 |
| 17th St S | BRN | 14 | L-25 |
| 18th St | EKT | 38 | AB-54 |
| 18th St | ECO | 38 | AC-54 |
| 18th St E | MSH | 35 | AD-33 |
| 18th St N | NLS | 5 | F-26 |
| 18th St S | NLS | 5 | F-26 |
| 19th St | EKT | 38 | AB-54 |
| 19th St | ECO | 38 | AC-54 |
| 19th St S | BRN | 5 | F-26 |
| 20th Pl | BRN | 5 | G-26 |
| 20th Pl | BRN | 5 | G-26 |

| Name | City | Pg | Grid |
|---|---|---|---|
| 20th St | STB | 35 | AB-27 |
| 20th St | EKT | 38 | AB-53 |
| 20th St | GSH | 51 | AL-76 |
| 21st St | MSH | 35 | AB-28 |
| 21st St | BRN | 15 | L-26 |
| 21st St N | GSH | 51 | AL-76 |
| 21st St S | GSH | 51 | AL-76 |
| 21st St S | GSH | 51 | AL-76 |
| 22nd St | GSH | 51 | AL-76 |
| 22nd St | EKT | 28 | Y-53 |
| 22nd St N | GSH | 51 | AL-76 |
| 22nd St S | GSH | 51 | AL-76 |
| 23rd St | STB | 25 | X-28 |
| 23rd St N | GHS | 51 | AK-76 |
| 23rd St S | STB | 35 | AA-28 |
| 23rd St S | STB | 35 | AB-28 |
| 23rd St S | GSH | 51 | AL-76 |
| 24th St | GSH | 51 | AL-76 |
| 24th St S | MSH | 35 | AB-28 |
| 25th St S | STB | 35 | AA-28 |
| 25th St S | STB | 35 | AB-28 |
| 25th St S | STB | 35 | AB-28 |
| 26th St | ECO | 38 | AA-53 |
| 26th St | STB | 25 | X-28 |
| 26th St N | STB | 35 | AA-28 |
| 26th St N | STB | 35 | Z-28 |
| 26th St S | STB | 35 | AA-28 |
| 26th St S | GSH | 51 | AL-76 |
| 26th St S | GSH | 51 | AL-76 |
| 27th St | ECO | 38 | AA-53 |
| 27th St | GSH | 51 | AL-77 |
| 27th St | STB | 25 | X-28 |
| 27th St N | STB | 25 | Z-28 |
| 27th St S | STB | 35 | AA-28 |
| 27th St S | STB | 35 | AB-28 |
| 28th St | GSH | 51 | AL-77 |
| 28th St N | STB | 25 | X-28 |
| 28th St S | STB | 35 | AA-29 |
| 28th St S | STB | 35 | AB-29 |
| 28th St S | STB | 35 | AB-29 |
| 29th St | ECO | 51 | AK-77 |
| 29th St N | STB | 25 | X-29 |
| 29th St S | STB | 35 | AA-29 |
| 29th St S | STB | 35 | AB-29 |
| 29th St S | STB | 35 | AB-29 |
| 30th St N | SJO | 25 | W-29 |
| 30th St S | STB | 35 | AB-29 |
| 31st St | SJO | 25 | W-29 |
| 31st St S | STB | 35 | AB-29 |
| 32nd St N | SJO | 25 | W-29 |
| 32nd St S | STB | 35 | AB-29 |
| 33rd St | SJO | 25 | W-29 |
| 33rd St S | STB | 35 | AA-29 |
| 33rd St S | STB | 35 | AB-29 |
| 34th St | SJO | 25 | W-29 |
| 34th St N | SJO | 25 | U-29 |
| 34th St S | MSH | 35 | AA-30 |
| 34th St S | MSH | 35 | AB-30 |
| 35th St S | MSH | 35 | AB-30 |
| 36th St N | STB | 35 | AA-30 |
| 36th St S | MSH | 35 | AB-30 |
| 45th St | ECO | 37 | AA-49 |
| 46th St | ECO | 37 | Z-49 |
| 47th St | ECO | 37 | AA-48 |
| 48th | ECO | 37 | AA-48 |
| 49th | ECO | 37 | AA-48 |
| 50th St | ECO | 37 | AA-48 |

**A**

| Name | City | Pg | Grid |
|---|---|---|---|
| A Av | CSS | 18 | K-50 |
| A Ct | ECO | 28 | W-54 |
| A Ln | EKT | 38 | AC-56 |
| A St | ECO | 18 | R-57 |
| Aaron Dr | SJO | 41 | AD-76 |
| Abbey Ct | GSH | 50 | AM-71 |
| Abbey Ct | SJO | 25 | W-27 |
| Abbey Dr W | SJO | 16 | Q-35 |
| Abbey Dr W | SJO | 16 | Q-35 |
| Abbot Ct | SJO | 25 | S-27 |
| Abel Rd | BRN | 2 | C-1 |
| Aberdeen Av | EKT | 39 | AC-60 |
| Aberdeen Ct | STB | 45 | AH-27 |
| Aberdeen Dr | GSH | 51 | AQ-77 |
| Abor Crossing Dr | SJO | 25 | T-32 |
| Abshire Dr | STB | 35 | AH-26 |
| Acacia Ln Dr | SJO | 37 | AC-43 |
| Acacia Pl | SJO | 25 | S-16 |
| Academy Pl | STB | 24 | W-21 |
| Acorn Ct | SJO | 27 | W-45 |
| Acorn Ln | MSH | 36 | AD-34 |
| Acorn Ln | ECO | 29 | S-65 |
| Acorn St | CSS | 17 | N-44 |
| Ada Dr | ECO | 29 | U-63 |
| Adams Acres Ct | SJO | 27 | V-45 |
| Adams Rd | CSS | 9 | G-60 |
| Adams Rd | SJO | 13 | Q-12 |
| Adams Rd | SJO | 13 | Q-15 |
| Adams Rd | SJO | 14 | Q-23 |
| Adams Rd | SJO | 14 | Q-24 |
| Adams Rd | SJO | 15 | Q-30 |
| Adams Rd | SJO | 15 | Q-33 |
| Adams Rd | SJO | 17 | Q-43 |
| Adams Rd | ECO | 17 | Q-47 |
| Adams St | GSH | 51 | AN-75 |
| Adams St | BRN | 14 | N-22 |
| Adams St | BRN | 14 | P-22 |
| Adams St | ECO | 29 | W-58 |
| Adams St | STB | 34 | Z-21 |
| Adams St E | OCS | 37 | AB-45 |
| Adams St N | STB | 24 | X-21 |
| Adams St W | OCS | 37 | AB-44 |
| Adamsville Rd | CSS | 18 | N-53 |
| Adamsville Rd | ECO | 18 | P-53 |
| Adamville | CSS | 18 | N-53 |
| Addison St | STB | 34 | AE-24 |
| Airline Av | EKT | 29 | Z-58 |
| Airport Blvd | STB | 23 | X-16 |
| Airport Pkwy | ECO | 28 | T-51 |
| Airport Rd | NLS | 5 | D-27 |
| Airport Rd | EKT | 28 | U-54 |
| Al-Vir Ct | SJO | 27 | X-43 |
| Alabama St | MSH | 35 | AC-29 |
| Alan St | SJO | 33 | AB-10 |
| Alana Dr | GSH | 51 | AR-75 |
| Albany St | EKT | 38 | AA-55 |
| Albert Av | STB | 23 | Z-17 |
| Albert Av S | STB | 33 | AB-17 |
| Alcorn Dr | GSH | 51 | AQ-77 |
| Alden Rd | SJO | 12 | R-5 |
| Alderwood Ct | ECO | 29 | V-65 |
| Aldrich Ct | EKT | 38 | AA-57 |
| Alex Wy | MSH | 36 | Z-33 |
| Alex Wy | MSH | 36 | Z-34 |
| Alexander Dr | SJO | 16 | R-40 |
| Alexander St E | BCH | 3 | G-10 |
| Alexander St W | BCH | 3 | G-10 |
| Alfonsa Dr | SJO | 33 | AB-10 |
| Alfonsa Dr | SJO | 33 | AB-11 |
| Alford St S | MSH | 36 | AB-36 |
| Alfred Ct | ECO | 38 | AA-52 |
| Alfred St | EKT | 29 | Y-59 |
| Alice Av | SJO | 16 | Q-39 |
| Alice Ct | NLS | 5 | F-26 |
| Alice St | MSH | 35 | AB-33 |
| Alida Dr | SJO | 27 | W-44 |
| Alida Dr | SJO | 27 | W-45 |
| Aline Ct | STB | 35 | AE-26 |
| Allegheny Ct | SJO | 15 | P-28 |
| Allen Dr | ECO | 39 | AC-63 |
| Allen St | STB | 24 | X-22 |
| Allen St | STB | 24 | Y-22 |
| Allerton St | BRN | 14 | L-25 |
| Allison St | SJO | 23 | Y-12 |
| Allouez Av | BRN | 14 | K-21 |
| Alluvial Dr | SJO | 27 | W-44 |
| Alma Av | EKT | 39 | AC-60 |
| Alma Av | EKT | 28 | X-53 |
| Alma Dr | STB | 23 | X-16 |
| Alman Av | CSS | 5 | C-32 |
| Almaugus Dr | CSS | 5 | F-29 |
| Almond | BRN | 14 | K-24 |
| Almond Ct | STB | 24 | Y-25 |
| Almond Dr | EKT | 29 | V-62 |
| Alou Ln | SJO | 24 | T-23 |
| Alpine Dr | STB | 35 | AF-26 |
| Alpine Ln | ECO | 28 | X-51 |
| Alt Dr | EKT | 28 | T-56 |
| Altgeld St | STB | 34 | AD-24 |
| Altgeld St E | STB | 35 | AD-27 |
| Alvin Dr | SJO | 25 | T-28 |
| Alyssa Dr | SJO | 27 | X-45 |
| Amber Dr | SJO | 27 | V-46 |
| Amber Valley Dr | SJO | 13 | P-15 |
| Amberley Ln | SJO | 25 | T-27 |
| Amberwoo Dr | ECO | 30 | Y-72 |
| Amberwood | SJO | 25 | S-27 |
| Amberwood Dr | GSH | 50 | AM-70 |
| Amberwood Dr | GSH | 50 | AM-71 |
| Ambleside Dr | SJO | 24 | S-22 |
| American Way Cir | EKT | 29 | Z-60 |
| Ameritech Dr | STB | 23 | S-13 |
| Amherst St | EKT | 39 | AB-60 |
| Amherst St | CSS | 5 | D-31 |
| Amhurst Av | STB | 34 | AE-25 |
| Amsie Dr | EKT | 28 | W-57 |
| Amston Ct | SJO | 15 | Q-32 |
| Amy Av | ECO | 39 | AE-62 |
| Anchor Ct | MSH | 36 | AD-40 |
| Anchor Dr | MSH | 36 | AD-40 |
| Anchor Ln | SJO | 16 | R-40 |
| Anchorage St | STB | 35 | AG-28 |
| Anders Ct | MSH | 25 | W-31 |
| Anderson Av | STB | 24 | X-21 |
| Anderson Lake Dr | SJO | 27 | S-43 |
| Anderson Rd | CSS | 6 | A-38 |
| Anderson Rd | CSS | 6 | C-38 |
| Anderson Rd | CSS | 6 | E-38 |
| Anderson Rd | CSS | 16 | L-38 |
| Anderson Rd | SJO | 17 | R-42 |
| Anderson St | SJO | 24 | S-23 |
| Andover Ct | ECO | 29 | W-63 |
| Andover Tr | SJO | 15 | Q-29 |
| Andrea Ct | SJO | 36 | Z-41 |
| Andrew Dr | SJO | 41 | AD-75 |
| Andrews Ct E | SJO | 34 | AH-25 |
| Andrews Ct W | SJO | 34 | AH-25 |
| Andrews Rd | BRN | 2 | D-8 |
| Angela Blvd E | STB | 24 | X-24 |
| Angela Blvd W | STB | 24 | X-23 |
| Angela Dr | ECO | 50 | AL-67 |
| Anjou Ct | SJO | 14 | Q-20 |
| Ann St | MSH | 35 | AA-31 |
| Ann St | MSH | 35 | AB-31 |
| Ann St | MSH | 25 | Z-31 |
| Anna St | EKT | 28 | V-57 |
| Antler St | SJO | 16 | Q-41 |
| Antone Rd | ECO | 21 | R-78 |
| Anzio Av | STB | 25 | X-28 |
| Apache Dr | SJO | 24 | U-25 |
| Apollo St | BTL | 31 | L-76 |
| Apple Blossom Ln | ECO | 50 | AQ-73 |
| Apple Ln | ECO | 50 | AQ-73 |
| Apple Ln | BRN | 14 | N-24 |
| Apple Ln | SJO | 27 | S-45 |
| Apple Rd | SJO | 27 | Z-45 |
| Apple Rd E | SJO | 37 | AE-45 |
| Appletree Dr | SJO | 37 | AC-45 |
| Appletree Ln | STB | 35 | AA-29 |
| Appletree Ln | SJO | 37 | AC-45 |
| Applewood Ln | SJO | 14 | P-17 |
| Apricot Ct | SJO | 34 | AF-19 |
| Aqua Dr | ECO | 19 | R-68 |
| Arabian Dr | ECO | 40 | AB-68 |
| Arapaho Ln | SJO | 25 | U-26 |
| Arbola Rd | CSS | 21 | M-76 |
| Arbor Dr | NLS | 4 | F-21 |
| Arbor Dr | SJO | 25 | T-29 |
| Arbor Ln | MSH | 36 | AD-34 |
| Arbor Pointe Dr | SJO | 13 | P-15 |
| Arbor Pointe Dr | SJO | 13 | P-17 |
| Arbor St | CSS | 5 | D-32 |
| Arbor Vista Rd | ECO | 41 | AB-79 |
| Arborcrest Dr | ECO | 39 | AA-62 |
| Arbutus | ECO | 39 | AE-58 |
| Arcade Av | EKT | 28 | Z-54 |
| Arcade Av N | EKT | 28 | Y-54 |
| Arcadia Av | STB | 25 | X-28 |
| Arch Av | STB | 34 | AA-25 |
| Arch Ct | ECO | 39 | AA-64 |
| Arch St | EKT | 39 | AA-60 |
| Arch St | SJO | 16 | R-40 |
| Archer Av | SJO | 37 | AF-43 |
| Arctic St | BCH | 3 | E-10 |
| Ardennes Av | MSH | 25 | X-33 |
| Ardith Av | SJO | 27 | X-44 |
| Ardmore Dr | ECO | 38 | AD-57 |
| Ardmore Tr | SJO | 23 | Y-12 |
| Ardmore Tr | SJO | 23 | Y-16 |
| Ardmore Tr | SJO | 23 | Y-17 |
| Arehart St | GHS | 50 | AK-74 |
| Argyle Ln | STB | 35 | AF-26 |
| Aric Way | ECO | 39 | AE-61 |
| Arizona Av | ECO | 39 | AA-49 |
| Arizona Av | SJO | 37 | Z-44 |
| Arlene Av | ECO | 39 | AF-63 |
| Arlington Av | SJO | 24 | T-24 |
| Arlington Dr | OCS | 37 | AA-44 |
| Arlington St | ECO | 28 | U-57 |
| Armour Dr | SJO | 27 | Y-42 |
| Armstrong Ct | BRN | 14 | M-24 |
| Arnold Ct | BRN | 14 | D-24 |
| Arnold St | SJO | 25 | U-26 |
| Arnold St S | STB | 34 | AB-22 |
| Arnold St S | STB | 34 | AC-21 |
| Arnold St S | STB | 34 | AC-22 |
| Arrowhead Cir | SJO | 27 | S-42 |
| Arrowhead Dr | ECO | 30 | U-73 |
| Arrowhead Dr | STB | 24 | V-18 |
| Arrowood Ct | SJO | 14 | Q-20 |
| Arrowwood Dr | ECO | 29 | V-65 |
| Arther St | SJO | 25 | T-29 |
| Arthur St | SJO | 24 | T-25 |
| Arthur St | SJO | 25 | T-31 |
| Arthur St | SJO | 25 | T-33 |
| Arthur St N | STB | 25 | Y-26 |
| Arthur St N | STB | 25 | Z-26 |
| Asbury Ct | SJO | 14 | R-21 |
| Asbury Ln | EKT | 28 | S-56 |
| Asford Ct | SJO | 15 | Q-28 |
| Asford Ln | SJO | 15 | Q-28 |
| Ash | BRN | 14 | K-24 |
| Ash Cir | ECO | 38 | AE-53 |
| Ash Ct | GSH | 50 | AL-70 |
| Ash Dr | EKT | 29 | W-61 |
| Ash Dr | EKT | 29 | W-62 |
| Ash Ln | STB | 35 | AD-27 |
| Ash Maple Ct | STB | 24 | U-18 |
| Ash Rd | OCS | 37 | AA-46 |
| Ash Rd | SJO | 37 | AF-46 |
| Ash Rd | SJO | 47 | AM-46 |
| Ash Rd | SJO | 47 | AQ-46 |
| Ash Rd | SJO | 27 | U-46 |
| Ash Road | SJO | 17 | R-46 |
| Ash St | NLS | 4 | E-23 |
| Ashard Dr | STB | 23 | S-16 |
| Ashby Ct | ECO | 39 | AA-64 |
| Ashdale Ct | SJO | 15 | P-29 |
| Ashland Av | EKT | 38 | AA-54 |
| Ashland Av | STB | 24 | Y-22 |
| Ashland St | SJO | 16 | R-41 |
| Ashley Ct | GSH | 50 | AL-70 |
| Ashley Dr | SJO | 17 | Q-45 |
| Ashleys Meadow Dr | SJO | 27 | S-45 |
| Ashmont Ct | SJO | 25 | S-28 |
| Ashmont Dr | SJO | 25 | S-28 |
| Ashton Ct | GSH | 51 | AN-76 |
| Ashton Ct | SJO | 15 | R-30 |
| Ashton Rd | CSS | 7 | F-49 |

| Name | City | Pg | Grid | Name | City | Pg | Grid | Name | City | Pg | Grid | Name | City | Pg | Grid |
|---|---|---|---|---|---|---|---|---|---|---|---|---|---|---|---|
| Beth Ann Dr | SJO | 33 | AB-10 | Bluebell Cir | SJO | 27 | S-42 | Branch Water Way | MSH | 25 | W-32 | Brink Av | SJO | 27 | Y-46 |
| Bethany Dr | SJO | 26 | W-41 | Bluebonnet Ln | SJO | 26 | R-41 | Branchwood Ln | SJO | 25 | T-31 | Brions Wy | SJO | 17 | Q-42 |
| Beutter Ln | STB | 25 | X-29 | Bluejay Dr | SJO | 22 | Y-9 | Brande Creek Dr | CSS | 17 | N-44 | Bristol Av | SJO | 14 | Q-24 |
| Beveridge Av | EKT | 39 | AB-59 | Bluff Crest Dr | ECO | 39 | AB-64 | Brandel Av | SJO | 25 | T-28 | Bristol St | ECO | 30 | W-66 |
| Beverly Ct | OCS | 37 | AA-44 | Bluff Dr | ECO | 50 | AP-72 | Brandle Av | SJO | 25 | U-29 | Bristol St | SJO | 23 | Z-12 |
| Beverly Dr | ECO | 37 | AB-48 | Bluff Rd | GSH | 50 | AP-73 | Brandon Dr | CSS | 7 | H-50 | Bristol St E | ECO | 30 | V-67 |
| Beverly Pl | STB | 24 | W-21 | Bluff St | BRN | 4 | C-24 | Brandon Ln | SJO | 25 | S-31 | Bristol St E | EKT | 29 | W-59 |
| Beyer Av | STB | 35 | AB-25 | Bluff St | BCH | 3 | E-11 | Brandy Wood Ct | SJO | 25 | S-29 | Bristol St E | ECO | 30 | W-67 |
| Beywood Ln | SJO | 15 | Q-32 | Bluffside Ct | SJO | 25 | R-33 | Brandychase N | SJO | 16 | Q-34 | Bristol St W | EKT | 28 | W-54 |
| Bicknell Av | BRN | 14 | M-24 | Blyler Pl | STB | 24 | W-21 | Brandychase W | SJO | 16 | R-35 | Britt Av | ECO | 27 | Y-48 |
| Bicknell Dr N | SJO | 27 | U-45 | Blyly Rd | CSS | 21 | M-82 | Brandywine Dr | GSH | 50 | AL-69 | Brittany Ct | SJO | 25 | S-31 |
| Billington Ct | SJO | 15 | R-33 | Blyly Rd | CSS | 21 | M-82 | Brandywine St | BRN | 4 | H-24 | Britton Rd | BTL | 30 | U-74 |
| Birch Dr | EKT | 29 | W-62 | Bob White Ct | SJO | 34 | AG-20 | Brattleboro | SJO | 35 | AH-29 | Brixworth Ln | GSH | 50 | AN-71 |
| Birch Lake Dr | SJO | 17 | Q-43 | Boca Raton | BRN | 14 | J-25 | Braxton Ct | GSH | 50 | AM-70 | Brizandine Rd | CSS | 16 | L-42 |
| Birch Ln | GSH | 50 | AJ-68 | Bohlsen St | SJO | 36 | Z-39 | Brayton Av | SJO | 25 | V-26 | Broad St | ECO | 38 | AC-53 |
| Birch Ln | SJO | 27 | Y-43 | Boland Dr | STB | 23 | V-17 | Breckenridge Ct | SJO | 25 | S-29 | Broad St | CSS | 5 | D-31 |
| Birch Rd | CSS | 10 | B-71 | Boland Dr | STB | 24 | V-20 | Breden Rise Ln | SJO | 26 | Z-42 | Broadmoor Dr | EKT | 29 | X-60 |
| Birch Rd | CSS | 10 | E-71 | Boles Av N | OCS | 37 | AB-43 | Breezewood Dr | MSH | 36 | AA-41 | Broadway | NLS | 4 | F-23 |
| Birch Rd | CSS | 10 | H-73 | Bolton Ct | ECO | 39 | AA-64 | Breezy Beach | CSS | 5 | D-32 | Broadway | NLS | 4 | F-25 |
| Birch Rd | CSS | 20 | J-74 | Bolton Ct | ECO | 39 | AA-65 | Breezy Ln | GSH | 50 | AJ-67 | Broadway Blvd | ECO | 39 | AD-63 |
| Birch Rd | CSS | 20 | K-73 | Bonanza Ct | SJO | 26 | S-35 | Bremen Hwy | SJO | 35 | AE-32 | Broadway St | STB | 34 | AB-25 |
| Birch Rd | SJO | 17 | R-43 | Bonanza Ct E | SJO | 26 | S-35 | Bremen Hwy | SJO | 35 | AH-32 | Broadway St E | MSH | 35 | AA-33 |
| Birch Rd | SJO | 27 | Z-43 | Bonanza Ct W | SJO | 26 | S-35 | Bremen Hwy | SJO | 45 | AK-32 | Broadway St E | STB | 34 | AB-24 |
| Birch St | NLS | 4 | G-21 | Bond St | NLS | 4 | H-22 | Bremen Hwy | SJO | 45 | AN-32 | Broadway St E | STB | 34 | AB-25 |
| Birch Wy | STB | 35 | AB-25 | Bond St | BRN | 14 | L-22 | Bremen Hwy | SJO | 45 | AQ-32 | Broadway St W | MSH | 35 | AA-31 |
| Birchfield Ct | SJO | 27 | Y-43 | Bonds Av | STB | 24 | Y-18 | Brems Ct | SJO | 27 | W-44 | Broadway St W | STB | 34 | AB-23 |
| Birchtree Dr | SJO | 27 | Y-43 | Bonds Av | STB | 24 | Y-19 | Brendon Ct | ECO | 38 | AC-50 | Broadwood Dr | ECO | 29 | V-64 |
| Birchway Ct | SJO | 27 | Z-43 | Bonfield Pl | STB | 33 | AA-17 | Brendon Hills Dr | SJO | 25 | T-33 | Broceus School Rd | BRN | 2 | D-7 |
| Birchway Dr | SJO | 27 | Z-43 | Bonnethill Tr | MSH | 25 | X-33 | Brenshire Ct | SJO | 15 | Q-33 | Brockton Ct | SJO | 15 | Q-32 |
| Birchwood Av | STB | 33 | AA-16 | Bontrager Av | ECO | 39 | AC-58 | Brentwood Av | EKT | 29 | X-61 | Broderick Hill | SJO | 15 | P-29 |
| Birchwood Ct | SJO | 27 | Y-42 | Bontrager Av | EKT | 39 | AC-59 | Brentwood Ct | STB | 24 | X-18 | Broken Arrow Dr | SJO | 26 | S-40 |
| Birchwood Dr | MSH | 25 | Y-31 | Bontrager Av | EKT | 39 | AC-60 | Brentwood Dr | STB | 23 | Y-17 | Brokton Ct | MSH | 25 | X-33 |
| Birchwood Ln | STB | 24 | S-22 | Bonvale Dr | SJO | 25 | U-29 | Bresseau St | EKT | 28 | Y-55 | Bromley Chase Ct | SJO | 35 | AH-28 |
| Birdsell St | STB | 24 | Z-21 | Booker Av | SJO | 33 | Z-13 | Brewster Dr | ECO | 31 | S-75 | Bromley Chase Ctaaa | SJO | 35 | AG-28 |
| Birkdale Ct | SJO | 15 | Q-33 | Bordeaux Ct | EKT | 29 | W-63 | Briar Gate Ct | SJO | 17 | Q-46 | Bromley Ct | SJO | 16 | Q-37 |
| Birner St | STB | 24 | Z-22 | Borg Rd | ECO | 29 | U-58 | Briar Rd | BRN | 13 | L-17 | Brompton Rd | SJO | 45 | AK-26 |
| Biscayne Dr | SJO | 25 | U-28 | Borley Av E | MSH | 35 | AA-32 | Briar Rd | BRN | 14 | L-18 | Bronson St E | STB | 34 | AA-24 |
| Bishop Ct | ECO | 39 | AA-64 | Borley Av E | MSH | 36 | AA-34 | Briar Wy | STB | 35 | AD-27 | Bronson St E | STB | 34 | AA-25 |
| Bismark Av | EKT | 39 | AB-60 | Borley Av W | MSH | 35 | AA-30 | Briarcliff Ct | SJO | 25 | T-28 | Bronson St W | STB | 34 | AA-23 |
| Bison Ridge | ECO | 28 | S-54 | Borneman Av | EKT | 38 | AB-53 | Briarcliff Ln | SJO | 25 | T-28 | Brook Av | SJO | 36 | AD-37 |
| Bissell St | STB | 25 | Y-26 | Borwood Dr | SJO | 34 | AH-24 | Briarhill Dr | ECO | 40 | AF-66 | Brook Av N | MSH | 36 | AB-37 |
| Bitterfly Ct | SJO | 16 | R-40 | Boss Blvd | ECO | 38 | AA-52 | Briarton Dr | SJO | 26 | W-34 | Brook Av S | MSH | 36 | AB-37 |
| Bittersweet Ln | ECO | 28 | S-54 | Bosse Av | MSH | 36 | AB-38 | Briarwood Blvd | GSH | 50 | AJ-69 | Brook Av S | MSH | 36 | AC-37 |
| Bittersweet Rd | SJO | 16 | R-40 | Boston Ct | MSH | 36 | AD-36 | Briarwood Ct | EKT | 39 | AD-59 | Brook Haven Dr | SJO | 16 | P-36 |
| Bittersweet Rd | SJO | 26 | U-40 | Boston Dr | STB | 23 | Z-16 | Briarwood Ct | SJO | 15 | Q-29 | Brook Ln | ECO | 30 | W-69 |
| Bittersweet Tr | SJO | 16 | Q-40 | Boulder Av | GSH | 50 | AJ-67 | Briarwood Dr | EKT | 29 | X-63 | Brook Run Dr | MSH | 36 | AF-33 |
| Black Friars Ln | SJO | 36 | Z-42 | Bow Ct | STB | 24 | U-19 | Brick Church Rd | CSS | 8 | D-53 | Brook Run Dr | MSH | 36 | AG-34 |
| Black Maple Ct | STB | 24 | U-18 | Bowdoin Dr | MSH | 36 | AF-34 | Brick Rd | SJO | 23 | S-10 | Brook Run Dr | MSH | 36 | AG-34 |
| Black Oak Dr | STB | 25 | Y-27 | Bowen St | STB | 34 | AF-25 | Brick Rd | SJO | 23 | S-16 | Brook Run Dr | MSH | 36 | AG-34 |
| Black Pheasant Dr | SJO | 27 | Z-44 | Bower Crest Ct | SJO | 25 | U-29 | Brick Rd | SJO | 24 | S-28 | Brook St | SJO | 24 | S-23 |
| Blackberry Rd | SJO | 36 | AE-40 | Bower St | EKT | 28 | Y-54 | Brick Rd | SJO | 25 | S-28 | Brookdale Ct W | SJO | 24 | T-23 |
| Blackford Ct | STB | 35 | AG-27 | Bowers Ct | EKT | 29 | Y-58 | Brick Rd | SJO | 25 | S-32 | Brookdale Dr | SJO | 24 | T-23 |
| Blackford Dr | STB | 35 | AG-27 | Bowman St | SJO | 26 | Z-42 | Brick Rd | SJO | 26 | S-34 | Brookfield | NLS | 4 | G-22 |
| Blackford Dr E | STB | 35 | AG-27 | Bowman St E | STB | 34 | AC-24 | Brick Rd | SJO | 26 | S-40 | Brookfield | ECO | 29 | U-58 |
| Blackford Dr W | STB | 35 | AG-27 | Bowman St E | STB | 34 | AC-25 | Brick Rd | SJO | 26 | S-40 | Brookfield Ct | GSH | 50 | AN-77 |
| Blackhawk Ct | SJO | 17 | Q-43 | Bowman St E | STB | 35 | AC-26 | Brick St | BRN | 14 | N-22 | Brookfield Dr | ECO | 29 | U-58 |
| Blackport Dr | GSH | 51 | AL-76 | Bowman St W | STB | 34 | AC-24 | Brick St | BRN | 14 | P-23 | Brookfield St N | STB | 24 | X-20 |
| Blacksmith Ln | SJO | 32 | AC-8 | Bowood Ct | SJO | 26 | R-41 | Bridge | STB | 34 | AA-24 | Brookfield St S | STB | 34 | AA-20 |
| Blaine Av | ECO | 37 | AA-48 | Boxwood Ct | EKT | 29 | V-62 | Bridge Dr | SJO | 17 | P-42 | Brookfield St S | STB | 34 | AB-20 |
| Blaine Av | STB | 24 | Y-21 | Boxwood Dr | SJO | 44 | AH-25 | Bridge St | GSH | 51 | AL-74 | Brookfield St S | STB | 34 | AC-20 |
| Blaine Av | STB | 24 | Z-22 | Boxwood Dr | GSH | 50 | AJ-67 | Bridge St | EKT | 28 | Z-55 | Brookfield St S | STB | 34 | AD-20 |
| Blaine Av E | EKT | 39 | AA-58 | Boyland | ECO | 29 | U-59 | Bridge Town Rd | ECO | 30 | V-72 | Brookhurst Pl | STB | 25 | Y-30 |
| Blaine Av W | EKT | 38 | AA-55 | Boynton Av | STB | 25 | Y-29 | Bridge Water Wy | MSH | 26 | X-34 | Brooklane Dr | ECO | 51 | AK-79 |
| Blaine Av W | EKT | 38 | AA-56 | Bracken Fern Ct | SJO | 25 | U-26 | Bridgeton Ln S | STB | 45 | AH-27 | Brooklyn Av | ECO | 17 | P-47 |
| Blair Ct | ECO | 29 | W-64 | Bracken Fern Dr | SJO | 25 | U-26 | Bridgetown Cir | MSH | 36 | AD-38 | Brookmede Dr | STB | 35 | AE-27 |
| Blair Hills Av | MSH | 36 | AF-34 | Bradford Ct | ECO | 39 | AA-64 | Bridgeview Dr | SJO | 25 | U-28 | Brooks St | BRN | 14 | P-23 |
| Blair Hills Ct | MSH | 36 | AE-34 | Bradford Dr | STB | 35 | AG-27 | Bridgeview Tr | STB | 25 | W-27 | Brookside Dr | BRN | 3 | F-12 |
| Blanchard Dr | MSH | 36 | AD-38 | Bradford St | MSH | 36 | AC-34 | Bridgewater | ECO | 18 | R-56 | Brookside Dr | ECO | 30 | X-63 |
| Blanchard Dr | CSS | 5 | F-29 | Bradford St | MSH | 36 | AC-35 | Bridgewater Ct | SJO | 14 | R-21 | Brookston Dr W | SJO | 27 | W-44 |
| Blarney Ct | BRN | 4 | F-19 | Bradie Wy | SJO | 27 | W-45 | Bridgewood Dr E | ECO | 30 | U-67 | Brookton Dr | STB | 35 | AE-26 |
| Blazer Blvd | EKT | 39 | Y-59 | Bradley Ct | SJO | 22 | V-7 | Bridgewood Dr W | ECO | 29 | U-66 | Brookton Dr | STB | 35 | AF-26 |
| Bloomfield Pl | STB | 33 | AA-15 | Bradley St | EKT | 39 | AC-60 | Bridlewood Dr | SJO | 16 | P-35 | Brookton Dr | STB | 35 | AF-26 |
| Bloomingdale Rd | BTL | 31 | V-76 | Bradley St | ECO | 27 | X-48 | Briggs Av | EKT | 29 | X-62 | Brooktrails Dr | SJO | 24 | T-22 |
| Blue Bird | SJO | 34 | AF-20 | Brady Ln | MSH | 36 | AC-36 | Brightlingsea Pl | SJO | 25 | T-27 | Brooktree Ct | EKT | 29 | V-61 |
| Blue Grass Ct | GHS | 50 | AK-72 | Brady Rd | CSS | 18 | K-50 | Brighton Ct | SJO | 16 | R-34 | Brookview Ct | SJO | 25 | S-26 |
| Blue Jay Ln | MSH | 25 | W-30 | Brady St | CSS | 18 | J-50 | Brighton Park | SJO | 25 | S-26 | Brookwillow Ct | SJO | 15 | R-28 |
| Blue Ribbon Ln | ECO | 19 | R-60 | Brady St | EKT | 28 | Y-56 | Brighton Pl | STB | 25 | Y-30 | Brookwood Dr | BRN | 3 | G-13 |
| Blue Smoke Tr | MSH | 36 | AE-34 | Brady St | EKT | 28 | Y-56 | Brightwood Blvd | ECO | 39 | AA-64 | Brookwood Dr | SJO | 24 | U-23 |
| Blue Spruce Dr | ECO | 27 | V-48 | Braewick Ln | SJO | 45 | AK-26 | Brightwood Ln | SJO | 44 | AK-25 | Brookwood Dr | EKT | 29 | V-61 |
| Blue Spurce Tr | SJO | 26 | S-37 | Branch Water Ct | MSH | 25 | W-32 | Brimmer St | SJO | 26 | X-41 | Brookwood Dr | EKT | 29 | W-61 |

| Name | City | Pg | Grid | Name | City | Pg | Grid | Name | City | Pg | Grid | Name | City | Pg | Grid |
|---|---|---|---|---|---|---|---|---|---|---|---|---|---|---|---|
| Centennial Dr | ECO | 28 | S-54 | Chaucer Ln | SJO | 25 | S-27 | Christian Av | EKT | 38 | AB-56 | Cleveland Av | STB | 24 | Y-21 |
| Center Av | CSS | 5 | C-32 | Chauncey | MSH | 25 | W-31 | Christiana Creek Rd | CSS | 18 | L-54 | Cleveland Av | STB | 24 | Z-21 |
| Center Dr | BRN | 3 | G-13 | Chelle Ln | SJO | 26 | U-35 | Christiana Cres | NLS | 4 | E-20 | Cleveland Av E | EKT | 39 | AA-58 |
| Center Dr N | CSS | 10 | D-68 | Chelsea Av | SJO | 32 | AA-8 | Christiana Cres | NLS | 4 | E-21 | Cleveland Av W | EKT | 38 | AA-56 |
| Center Dr S | CSS | 10 | E-69 | Chelsea Ct | ECO | 39 | AA-64 | Christiana Dr | BRN | 4 | F-20 | Cleveland Estates Dr | ECO | 27 | V-49 |
| Center Field Av | CSS | 5 | E-30 | Chelsea Ct | STB | 35 | AE-27 | Christiana Dr | CSS | 18 | J-54 | Cleveland Rd | STB | 23 | T-15 |
| Center St | GHS | 51 | AK-74 | Chelsea Ct | ECO | 30 | X-68 | Christiana Lake Rd | CSS | 18 | K-54 | Cleveland Rd | STB | 24 | U-20 |
| Center St | CSS | 10 | E-68 | Chelsea Dr | SJO | 27 | W-44 | Christiana Ln | ECO | 28 | S-55 | Cleveland Rd | SJO | 26 | U-36 |
| Center St | EDW | 17 | K-43 | Chelsea Ln | ECO | 30 | X-68 | Christiana St | CSS | 18 | K-54 | Cleveland Rd E | RSL | 24 | U-23 |
| Center St | CSS | 17 | M-47 | Chelsen Ct | SJO | 44 | AH-21 | Christiana St | EKT | 28 | X-56 | Cleveland Rd E | MSH | 25 | U-33 |
| Center St | EKT | 29 | Z-59 | Chelsielee Ct | ECO | 39 | AE-63 | Christine Dr | SJO | 35 | AF-32 | Cleveland St | MSH | 35 | AC-30 |
| Center St | EKT | 29 | Z-60 | Cheri Ln | ECO | 30 | V-68 | Christopher Dr | ECO | 30 | X-67 | Clifden Dr | SJO | 16 | R-34 |
| Center St N | MSH | 35 | AB-31 | Cherokee Dr | SJO | 25 | V-29 | Christyann St | MSH | 35 | AA-32 | Clifford St | SJO | 24 | S-24 |
| Center St S | MSH | 35 | AB-31 | Cherokee Ln | SJO | 24 | U-25 | Church Ct | EKT | 29 | Y-59 | Climbing Rose Ln | MSH | 36 | AE-34 |
| Central | SJO | 22 | V-8 | Cherry Farm Tr | SJO | 16 | Q-37 | Church Ct N | GHS | 50 | AK-68 | Clinton Av | EKT | 28 | Z-54 |
| Central Av | SJO | 24 | S-24 | Cherry Ln | ECO | 38 | AD-54 | Church Gate Dr | SJO | 25 | S-28 | Clinton Av | STB | 34 | AB-24 |
| Central Ct | BCH | 3 | G-10 | Cherry Ln | ECO | 50 | AQ-73 | Church Rd | ECO | 20 | Q-73 | Clinton St | GSH | 50 | AL-68 |
| Central Dr | MSH | 36 | AA-34 | Cherry Ln | CSS | 7 | H-49 | Church St | MSH | 35 | AB-32 | Clinton St E | GSH | 50 | AL-73 |
| Central St | NLS | 4 | E-23 | Cherry Ln | BRN | 14 | K-24 | Church St | GHS | 51 | AK-76 | Clinton St W | GSH | 50 | AL-71 |
| Central St | CSS | 21 | N-76 | Cherry Pointe | STB | 23 | S-16 | Church St | EDW | 17 | K-43 | Clinton St W | GSH | 50 | AL-73 |
| Century Dr | GSH | 51 | AP-79 | Cherry Rd | SJO | 16 | Q-38 | Church St | BRN | 14 | P-23 | Clinton Woods | GSH | 50 | AL-70 |
| Century Dr | ECO | 29 | W-64 | Cherry Rd | SJO | 16 | R-38 | Church St | STB | 25 | Y-27 | Cloister Ct | SJO | 25 | S-27 |
| Chadwick Ct | SJO | 15 | R-32 | Cherry St | STB | 34 | AA-21 | Churchill Dr | EKT | 29 | W-61 | Clona Ct | SJO | 33 | AB-11 |
| Chain Lake St | CSS | 9 | B-60 | Cherry St | NLS | 4 | G-24 | Churchill Dr | STB | 25 | Y-27 | Clover Dr | SJO | 16 | Q-35 |
| Chain Lake St | CSS | 9 | B-65 | Cherry St | NLS | 4 | G-25 | Cindy Dr | ECO | 39 | AB-64 | Clover Dr | SJO | 26 | X-35 |
| Chain Lake St | CSS | 10 | B-67 | Cherry St | CSS | 17 | N-47 | Cinnamon Teral Ct | SJO | 15 | Q-30 | Clover Ln | ECO | 29 | U-58 |
| Chain O Lakes Dr | SJO | 22 | X-9 | Cherry St | EKT | 28 | X-55 | Cinnamon Tree Ct | SJO | 17 | R-45 | Clover Rd | MSH | 36 | AE-35 |
| Chalet Ct | STB | 35 | AH-27 | Cherry Tree Ln | STB | 25 | Y-27 | Cinnamon Tree Dr | SJO | 17 | R-45 | Clover Rd | SJO | 36 | Z-35 |
| Chalfant St | STB | 25 | Y-26 | Cherry Tree Ln | STB | 25 | Z-27 | Circle Av | STB | 34 | AA-21 | Clover Rd | MSH | 26 | Z-35 |
| Chalk Maple Ct | STB | 24 | V-19 | Cherrytree Ln | EKT | 29 | V-62 | Circle Dr | BCH | 3 | E-10 | Clover Ridge Dr | SJO | 16 | Q-35 |
| Chalmers Dr | SJO | 27 | X-44 | Cheryl Dr | SJO | 26 | S-40 | Circle Dr | EDW | 17 | K-43 | Clover St | STB | 35 | AB-26 |
| Chamberlain Rd | BRN | 3 | H-11 | Cheryl St | GHS | 50 | AK-69 | Circle Ln | ECO | 29 | W-64 | Clover Tr | SJO | 26 | S-35 |
| Chamberlain Rd | BRN | 2 | H-8 | Cheshire Dr | MSH | 35 | AG-28 | Circle Oak Ct | SJO | 17 | R-42 | Clover Trails Blvd | GSH | 50 | AN-72 |
| Chamberlain St | SJO | 23 | Y-14 | Chesnut Rd | SJO | 16 | R-37 | Circle R Ln | ECO | 39 | AG-61 | Cloverdale Dr | ECO | 19 | R-61 |
| Chamberlin Dr | SJO | 33 | AB-9 | Chesnut Ridge Dr | SJO | 16 | Q-35 | Circle Ridge Dr | BRN | 3 | G-14 | Cloverdale Ln Rd | SJO | 36 | AF-35 |
| Chamberlin Dr | STB | 25 | Z-29 | Chessington Dr | MSH | 36 | AD-36 | Circle W | ECO | 29 | X-64 | Cloverhill Ct | SJO | 44 | AH-20 |
| Champlain Dr | BRN | 14 | K-21 | Chester Dr | EKT | 29 | Z-65 | Citizens Av E | GHS | 50 | AK-74 | Cloverleaf North Dr | SJO | 25 | S-27 |
| Chan-Oak Ct | ECO | 28 | W-50 | Chester St | EKT | 38 | AA-57 | Citizens Av W | GHS | 50 | AK-73 | Clovis St | MSH | 25 | U-30 |
| Chandler Blvd | MSH | 35 | AE-31 | Chester St | STB | 35 | AB-26 | City Hall Ct | STB | 34 | Z-23 | Cloyd St | SJO | 33 | AE-15 |
| Chandler Blvd | MSH | 35 | AE-32 | Chestnut | BRN | 14 | K-24 | Claffey St | SJO | 14 | Q-23 | Club Blvd | MSH | 36 | AB-34 |
| Channel Ct | ECO | 19 | Q-60 | Chestnut Ct | EKT | 29 | W-62 | Claire St | EDW | 17 | J-42 | Club Dr | STB | 25 | Z-28 |
| Channel Ln | CSS | 8 | G-54 | Chestnut Ln | ECO | 39 | AB-65 | Clairmont Dr | SJO | 25 | T-27 | Clubhouse Ct | SJO | 22 | S-8 |
| Channel Pkwy | CSS | 18 | J-55 | Chestnut Rd | SJO | 16 | Q-37 | Clara Av | STB | 34 | AG-24 | Clubhouse Dr | SJO | 22 | R-8 |
| Channel Pkwy N | CSS | 18 | J-55 | Chestnut St | MSH | 35 | AA-33 | Clare | BRN | 4 | D-25 | Clyde Ct | SJO | 22 | Y-8 |
| Channel View Dr | ECO | 28 | Z-50 | Chestnut St | MSH | 35 | AB-33 | Clare Rd | CSS | 21 | N-75 | Clyde St | STB | 35 | AD-26 |
| Chapel Hill St | CSS | 9 | H-63 | Chestnut St | BTL | 31 | U-75 | Clare Rd | CSS | 21 | P-75 | Clyde St | EKT | 28 | Y-56 |
| Chapel Hill St | CSS | 10 | H-67 | Chestnut St N | OCS | 37 | AB-45 | Claredon Dr | EKT | 29 | X-60 | Clydesdale Dr | ECO | 40 | AB-68 |
| Chapel Hill St | CSS | 10 | H-72 | Chestnut St S | STB | 34 | AA-21 | Claredon Hills Dr | SJO | 25 | S-33 | Coachman Dr | SJO | 44 | AH-19 |
| Chapel Ln | SJO | 33 | AA-14 | Chestnut St S | OCS | 37 | AB-45 | Claremont St | BCH | 3 | G-11 | Coachmans Tr | SJO | 25 | T-27 |
| Chapin St | STB | 24 | Z-23 | Chestwick Ct | SJO | 34 | AH-20 | Clarendon Av | NLS | 4 | E-25 | Coast Ct | EKT | 28 | T-57 |
| Chapin St | STB | 34 | AA-22 | Chevy Chase Av | BRN | 14 | N-20 | Clarewood Ct | EKT | 29 | Z-62 | Cobblestone Cir | MSH | 36 | AD-35 |
| Chapin St | STB | 34 | AC-22 | Chevy Chase Dr | SJO | 17 | Q-46 | Claridge Ct | EKT | 29 | Y-58 | Cobblestone Ct | SJO | 25 | S-28 |
| Chaplegate Av | BRN | 14 | N-20 | Chevy Chase St | STB | 25 | Z-30 | Clarinet Blvd E | EKT | 29 | Z-61 | Cobblestone Dr | SJO | 41 | AD-20 |
| Chapman Av | EKT | 28 | Z-57 | Chicago Av | EKT | 39 | AB-59 | Clarinet Blvd S | EKT | 29 | Z-61 | Cobblestone Wy | ECO | 28 | T-54 |
| Chaptula St | BTL | 31 | U-76 | Chicago Av | GHS | 50 | AK-71 | Clarinet Blvd W | EKT | 29 | Z-60 | Cobus Creek Dr | ECO | 27 | U-48 |
| Charla Ln | ECO | 27 | W-46 | Chicago Av | GSH | 50 | AL-72 | Clarion Ct | ECO | 39 | AB-64 | Cobus Ct | ECO | 27 | U-48 |
| Charlatte St | MSH | 25 | Y-31 | Chicago Rd | NLS | 4 | G-21 | Clark Dr | STB | 23 | T-12 | Cobus Lake Dr | ECO | 27 | V-48 |
| Charles Av | STB | 23 | X-15 | Chicago Rd | BRN | 14 | J-18 | Clark St | BRN | 4 | C-24 | Cobus Ln | ECO | 27 | X-47 |
| Charles Av S | MSH | 36 | AB-40 | Chicago Rd | BRN | 13 | K-16 | Clark St | BCH | 3 | F-10 | Cobus Ln | ECO | 27 | X-48 |
| Charles St | ECO | 38 | AD-54 | Chicago Rd | BRN | 13 | M-11 | Clark St S | EKT | 28 | Y-57 | Cobus Oaks Dr | ECO | 27 | U-47 |
| Charles St | BCH | 3 | G-10 | Chicago St | BCH | 3 | G-11 | Clark St W | RSL | 24 | U-23 | Cogic St | CSS | 5 | G-28 |
| Charles St | BTL | 31 | U-76 | Chicago St E | BCH | 3 | G-10 | Clarmont Ct | GSH | 50 | AL-68 | Coguillard Dr | STB | 35 | AA-27 |
| Charles St | STB | 25 | X-27 | Chicago St N | STB | 23 | X-17 | Clave St | SJO | 34 | AH-25 | Coguillard Dr | STB | 25 | Y-27 |
| Charles St | STB | 25 | X-30 | Chicago St N | STB | 23 | Z-17 | Clay St | MSH | 35 | AA-30 | Coguillard Dr | STB | 35 | Z-27 |
| Charles St | EKT | 29 | Z-58 | Chicago St S | STB | 23 | Z-17 | Clay St | ECO | 38 | AB-53 | Col Fax Av | STB | 35 | Z-28 |
| Charles St E | OCS | 37 | AA-45 | Chicago St W | BCH | 3 | G-9 | Clay St | NLS | 4 | F-22 | Col Fax Av | STB | 35 | Z-29 |
| Charles St N | MSH | 36 | AB-40 | Chicago Tr | SJO | 12 | Q-1 | Clay St | SJO | 34 | X-1 | Colby Dr | SJO | 26 | W-40 |
| Charleston Dr | MSH | 25 | Y-32 | Chicago Tr | ECO | 17 | Q-49 | Clayton Dr | STB | 35 | AE-26 | Coldspring Ct | SJO | 25 | R-33 |
| Charlotte Av | ECO | 38 | AC-52 | Chickadee Ct | ECO | 37 | AD-48 | Clayton St | ECO | 39 | AD-61 | Cole St | ECO | 39 | AE-63 |
| Charlotte Av | ECO | 38 | AD-52 | Chickory Ct | SJO | 25 | T-31 | Clear Lake Rd E | BRN | 2 | F-5 | Coleman Dr | STB | 33 | AB-15 |
| Charlotte St | MSH | 35 | AA-31 | Chicory Ln | SJO | 27 | S-42 | Clear Lake Rd W | BRN | 2 | D-2 | Colfax Av | STB | 25 | Z-29 |
| Charlotte St | MSH | 25 | Y-31 | Chimes Blvd | STB | 25 | X-28 | Clear Lake Rd W | BRN | 2 | G-2 | Colfax Av E | STB | 35 | Z-26 |
| Charlotte St | MSH | 35 | Z-31 | Chinguapin Dr | SJO | 23 | U-10 | Clear Water Ln | SJO | 14 | R-18 | Colfax Av E | MSH | 35 | Z-32 |
| Chase St | EKT | 39 | AA-59 | Chippewa Av E | STB | 34 | AE-24 | Clearview Pl | STB | 33 | AA-15 | Colfax Av W | STB | 23 | Z-19 |
| Chase Tr | ECO | 39 | AE-64 | Chippewa Av W | STB | 34 | AE-22 | Clearview Pl | STB | 33 | AA-15 | Colfax Av W | STB | 24 | Z-19 |
| Chateau Ct | SJO | 14 | Q-19 | Chippewa Blvd | SJO | 26 | Z-38 | Clearwater Ct | ECO | 29 | S-62 | Colfax Av W | STB | 34 | Z-21 |
| Chaten Ct | SJO | 25 | S-31 | Chippewa Dr | EKT | 38 | AB-57 | Clemens St | STB | 25 | Y-27 | Colfax Av W | MSH | 35 | Z-31 |
| Chatham Pl | ECO | 31 | S-75 | Chippewa St | BCH | 2 | E-9 | Clemens St | STB | 23 | Z-15 | Colleen Ct | SJO | 15 | R-29 |
| Chatsworth Ln | SJO | 16 | R-41 | Chippewa Tr | NLS | 4 | G-21 | Clermont St | STB | 35 | AG-28 | College Av | GSH | 51 | AP-76 |
| Chaucer Ct | STB | 45 | AJ-26 | Chipstead Dr | SJO | 25 | T-27 | Clermont St | STB | 25 | Y-28 | College Av | GSH | 51 | AP-78 |
|  |  |  |  |  |  |  |  | Cleveland Av | ECO | 37 | AA-48 |  |  |  |  |

| Name | City | Pg | Grid |
|------|------|----|----|
| Faun Ridge Dr | SJO | 33 | AC-10 |
| Fawn Ct | STB | 24 | T-20 |
| Fawn Dale Ct | SJO | 17 | Q-45 |
| Fawn Ln | ECO | 19 | Q-59 |
| Fawn River Ct | ECO | 39 | AC-63 |
| Fawn River Ct | ECO | 39 | AD-63 |
| Fawn River Ct | ECO | 39 | AD-64 |
| Fawn Woods Ct | SJO | 17 | Q-45 |
| Faye Ct | SJO | 27 | W-46 |
| Faye Dr | SJO | 27 | W-46 |
| Federal Ct | NLS | 4 | G-25 |
| Fedore Rd | BRN | 2 | C-5 |
| Felicity Dr | SJO | 26 | W-35 |
| Fellows St | STB | 34 | AC-24 |
| Fellows St | STB | 34 | AF-24 |
| Fellows St | STB | 34 | AG-24 |
| Fellows St | SJO | 34 | AH-24 |
| Fellows St | SJO | 44 | AH-24 |
| Fellows St | STB | 44 | AJ-24 |
| Fellows St | SJO | 44 | AK-24 |
| Fellows St | SJO | 44 | AK-24 |
| Fenmore Av | ECO | 40 | AG-67 |
| Fenner Ln | SJO | 37 | AD-45 |
| Fenton Ln | SJO | 25 | W-29 |
| Fergus Dr | SJO | 25 | T-29 |
| Fern Dr | ECO | 18 | Q-56 |
| Fern Hill Dr | MSH | 36 | AD-39 |
| Fern Ln | GSH | 50 | AJ-67 |
| Fern Rd | SJO | 46 | AK-34 |
| Fern Wy | STB | 35 | Z-28 |
| Ferndale Blvd | BRN | 14 | J-24 |
| Fernlake Dr | MSH | 36 | AD-35 |
| Fernwood Av | ECO | 38 | AA-53 |
| Fernwood Ct | SJO | 14 | Q-20 |
| Fernwood Dr | SJO | 25 | U-26 |
| Ferrettie Ct | SJO | 36 | AA-38 |
| Ferris Av | MSH | 36 | AA-36 |
| Ferry St | NLS | 4 | F-22 |
| Ferry St | NLS | 4 | F-23 |
| Ferry St | NLS | 4 | F-25 |
| Fescue Ct | GSH | 50 | AJ-72 |
| Fetters Ct | EKT | 39 | AA-58 |
| Fiddle Head Ct | SJO | 25 | U-26 |
| Field Ct | SJO | 25 | S-27 |
| Field Farm Tr | ECO | 18 | R-56 |
| Field Gate Dr | STB | 24 | S-18 |
| Field Pointe Ln | SJO | 16 | R-34 |
| Field Stone Dr | ECO | 27 | R-46 |
| Fieldcrest Ct | SJO | 15 | R-33 |
| Fieldhouse Av | EKT | 38 | AB-54 |
| Fieldsfarm Ct | SJO | 16 | R-41 |
| Fieldsfarm Tr | ECO | 18 | R-56 |
| Fieldstone Dr | ECO | 27 | S-47 |
| Fieldstone Ln | SJO | 25 | S-29 |
| Fifth St N | BRN | 4 | A-25 |
| Filbert Rd | SJO | 25 | Y-33 |
| Filbert Road | SJO | 25 | T-33 |
| Filbert Way | EKT | 29 | V-62 |
| Fillmore Av | CSS | 17 | M-47 |
| Fillmore Rd | SJO | 33 | Z-14 |
| Filmore St | SJO | 26 | Z-40 |
| Finch Dr | STB | 34 | AG-25 |
| Fir Ln | STB | 35 | Z-29 |
| Fir Rd | SJO | 36 | AH-35 |
| Fir Rd | SJO | 46 | AJ-35 |
| Fir Rd | SJO | 46 | AQ-35 |
| Fir Rd | SJO | 46 | AR-35 |
| Fir Rd | CSS | 16 | N-35 |
| Fir Rd | CSS | 16 | P-35 |
| Fir Rd | SJO | 16 | R-34 |
| Fir Rd | MSH | 26 | Y-35 |
| Fir Rd S | MSH | 36 | AD-35 |
| Fireside Ct | SJO | 32 | AB-9 |
| Fireside Dr | ECO | 40 | AF-66 |
| Firethorn Dr | GSH | 51 | AR-79 |
| First Ct | NLS | 4 | F-22 |
| First St | ECO | 29 | S-64 |
| Firwood Ln | ECO | 29 | S-65 |
| Fish Ladder Ln | MSH | 35 | AB-32 |
| Fisher Ct | MSH | 35 | AC-32 |
| Fisher St W | STB | 34 | AB-19 |
| Fisher St W | STB | 34 | AB-21 |
| Fisk Av | CSS | 15 | E-31 |
| Five Points Rd | CSS | 19 | N-59 |
| Flag Av | STB | 25 | Y-28 |
| Flake St | EKT | 38 | AA-55 |
| Flamingo Ct | SJO | 26 | W-36 |
| Flat Creek Rd | STB | 24 | S-20 |
| Fleetwood Dr | SJO | 25 | V-29 |
| Flicker Dr | ECO | 39 | AB-65 |
| Flicker Ln | SJO | 25 | U-27 |
| Flint Ct | STB | 24 | U-19 |
| Flora Av | EKT | 29 | Z-63 |
| Flora St | MSH | 36 | AA-40 |
| Floral Ct | BRN | 14 | L-24 |
| Floral Ct | EKT | 29 | Z-59 |
| Floral Dr | BRN | 14 | M-24 |
| Floral Pl | STB | 33 | AB-15 |
| Florence Av | ECO | 39 | AD-62 |
| Florence Av | ECO | 39 | AD-63 |
| Florence Av | BRN | 14 | M-25 |
| Florence Ln | ECO | 28 | U-57 |
| Florence Ln | ECO | 28 | U-57 |
| Florence St | ECO | 38 | AB-53 |
| Florence St | EKT | 28 | Y-54 |
| Florence St | STB | 24 | Z-20 |
| Florida Av | ECO | 37 | Z-49 |
| Florine Ct | STB | 33 | AC-27 |
| Floyd St | EKT | 28 | X-56 |
| Folkstone Ct | MSH | 36 | AD-35 |
| Follmer St | CSS | 16 | K-37 |
| Folsom St | EKT | 29 | AA-59 |
| Fop Dr | NLS | 4 | F-22 |
| Ford St | SJO | 33 | AA-11 |
| Ford St | SJO | 33 | AA-14 |
| Ford St | SJO | 33 | AA-15 |
| Ford St | STB | 34 | AA-19 |
| Ford St | STB | 34 | AA-21 |
| Ford St | SJO | 32 | AA-8 |
| Ford St | SJO | 33 | AB-13 |
| Ford St | CSS | 6 | D-34 |
| Ford St W | STB | 33 | AA-16 |
| Ford St W | STB | 33 | AA-17 |
| Forest Av | NLS | 4 | G-23 |
| Forest Av | STB | 24 | Y-23 |
| Forest Av | MSH | 25 | Y-31 |
| Forest Av | MSH | 25 | Y-31 |
| Forest Av | MSH | 25 | Z-31 |
| Forest Ct | GSH | 51 | AR-74 |
| Forest Edge Dr | MSH | 36 | AE-34 |
| Forest Glen Dr | SJO | 14 | P-20 |
| Forest Grove Av | ECO | 29 | W-64 |
| Forest Ln | ECO | 29 | AA-63 |
| Forest Ln | ECO | 39 | AD-65 |
| Forest Rd | ECO | 19 | R-59 |
| Forest St | MSH | 35 | AA-31 |
| Forest View Tr | STB | 45 | AJ-26 |
| Forestbrook Av | SJO | 14 | R-24 |
| Forestbrook Av | SJO | 24 | S-24 |
| Forestbrook Av | SJO | 24 | S-24 |
| Forestview Av | ECO | 39 | AF-63 |
| Forestview Av | ECO | 39 | AF-64 |
| Forglove Ct | MSH | 36 | AA-36 |
| Forrest Hill Av | ECO | 29 | V-58 |
| Forshire Ln | SJO | 25 | R-32 |
| Fort St | NLS | 4 | H-23 |
| Fortino Ct | EKT | 29 | W-63 |
| Foster | BCH | 3 | G-12 |
| Foster Av | EKT | 29 | Y-60 |
| Foster St | STB | 24 | Y-24 |
| Foundation Ct | STB | 23 | V-17 |
| Foundation Dr | BRN | 13 | K-15 |
| Foundation Dr | STB | 23 | V-17 |
| Fountain Ct | SJO | 16 | Q-38 |
| Fountain Row | ECO | 38 | AA-52 |
| Fourteenth St | NLS | 4 | H-24 |
| Fourth | NLS | 4 | D-23 |
| Fourth St | BCH | 2 | F-8 |
| Fourth St | ECO | 29 | T-64 |
| Fox Chase | ECO | 30 | U-73 |
| Fox Chase Dr | SJO | 16 | Q-37 |
| Fox Chase Dr | ECO | 31 | W-76 |
| Fox Ct | SJO | 24 | U-25 |
| Fox Den Dr | SJO | 15 | R-28 |
| Fox Fire Dr | STB | 24 | S-20 |
| Fox Pointe Ln | SJO | 15 | R-32 |
| Fox Run | SJO | 25 | R-32 |
| Fox Run Tr | ECO | 27 | S-48 |
| Fox Run Tr | SJO | 26 | W-34 |
| Fox St | STB | 34 | AC-24 |
| Fox St | STB | 34 | AC-25 |
| Fox St | STB | 35 | AC-26 |
| Fox Tr | SJO | 16 | P-38 |
| Fox Trail Ct | SJO | 26 | W-35 |
| Fox Trail Dr | SJO | 26 | W-36 |
| Fox Trail Tr | SJO | 22 | T-9 |
| Fox Valley Ct | SJO | 25 | S-29 |
| Foxboro Ct | MSH | 36 | AA-36 |
| Foxboro Dr | ECO | 27 | R-47 |
| Foxbriar Ln | GSH | 50 | AM-70 |
| Foxbriar Ln | GSH | 50 | AN-70 |
| Foxcross Dr | SJO | 15 | Q-31 |
| Foxdale Ln | SJO | 25 | S-32 |
| Foxfire Dr | STB | 24 | T-19 |
| Foxfire Dr | ECO | 29 | V-65 |
| Foxhollow Ct | SJO | 16 | R-40 |
| Frailey Rd | ECO | 28 | Y-50 |
| Frances Av | EKT | 39 | AB-58 |
| Frances St | BRN | 4 | B-24 |
| Frances St N | STB | 24 | Y-25 |
| Frances St N | STB | 34 | Z-25 |
| Frances St S | STB | 34 | AA-25 |
| Francis Av | SJO | 36 | AA-38 |
| Francis St | SJO | 24 | T-25 |
| Frank Ct | ECO | 38 | AA-51 |
| Franklin | CSS | 18 | L-54 |
| Franklin Av | MSH | 36 | AB-40 |
| Franklin Ct | ECO | 41 | AE-74 |
| Franklin Ct | EKT | 28 | Z-56 |
| Franklin Pl | STB | 34 | Z-23 |
| Franklin Rd | BRN | 2 | H-9 |
| Franklin Rd | BRN | 12 | J-8 |
| Franklin Rd | BRN | 12 | J-9 |
| Franklin St | STB | 34 | AA-23 |
| Franklin St | SJO | 33 | AB-42 |
| Franklin St | STB | 34 | AD-23 |
| Franklin St | GSH | 51 | AN-74 |
| Franklin St E | EKT | 28 | Y-57 |
| Franklin St W | ECO | 38 | AA-51 |
| Frantz Dr | CSS | 15 | J-28 |
| Freda Dr | ECO | 29 | T-58 |
| Fredericksbur Ct | SJO | 34 | AH-25 |
| Frederickson St | STB | 24 | Y-19 |
| Frederickson St | STB | 24 | Y-20 |
| Fredrick | ECO | 39 | AG-64 |
| Fredrick Cir | ECO | 39 | AH-64 |
| Freight St | EKT | 28 | Z-57 |
| Fremont St | STB | 24 | X-19 |
| Fremont St | STB | 24 | Z-19 |
| Fremont St | EKT | 28 | Z-55 |
| French St | NLS | 4 | G-22 |
| Fresno St | SJO | 22 | Y-9 |
| Friars Ct | SJO | 25 | S-27 |
| Friars Ct | SJO | 25 | S-27 |
| Front St | NLS | 4 | E-22 |
| Front St E | MSH | 35 | AB-32 |
| Front St E | BCH | 3 | F-11 |
| Front St W | BCH | 2 | F-7 |
| Frontier Ct | SJO | 26 | S-40 |
| Frostfield Dr | MSH | 35 | AG-33 |
| Frostfield Dr | MSH | 36 | AG-34 |
| Fuerbringer St | STB | 24 | Z-22 |
| Fulkerson Rd | BRN | 14 | M-23 |
| Fulmer Rd | MSH | 35 | AF-33 |
| Fulmer Rd | MSH | 36 | AF-34 |
| Fulton Ct | STB | 34 | Z-22 |
| Fulton St | BCH | 3 | E-10 |
| Fulton St | EKT | 28 | Y-54 |
| Fulton St | EKT | 28 | Y-55 |
| Furrow Dr | SJO | 25 | S-27 |

**G**

| Name | City | Pg | Grid |
|------|------|----|----|
| G Ln | EKT | 38 | AC-56 |
| G St | EKT | 28 | W-52 |
| Gage Av | EKT | 29 | Y-60 |
| Gagnon St | STB | 23 | U-17 |
| Galaxy Dr | SJO | 15 | Q-28 |
| Gale Rd | SJO | 33 | Z-12 |
| Galien-Buchanan Rd | BRN | 2 | H-4 |
| Galway Ct | STB | 35 | AE-27 |
| Galway Dr | STB | 35 | AF-27 |
| Galya Dr | CSS | 19 | P-60 |
| Gano St | ECO | 38 | AC-52 |
| Garden Av | GHS | 50 | AK-73 |
| Garden Blvd | EKT | 39 | AC-60 |
| Garden Dr | ECO | 39 | AB-63 |
| Garden Ln | STB | 33 | AB-15 |
| Garden Pl | STB | 23 | Z-17 |
| Garden Rd | SJO | 37 | AA-42 |
| Garden St | EKT | 28 | W-57 |
| Gardena Pl | ECO | 29 | X-64 |
| Gardenia Dr | SJO | 25 | U-26 |
| Gardner Ct | EKT | 28 | Z-56 |
| Garfield Av | ECO | 37 | AA-48 |
| Garfield Av E | EKT | 39 | AA-58 |
| Garfield Av W | EKT | 38 | AA-56 |
| Garfield Av W | GSH | 50 | AM-73 |
| Garfield Ct | STB | 34 | Z-22 |
| Garfield St | OCS | 37 | AA-44 |
| Garland Cir | STB | 35 | AD-26 |
| Garland Dr | GSH | 50 | AN-76 |
| Garland Rd | STB | 35 | AE-26 |
| Garland St | EKT | 28 | X-57 |
| Garland St N | SJO | 25 | X-26 |
| Garnet Dr E | STB | 34 | AG-22 |
| Garnet Dr N | STB | 34 | AG-22 |
| Garnsey | BRN | 14 | N-22 |
| Garst St W | STB | 34 | AB-23 |
| Gartner Av | STB | 35 | Y-27 |
| Garver Av | ECO | 39 | AF-63 |
| Garver Av | CSS | 17 | M-47 |
| Garver Lake Rd | CSS | 17 | L-48 |
| Garver Lake Rd N | CSS | 17 | J-48 |
| Garvin St | EKT | 28 | W-53 |
| Garway Common St | SJO | 45 | AH-25 |
| Garwood Ct | SJO | 25 | S-26 |
| Gary Ct | BRN | 14 | N-23 |
| Gary Ct | EKT | 27 | Z-60 |
| Gary Dr | ECO | 39 | AD-65 |
| Gatehouse Dr E | STB | 24 | S-22 |
| Gatehouse Dr N | SJO | 24 | R-21 |
| Gatehouse Dr S | SJO | 24 | S-21 |
| Gatehouse Dr W | SJO | 24 | S-21 |
| Gateway Ct | SJO | 33 | AB-11 |
| Gateway Rd | EDW | 17 | K-44 |
| Geary Ct | SJO | 25 | S-26 |
| Gee Ct | SJO | 14 | R-18 |
| Geiger Rd | BRN | 4 | B-18 |
| Gene | NLS | 4 | D-24 |
| Generations Dr | SJO | 25 | V-28 |
| Generations Dr | SJO | 25 | V-28 |
| Genes Cir | CSS | 5 | D-32 |
| Gentian Ln | SJO | 27 | S-42 |
| Gentle Run Ct | SJO | 34 | AH-21 |
| George Av S | STB | 34 | AA-25 |
| George Dr | ECO | 18 | Q-56 |
| George F Smith Ct | CSS | 18 | J-55 |
| George St | BRN | 5 | G-26 |
| George St | SJO | 25 | W-27 |
| George St N | MSH | 36 | AB-35 |
| Georgia Blvd | EKT | 28 | X-51 |
| Georgia St | GSH | 50 | AJ-70 |
| Georgian Ct | STB | 35 | AH-27 |
| Georgian Dr | STB | 35 | AH-27 |
| Georgiana St | STB | 24 | Y-25 |
| Gerald St | SJO | 25 | S-30 |
| Gerald St | ECO | 28 | U-57 |
| Geranium Ct | SJO | 15 | Q-28 |
| Gerencser Ct | SJO | 43 | AL-13 |

| Name | City | Pg | Grid |
|---|---|---|---|
| Hatcher Av | CSS | 5 | G-27 |
| Hausman St | SJO | 24 | U-25 |
| Haven Ct | MSH | 26 | Z-34 |
| Haven Hill Dr | SJO | 15 | Q-31 |
| Haverford Ct | SJO | 45 | AK-25 |
| Haverhill Ct | SJO | 14 | R-21 |
| Haviland Av | SJO | 14 | Q-24 |
| Hawbaker St | STB | 34 | AF-24 |
| Hawkins Ct | STB | 35 | AH-26 |
| Hawks St | CSS | 9 | G-65 |
| Hawks St | CSS | 10 | G-67 |
| Hawthorne | ECO | 38 | AC-53 |
| Hawthorne | BRN | 14 | M-21 |
| Hawthorne Dr | STB | 35 | AD-27 |
| Hawthorne Dr | EKT | 38 | AB-57 |
| Hawthorne Dr | GSH | 50 | AL-69 |
| Hawthorne Ln | NLS | 4 | H-21 |
| Hawthorne Tr | SJO | 45 | AK-29 |
| Hayfield Dr | SJO | 23 | R-12 |
| Haymaker Dr | SJO | 25 | S-29 |
| Haynes Av | SJO | 36 | AA-37 |
| Haynes Av | SJO | 36 | AA-38 |
| Haynes Av | SJO | 36 | AA-38 |
| Hays Ct | STB | 35 | AE-27 |
| Hazel Rd | SJO | 35 | AF-29 |
| Hazel Rd | CSS | 20 | M-69 |
| Hazel Rd | SJO | 15 | R-29 |
| Hazel St | EKT | 39 | AB-60 |
| Hazelhurst Ct | ECO | 39 | AA-62 |
| Hazelwood Ct | STB | 23 | Z-15 |
| Hearthside Ct | SJO | 16 | Q-37 |
| Hearthside Dr | SJO | 16 | P-37 |
| Hearthside Dr | SJO | 16 | Q-37 |
| Hearthstone Dr | SJO | 25 | W-33 |
| Heath Dr | CSS | 5 | E-30 |
| Heather | SJO | 25 | S-26 |
| Heather Cv | SJO | 25 | S-28 |
| Heather Hill Ln | SJO | 15 | Q-32 |
| Heather Ln | STB | 35 | AG-27 |
| Heather Ln | ECO | 18 | Q-55 |
| Heather Ridge Ct | SJO | 33 | AA-11 |
| Heather Wood Ct | SJO | 26 | W-34 |
| Heather Wood Dr | SJO | 25 | W-33 |
| Heatherfield Dr | SJO | 25 | S-27 |
| Heatherridge Dr | SJO | 13 | P-15 |
| Heaton Vista | ECO | 29 | S-64 |
| Heaton Vista | ECO | 29 | T-65 |
| Heatwood Dr | SJO | 16 | P-35 |
| Hebron Rd | CSS | 11 | E-80 |
| Hebron Rd | CSS | 11 | H-81 |
| Hedge Ln | SJO | 25 | R-32 |
| Hedge Maple Ct | STB | 24 | U-18 |
| Hedgect | SJO | 25 | S-31 |
| Hedgewood Ct | SJO | 16 | P-35 |
| Helen Av | SJO | 24 | R-25 |
| Helen Av S | MSH | 36 | AB-36 |
| Helen St | ECO | 39 | AD-62 |
| Helen St | ECO | 31 | T-81 |
| Helena Dr | SJO | 27 | V-46 |
| Helman Av | SJO | 14 | R-24 |
| Helman Av | SJO | 24 | T-24 |
| Helman Ct | STB | 34 | AA-24 |
| Helman Dr | STB | 25 | Y-30 |
| Helvie Dr | SJO | 25 | T-28 |
| Hemlock Ct | GSH | 50 | AJ-69 |
| Hemlock Dr | SJO | 37 | AD-43 |
| Hemlock Ln | EKT | 29 | W-62 |
| Hemlock Rd | STB | 35 | AF-28 |
| Hemlock Wy | STB | 35 | Z-28 |
| Hendricks St | MSH | 35 | AC-30 |
| Henning St | SJO | 33 | AB-10 |
| Henry Rd | SJO | 32 | AD-2 |
| Henry Rd | SJO | 37 | AD-45 |
| Henry St | MSH | 35 | AB-31 |
| Hepler St | SJO | 25 | W-28 |
| Hepler St | SJO | 25 | W-29 |
| Herbert St | BRN | 5 | H-8 |
| Herbert St | SJO | 16 | Q-40 |
| Heritage Ct | MSH | 25 | Y-32 |
| Heritage Dr | SJO | 25 | W-33 |
| Heritage Ln | EKT | 28 | X-51 |
| Heritage Way | ECO | 40 | AB-72 |
| Herman St | GHS | 51 | AK-75 |
| Herman St | EKT | 29 | Z-65 |
| Hermitage Dr | STB | 34 | AG-25 |
| Hermosa Pl | STB | 34 | AB-24 |
| Heron Cove Ln | ECO | 29 | W-66 |
| Heron Cv | ECO | 30 | W-66 |
| Herrold Av | EKT | 38 | AB-57 |
| Herrold Av E | EKT | 38 | AB-58 |
| Herrold Av W | EKT | 38 | AB-57 |
| Hess Rd | CSS | 7 | E-45 |
| Hess Rd | CSS | 7 | H-45 |
| Hester St | EKT | 28 | Z-55 |
| Hiawatha Dr | EKT | 38 | AB-56 |
| Hiawatha Dr | EKT | 38 | AB-57 |
| Hiawatha Tr | STB | 34 | AG-22 |
| Hickory Cir | ECO | 38 | AD-53 |
| Hickory Dr | MSH | 25 | U-30 |
| Hickory Hills Ct | SJO | 27 | Z-45 |
| Hickory Ln | BCH | 2 | E-8 |
| Hickory Ln | ECO | 29 | V-63 |
| Hickory Ln | ECO | 27 | Y-49 |
| Hickory Ln | STB | 35 | Z-29 |
| Hickory Pl | GSH | 50 | AL-71 |
| Hickory Rd | SJO | 35 | AF-30 |
| Hickory Rd | SJO | 45 | AH-30 |
| Hickory Rd | SJO | 45 | AP-30 |
| Hickory Rd | SJO | 25 | R-30 |
| Hickory Rd | SJO | 25 | S-30 |
| Hickory Rd | MSH | 25 | X-30 |
| Hickory Rd | STB | 25 | Y-30 |
| Hickory Rd N | STB | 25 | Z-30 |
| Hickory St | GSH | 50 | AL-71 |
| Hickory St | NLS | 4 | F-23 |
| Hickory St | NLS | 4 | F-24 |
| Hidden Lakes Dr | MSH | 36 | AF-34 |
| Hidden Oaks Ct | STB | 24 | S-20 |
| Hidden Pines Ct | SJO | 15 | R-30 |
| Hidden Valley Ct | SJO | 25 | T-30 |
| Hidden Valley Dr | SJO | 25 | T-30 |
| Higgins Blvd | ECO | 29 | U-58 |
| Higgins St | BRN | 14 | M-23 |
| High Bridge Rd | BRN | 2 | H-5 |
| High Bridge Rd | BRN | 12 | J-5 |
| High Park Av | GSH | 51 | AP-74 |
| High Pointe Dr | SJO | 34 | AF-18 |
| High St | STB | 34 | AB-25 |
| High St | STB | 34 | AC-25 |
| High St | STB | 34 | AE-25 |
| High St | GSH | 50 | AL-72 |
| High St | CSS | 17 | J-50 |
| High St N | CSS | 21 | L-75 |
| High St S | STB | 34 | AF-25 |
| High St W | EKT | 28 | Y-56 |
| Highland Av | EKT | 28 | Y-54 |
| Highland Av N | EKT | 28 | Y-54 |
| Highland Blvd | ECO | 28 | V-54 |
| Highland Blvd | ECO | 28 | W-54 |
| Highland Ct | ECO | 27 | Z-47 |
| Highland Dr | GHS | 51 | AK-75 |
| Highland Dr | SJO | 25 | T-29 |
| Highland Shore Dr | SJO | 15 | Q-30 |
| Highmeadow Dr | SJO | 15 | Q-28 |
| Highland Av | SJO | 33 | AB-42 |
| Hilbish Blvd | BTL | 30 | U-74 |
| Hilde Ct | STB | 35 | AC-26 |
| Hildebrand St | STB | 34 | AH-23 |
| Hildreth St | STB | 35 | AB-27 |
| Hill Dr | ECO | 18 | Q-56 |
| Hill St | STB | 34 | AA-24 |
| Hill St | EKT | 38 | AA-54 |
| Hill St | SJO | 36 | AF-37 |
| Hill St | GSH | 51 | AL-77 |
| Hill St | NLS | 4 | D-23 |
| Hill St | BCH | 2 | G-9 |
| Hill St N | MSH | 35 | AB-31 |
| Hill St N | STB | 34 | Y-24 |
| Hill St N | STB | 34 | Z-24 |
| Hill Tr | SJO | 23 | U-10 |
| Hillcrest | ECO | 38 | AD-57 |
| Hillcrest Av | ECO | 39 | AG-60 |
| Hillcrest Dr | ECO | 38 | AE-53 |
| Hillcrest Dr | CSS | 11 | G-75 |
| Hillcrest Rd | NLS | 4 | G-21 |
| Hillcrest Rd | STB | 34 | X-23 |
| Hillsdale Rd | STB | 35 | AE-27 |
| Hillside Av | STB | 34 | AC-20 |
| Hillside Ct | EKT | 28 | Z-56 |
| Hillside Dr | SJO | 22 | V-9 |
| Hillside St | STB | 34 | AC-20 |
| Hillst | MSH | 35 | AB-31 |
| Hilltop Dr | STB | 35 | AD-27 |
| Hilltop Dr | BRN | 3 | H-10 |
| Hilltop Dr | CSS | 20 | M-73 |
| Hilltop Rd | SJO | 12 | Q-5 |
| Hilltop St | GHS | 50 | AK-74 |
| Hilltop Tr | BRN | 3 | G-13 |
| Hillview Av | BCH | 2 | G-8 |
| Hillview Dr | ECO | 38 | AE-51 |
| Hillview Dr | CSS | 17 | P-44 |
| Hilly Ln | ECO | 38 | AD-57 |
| Himebaugh Av | ECO | 39 | AD-62 |
| Hine St | STB | 34 | Z-21 |
| Hinton Ln | SJO | 26 | S-39 |
| Hively Av | ECO | 38 | AB-53 |
| Hively Av E | EKT | 39 | AB-59 |
| Hively Av E | ECO | 39 | AB-62 |
| Hively Av W | ECO | 38 | AB-53 |
| Hively Av W | EKT | 38 | AB-55 |
| Hively St | ECO | 39 | AB-65 |
| Hobart St | BRN | 3 | G-10 |
| Hodson Av | MSH | 36 | AC-37 |
| Hodson Av | SJO | 36 | AD-37 |
| Hodson St | MSH | 36 | AB-37 |
| Hoffman Ct | STB | 34 | AB-25 |
| Hoffman St | EKT | 29 | Y-66 |
| Hoke St | STB | 35 | AC-27 |
| Holaway Ct | GSH | 50 | AL-71 |
| Holiday Dr | ECO | 29 | X-64 |
| Holiday Dr N | STB | 35 | Z-28 |
| Holiday Dr S | STB | 35 | AA-28 |
| Holiday Pl | ECO | 38 | AC-51 |
| Holland St | STB | 34 | Z-19 |
| Holler St | SJO | 32 | AG-4 |
| Holley St | CSS | 5 | D-31 |
| Hollingshead Dr | SJO | 27 | Z-43 |
| Hollow Tr | SJO | 32 | T-10 |
| Holly Brook Ct | SJO | 16 | Q-36 |
| Holly Brook Dr | SJO | 16 | P-36 |
| Holly Ct | SJO | 25 | T-26 |
| Holly Ct W | GSH | 50 | AL-70 |
| Holly Dr | ECO | 29 | X-63 |
| Holly Fern Ct | SJO | 25 | U-26 |
| Holly Ln | EKT | 29 | X-60 |
| Hollyhock Rd | SJO | 14 | Q-25 |
| Hollyhock Rd | SJO | 24 | S-25 |
| Hollyhock Rd | SJO | 24 | T-25 |
| Hollywood Av | EKT | 29 | Y-63 |
| Hollywood Blvd | STB | 33 | AB-15 |
| Hollywood Blvd | SJO | 33 | AF-15 |
| Hollywood Blvd | SJO | 23 | X-14 |
| Hollywood Pl | STB | 24 | W-21 |
| Hollywood Shores Rd | CSS | 20 | N-73 |
| Holmes Dr | BRN | 3 | F-13 |
| Holmes St | SJO | 36 | Y-13 |
| Holstein St | BRN | 14 | N-21 |
| Holub Ln | GSH | 51 | AJ-75 |
| Homan Av | EKT | 29 | Y-62 |
| Home Av | EKT | 29 | Y-60 |
| Home St N | MSH | 36 | AA-36 |
| Home St N | MSH | 36 | AB-36 |
| Home St N | MSH | 26 | Z-36 |
| Home St S | MSH | 36 | AB-36 |
| Homeacres St | GHS | 50 | AK-69 |
| Homeland Rd | ECO | 29 | W-64 |
| Homer Av | EKT | 39 | AC-60 |
| Homer Av | STB | 34 | AF-23 |
| Homestead Av | ECO | 29 | V-58 |
| Homestead Tr | SJO | 15 | Q-32 |
| Homewood Av | MSH | 36 | AB-33 |
| Homewood Av | MSH | 36 | AB-34 |
| Homewood Av | ECO | 29 | V-58 |
| Homewood Av | EKT | 29 | Y-61 |
| Honan Dr | STB | 35 | AE-26 |
| Hondon Hall | SJO | 15 | R-31 |
| Honey Suckle Ln | MSH | 36 | AB-41 |
| Honeysuckle Ln | ECO | 38 | AD-54 |
| Honeysuckle St | CSS | 5 | G-28 |
| Hook Ln | MSH | 36 | AE-34 |
| Hoose Ct | STB | 34 | AA-22 |
| Hoosier Av | SJO | 36 | AA-38 |
| Hoover Av | STB | 35 | AA-27 |
| Hoover Av | ECO | 38 | AE-50 |
| Hoover Av | SJO | 36 | Z-40 |
| Hoover Rd | EKT | 28 | X-57 |
| Hoover St | STB | 34 | AF-23 |
| Hope Av | STB | 25 | Y-29 |
| Horne Ct | STB | 35 | AA-29 |
| Horseshoe Ct | ECO | 40 | AB-67 |
| Horton Ct | CSS | 5 | D-33 |
| Hound Tr | SJO | 22 | U-9 |
| Hovey St | EKT | 39 | AA-58 |
| Howard Ct | GSH | 50 | AL-70 |
| Howard Ct | STB | 25 | Y-27 |
| Howard St | MSH | 35 | AA-31 |
| Howard St | NLS | 4 | E-23 |
| Howard St | NLS | 4 | F-25 |
| Howard St | EKT | 29 | X-58 |
| Howard St | STB | 24 | Y-25 |
| Howard St | STB | 25 | Y-26 |
| Howe Ln | BRN | 3 | G-11 |
| Howland Av N | EKT | 29 | X-58 |
| Hoyt Dr | CSS | 6 | B-36 |
| Hoyt St | CSS | 5 | B-33 |
| Hubbard Av E | EKT | 39 | AA-58 |
| Hubbard Av W | EKT | 38 | AA-56 |
| Hubbard Hill Ln | ECO | 38 | AD-53 |
| Hubbard Hill Ln | ECO | 38 | AE-53 |
| Hubbard St | STB | 35 | AD-28 |
| Hudson Av | STB | 24 | Y-22 |
| Hudson St | EKT | 28 | Z-55 |
| Huey St | STB | 24 | X-20 |
| Huey St | STB | 34 | Z-20 |
| Huff Av | CSS | 5 | D-32 |
| Huff Rd | CSS | 5 | D-32 |
| Huffman Dr | STB | 35 | AH-26 |
| Hug St | EKT | 28 | Z-57 |
| Hull St | STB | 24 | Y-25 |
| Humbolt Av | STB | 24 | Y-21 |
| Humbolt St | SJO | 23 | Y-13 |
| Humbolt St | STB | 24 | Y-20 |
| Humingbird Dr | SJO | 22 | Y-8 |
| Hummel Dr | MSH | 36 | AC-36 |
| Hummingbird Ct | ECO | 39 | AB-65 |
| Hummingbird Ct | GSH | 50 | AJ-67 |
| Humphreys Ct | STB | 34 | AB-21 |
| Hunt Tr | SJO | 22 | U-9 |
| Hunter Ct | SJO | 37 | AF-43 |
| Hunter Ct | ECO | 29 | W-65 |
| Hunter Run Cir | STB | 24 | T-20 |
| Hunters Cove Ct | SJO | 17 | Q-46 |
| Hunters Crossing Ct | SJO | 17 | R-44 |
| Hunting Ridge Tr | SJO | 16 | R-34 |
| Hunting Ridge Tr N | SJO | 16 | R-34 |
| Huntington | SJO | 15 | Q-31 |
| Huntington Pl | MSH | 36 | AF-34 |
| Huntington Ridge Tr | SJO | 15 | R-33 |
| Huntley Ct | STB | 35 | AG-27 |
| Huntly Rd | CSS | 5 | C-32 |
| Huntly Rd | CSS | 5 | C-32 |
| Huntly Rd | CSS | 5 | D-31 |
| Huntly Rd | CSS | 5 | D-31 |
| Huntly Rd | CSS | 5 | E-30 |
| Huntly Rd | CSS | 5 | F-30 |
| Hurd Rd | SJO | 32 | AD-1 |
| Huron Cir | STB | 33 | AA-16 |
| Huron Dr | BRN | 3 | H-12 |
| Huron Dr | SJO | 33 | AA-11 |
| Huron St | STB | 34 | AA-17 |

| Name | City | Pg | Grid |
|------|------|----|------|
| Huron St | STB | 34 | AA-19 |
| Huron St | STB | 34 | AA-21 |
| Huron St | EKT | 39 | AA-60 |
| Huron St | SJO | 32 | AA-8 |
| Huron St | GSH | 50 | AL-72 |
| Huron St | NLS | 4 | G-23 |
| Huron St | NLS | 4 | G-25 |
| Huron St W | SJO | 33 | AA-13 |
| Huron St W | SJO | 33 | AA-13 |
| Huron St W | SJO | 33 | AA-15 |
| Hush Breeze Ct | SJO | 34 | AH-21 |
| Hyde Park Dr | ECO | 29 | V-66 |
| Hydraulic Av | STB | 24 | Z-24 |
| Hynes Dr | SJO | 34 | AH-22 |
| Hyrne Av | CSS | 5 | E-31 |

**I**

| Name | City | Pg | Grid |
|------|------|----|------|
| I Ln | EKT | 38 | AC-57 |
| Ice Tr | SJO | 34 | AF-18 |
| Ida St | SJO | 24 | U-25 |
| Ida St | ECO | 28 | V-55 |
| Ideal Beach Rd | ECO | 29 | T-65 |
| Idlewild Av | ECO | 30 | AC-61 |
| Idlewilde St | CSS | 21 | N-77 |
| Idlewood Dr | SJO | 37 | AC-43 |
| Illinois Av | ECO | 38 | AA-52 |
| Illinois Av | EKT | 38 | AA-53 |
| Illinois St | GSH | 51 | AN-75 |
| Illinois St | BTL | 31 | U-75 |
| Illinois St N | STB | 23 | X-17 |
| Illinois St N | STB | 23 | Z-17 |
| Illinois St S | STB | 34 | AA-17 |
| Imus Ct | MSH | 25 | Y-31 |
| Imus St | MSH | 25 | Y-31 |
| Independence Dr | GSH | 50 | AL-69 |
| Independence Dr | RSL | 24 | V-24 |
| Independence St | EKT | 29 | W-59 |
| Independence St | EKT | 29 | X-59 |
| India Ct | STB | 34 | Z-22 |
| Indian East West Toll Road | STB | 24 | U-20 |
| Indian Ridge Blvd | MSH | 25 | V-31 |
| Indian Springs Rd | BRN | 3 | A-10 |
| Indian Springs Rd | BRN | 3 | A-10 |
| Indian Springs S | BRN | 3 | A-11 |
| Indiana Av | MSH | 36 | AA-34 |
| Indiana Av | SJO | 22 | X-9 |
| Indiana Av E | EKT | 39 | AA-59 |
| Indiana Av E | STB | 35 | AB-26 |
| Indiana Av E | STB | 34 | AC-24 |
| Indiana Av N | ECO | 40 | AF-71 |
| Indiana Av N | ECO | 50 | AJ-72 |
| Indiana Av N | GHS | 50 | AK-72 |
| Indiana Av N | GSH | 50 | AL-72 |
| Indiana Av S | GSH | 50 | AM-72 |
| Indiana Av W | STB | 34 | AC-20 |
| Indiana Av W | STB | 34 | AC-22 |
| Indiana Av W | ECO | 27 | Z-48 |
| Indiana East West Toll Rd | SJO | 14 | R-19 |
| Indiana East West Toll Road | SJO | 22 | R-6 |
| Indiana East West Toll Road | MSH | 25 | V-30 |
| Indiana East-West Toll Road | SJO | 27 | T-43 |
| Indiana East-West Toll Road | ECO | 29 | T-60 |
| Indiana East-West Toll Road | ECO | 30 | T-69 |
| Indiana East-West Toll Road | ECO | 31 | T-81 |
| Indiana Lake Rd | CSS | 20 | P-74 |
| Indiana Lake Rd | BTL | 31 | T-75 |
| Indiana St | BTL | 30 | U-74 |
| Indiana St | BTL | 30 | V-74 |
| Indigan Ln | CSS | 7 | E-42 |
| Industrial Dr | STB | 34 | AB-18 |
| Industrial Dr | MSH | 36 | AD-34 |
| Industrial Dr | NLS | 5 | D-26 |
| Industrial Dr | SJO | 16 | R-40 |
| Industrial Dr N | SJO | 16 | R-40 |
| Industrial Park Dr | GSH | 51 | AQ-75 |
| Industrial Pkwy | EKT | 29 | Y-62 |
| Inez St | BRN | 15 | N-26 |
| Ing Richards Wy | SJO | 17 | Q-44 |
| Inglewood Ct | STB | 24 | V-21 |
| Inglewood Pl | STB | 24 | W-21 |
| Inn's Brook Rd | SJO | 25 | S-28 |
| Inner Dr | NLS | 4 | G-25 |
| Instamatic Dr | EKT | 29 | Z-63 |
| Institution Dr | ECO | 41 | AH-78 |
| Interchange Dr | EKT | 28 | S-57 |
| International Dr | EKT | 28 | S-57 |
| Interurban St | OCS | 37 | AB-45 |
| Inverness Dr | SJO | 22 | R-8 |
| Inverness Ln | STB | 35 | AF-26 |
| Inwood Ct | ECO | 39 | AA-64 |
| Inwood Rd | STB | 35 | AE-27 |
| Inwood Rd | MSH | 35 | AE-30 |
| Inwood Rd | SJO | 32 | AE-4 |
| Inwood Rd | SJO | 37 | AE-46 |
| Iowa Av | EKT | 38 | AA-53 |
| Iowa St | MSH | 35 | AC-33 |
| Iowa St | MSH | 35 | AD-33 |
| Iowa St | GSH | 51 | AN-75 |
| Iowa St | STB | 24 | Y-18 |
| Iowa St N | STB | 24 | X-18 |
| Iowa St N | STB | 24 | Y-18 |
| Iowa St S | STB | 34 | AA-18 |
| Ireland Dr E | STB | 35 | AF-27 |
| Ireland Rd | SJO | 35 | AF-32 |
| Ireland Rd | SJO | 36 | AF-37 |
| Ireland Rd | SJO | 37 | AF-45 |
| Ireland Rd E | STB | 35 | AF-26 |
| Ireland Rd E | STB | 35 | AF-28 |
| Ireland Rd E | SJO | 35 | AF-31 |
| Ireland Rd S | SJO | 34 | AF-20 |
| Ireland Rd W | SJO | 34 | AF-17 |
| Ireland Rd W | STB | 34 | AF-22 |
| Ireland Tr | MSH | 35 | AE-31 |
| Iris Ct | ECO | 28 | S-54 |
| Iris St | STB | 34 | AB-24 |
| Irish Hills Dr | STB | 35 | AE-28 |
| Irish Hills Dr | STB | 35 | AF-28 |
| Irish Wy | STB | 25 | W-27 |
| Irma Av | BRN | 4 | A-19 |
| Iroavois Ln | MSH | 25 | Y-32 |
| Iron Forge Ct | SJO | 25 | T-30 |
| Iron Forge Ln | SJO | 25 | S-29 |
| Iron Gate Dr | ECO | 27 | X-48 |
| Irongate Ct | SJO | 25 | S-29 |
| Ironstone Dr | SJO | 25 | S-29 |
| Ironwood | ECO | 39 | AD-63 |
| Ironwood Cir | STB | 25 | X-28 |
| Ironwood Dr | ECO | 39 | AD-64 |
| Ironwood Dr N | MSH | 35 | AC-28 |
| Ironwood Dr N | SJO | 25 | T-27 |
| Ironwood Dr N | STB | 25 | Z-28 |
| Ironwood Dr S | STB | 35 | AD-28 |
| Ironwood Dr S | SJO | 45 | AJ-28 |
| Ironwood Dr S | SJO | 45 | AN-28 |
| Ironwood Dr S | STB | 35 | Z-28 |
| Ironwood Rd | STB | 35 | AF-28 |
| Ironwood Rd | CSS | 15 | L-27 |
| Ironwood Rd | CSS | 15 | N-27 |
| Ironwood Rd | CSS | 15 | P-27 |
| Ironwood Rd | SJO | 25 | R-26 |
| Iroquois St | STB | 24 | X-23 |
| Iroquois St | STB | 24 | Y-23 |
| Iroquois Tr | NLS | 4 | G-20 |
| Irvin St | ECO | 28 | V-57 |
| Irvington Av | STB | 35 | AD-27 |
| Irvington Av E | STB | 34 | AD-25 |
| Irvington St | SJO | 33 | AD-10 |
| Irvington St | STB | 34 | AD-19 |
| Irvington St | STB | 34 | AD-20 |
| Irvington St | STB | 34 | AD-24 |
| Irwing Dr | CSS | 17 | M-47 |
| Isaac Mc Coy Dr | BRN | 4 | F-19 |
| Isaac Mc Coy Dr | BRN | 4 | F-20 |
| Island Av | SJO | 37 | AA-42 |
| Island Dr | CSS | 17 | K-49 |
| Island Park Rd | CSS | 18 | J-53 |
| Island View Dr | GSH | 50 | AQ-74 |
| Iville Av | SJO | 27 | X-44 |
| Ivy Ct | CSS | 5 | F-29 |
| Ivy Ln | ECO | 27 | Z-49 |
| Ivy Rd | SJO | 25 | W-26 |
| Ivy Rd | STB | 25 | X-26 |

**J**

| Name | City | Pg | Grid |
|------|------|----|------|
| J. Hancock Ct | ECO | 31 | U-78 |
| J Ln | EKT | 38 | AC-57 |
| J. Q. Adams Ct | ECO | 31 | V-79 |
| Jackie Ln | SJO | 24 | T-23 |
| Jackie Ln | ECO | 29 | T-60 |
| Jackson Blvd E | ECO | 30 | W-68 |
| Jackson Blvd W | EKT | 28 | Y-56 |
| Jackson Pl W | EKT | 28 | Y-56 |
| Jackson Rd | SJO | 34 | AG-19 |
| Jackson Rd | STB | 34 | AG-23 |
| Jackson Rd | STB | 34 | AG-24 |
| Jackson Rd | SJO | 35 | AG-29 |
| Jackson Rd | SJO | 35 | AG-32 |
| Jackson Rd | SJO | 37 | AG-45 |
| Jackson Rd | SJO | 32 | AG-6 |
| Jackson Rd E | SJO | 36 | AG-38 |
| Jackson St | MSH | 35 | AC-30 |
| Jackson St | BRN | 4 | C-25 |
| Jackson St | BRN | 4 | D-25 |
| Jackson St | SJO | 26 | Z-39 |
| Jackson St E | GSH | 51 | AN-75 |
| Jackson St N | STB | 34 | Z-20 |
| Jackson St S | STB | 34 | AA-20 |
| Jackson St S | STB | 34 | AB-20 |
| Jackson St S | STB | 34 | AC-20 |
| Jackson St W | GSH | 50 | AA-73 |
| Jacob St | STB | 25 | Z-26 |
| Jacob St N | STB | 25 | Y-26 |
| Jacob St N | STB | 35 | Z-26 |
| Jacob St S | STB | 25 | Z-26 |
| James Ct | SJO | 32 | AF-5 |
| James Lawrence Pkwy | SJO | 16 | R-36 |
| James Pl | GSH | 50 | AL-71 |
| James Pl S | GSH | 50 | AM-71 |
| James St | NLS | 4 | S-22 |
| James St | EKT | 29 | Y-59 |
| Jameslawrence Ct | SJO | 26 | S-36 |
| Jamestown Av | ECO | 37 | AC-48 |
| Jamestown Ct | STB | 23 | Z-16 |
| Jamestown Ct S | MSH | 25 | Y-30 |
| Jamestown North | MSH | 25 | Y-30 |
| Jamestown Rd | ECO | 38 | AE-51 |
| Jami St | ECO | 28 | T-51 |
| Jamie Dr | SJO | 15 | P-33 |
| Jamie Ln | CSS | 8 | H-54 |
| Jane St | SJO | 24 | R-23 |
| Janellen Dr | CSS | 5 | F-28 |
| Janellen Dr | CSS | 5 | F-28 |
| Janet Dr | SJO | 25 | T-26 |
| Janet St | ECO | 27 | S-46 |
| Janice Ball Ct | SJO | 34 | AE-19 |
| Janice St | ECO | 31 | T-81 |
| Janiper Dr | ECO | 39 | AG-64 |
| Jasmine Ct | ECO | 39 | AE-60 |
| Jason Ct | ECO | 39 | AE-63 |
| Jaunita Av | EKT | 38 | AC-54 |
| Jauriet Ct | EKT | 29 | Y-58 |
| Jay Dee St | ECO | 28 | Y-51 |
| Jay St | BRN | 3 | C-16 |
| Jayne Dr | ECO | 28 | Z-51 |
| Jeanine Ct E | BRN | 5 | D-26 |
| Jeanine Place | SJO | 13 | P-16 |
| Jeannie Dr | SJO | 23 | S-10 |
| Jeannine Ct | NLS | 5 | E-26 |
| Jeanwood Dr | ECO | 29 | V-62 |
| Jefferson Blvd | SJO | 36 | AA-37 |
| Jefferson Blvd | SJO | 36 | Z-40 |
| Jefferson Blvd E | STB | 35 | AA-26 |
| Jefferson Blvd E | STB | 35 | AA-29 |
| Jefferson Blvd E | MSH | 35 | AA-33 |
| Jefferson Blvd W | STB | 34 | AA-17 |
| Jefferson Blvd W | STB | 34 | AA-21 |
| Jefferson Blvd W | STB | 34 | AA-21 |
| Jefferson Center St | CSS | 7 | C-43 |
| Jefferson Center St | CSS | 7 | C-44 |
| Jefferson Center St | CSS | 7 | C-48 |
| Jefferson Center St | CSS | 8 | C-52 |
| Jefferson Estates Ln | MSH | 35 | AA-31 |
| Jefferson Hwy | SJO | 27 | Z-46 |
| Jefferson Knolls Dr | SJO | 27 | Z-45 |
| Jefferson Ln | ECO | 41 | AE-74 |
| Jefferson Pkwy | ECO | 40 | AA-72 |
| Jefferson Pl | STB | 34 | AA-23 |
| Jefferson St | EDW | 17 | J-44 |
| Jefferson St E | GSH | 51 | AL-74 |
| Jefferson St W | GSH | 50 | AL-74 |
| Jefferson St W | EKT | 28 | Y-56 |
| Jefferson View Park | SJO | 41 | AD-76 |
| Jeffery Dr | SJO | 27 | X-42 |
| Jennifer Ct | SJO | 35 | AG-32 |
| Jennifer Ln | ECO | 29 | U-65 |
| Jennifer St | ECO | 50 | AL-67 |
| Jennings Av E | STB | 34 | AE-24 |
| Jennings Av W | STB | 34 | AE-23 |
| Jenny Ln | BRN | 4 | B-18 |
| Jenny Ln | ECO | 28 | S-54 |
| Jenny Ln | MSH | 25 | W-31 |
| Jeremy Ln | CSS | 5 | F-30 |
| Jeri Ann Dr | ECO | 39 | AD-65 |
| Jerome St | NLS | 4 | H-23 |
| Jesse Ln | SJO | 27 | S-46 |
| Jewell Av | STB | 34 | AG-23 |
| Jewell Av | STB | 34 | AG-24 |
| Jill St | CSS | 17 | M-46 |
| Jimmie St | ECO | 38 | AD-50 |
| Joan Av | SJO | 36 | AA-37 |
| Joan Dr | BRN | 4 | B-18 |
| Joanne Dr | EKT | 29 | Z-59 |
| Jodie Lynn Dr | SJO | 17 | R-45 |
| Johannes Ct | ECO | 29 | S-60 |
| John Glen Ct | MSH | 35 | AC-32 |
| John St | MSH | 35 | AB-33 |
| John St | ECO | 39 | AE-63 |
| John Weaver Pkwy | EKT | 28 | V-52 |
| Johnathan | SJO | 24 | S-22 |
| Johnny Ct | ECO | 19 | Q-66 |
| Johnson Rd | SJO | 34 | AG-21 |
| Johnson Rd | SJO | 32 | AG-3 |
| Johnson Rd | SJO | 33 | AH-17 |
| Johnson Rd | SJO | 34 | AH-25 |
| Johnson Rd | SJO | 35 | AH-30 |
| Johnson Rd | EKT | 29 | T-58 |
| Johnson Rd | EKT | 29 | W-58 |
| Johnson St | CSS | 20 | L-72 |
| Johnson St | STB | 24 | W-20 |
| Johnson St | STB | 24 | Z-20 |
| Johnston St | GSH | 50 | AJ-73 |
| Joilet Dr | BRN | 14 | K-21 |
| Jon Dr | EKT | 28 | V-57 |
| Jon Dr | EKT | 28 | W-57 |
| Jonathon Dr | ECO | 18 | Q-56 |
| Jones Av | ECO | 38 | AA-53 |
| Jones Dr | CSS | 15 | N-27 |
| Jordan St | BCH | 3 | G-10 |
| Jordan St | BCH | 3 | G-11 |
| Jordan St | EKT | 28 | X-55 |
| Joseph Ln | SJO | 33 | AB-12 |
| Joseph Rd | CSS | 10 | E-70 |
| Joseph St | MSH | 36 | AB-34 |
| Josephine Av | ECO | 37 | AB-48 |
| Joshua St | ECO | 38 | AD-51 |
| Joy Dr | SJO | 32 | AF-5 |
| Joyce Ct | EKT | 29 | Y-61 |
| Joyce Dr | STB | 24 | V-21 |
| Juanita Av | ECO | 29 | V-63 |
| Juday Creek Dr | SJO | 26 | U-35 |

| Name | City | Pg | Grid |
|---|---|---|---|
| Juday Lake Dr N | SJO | 25 | W-28 |
| Juday Lake Dr S | SJO | 25 | W-28 |
| Judie Av | SJO | 26 | Z-38 |
| Judy Ln | RSL | 24 | U-24 |
| Julep Ct | SJO | 33 | AF-14 |
| Juneberry Ct | ECO | 29 | V-65 |
| Junior Achievement Dr | EKT | 28 | Y-57 |
| Juniper | BRN | 14 | K-24 |
| Juniper Av | CSS | 5 | F-30 |
| Juniper Pl | STB | 33 | AB-17 |
| Juniper Rd | SJO | 45 | AR-25 |
| Juniper Rd | SJO | 14 | Q-25 |
| Juniper Rd | SJO | 24 | S-25 |
| Juniper Rd | SJO | 24 | T-25 |
| Juniper Rd | STB | 25 | X-26 |
| Juniper Woods Ct | SJO | 24 | S-25 |
| Juniperav | CSS | 5 | F-30 |
| Juno Ln | SJO | 15 | Q-28 |
| Juno St | CSS | 8 | G-53 |
| Juno St | CSS | 18 | J-55 |
| Justine Dr | SJO | 23 | S-16 |
| **K** | | | |
| K Ln | EKT | 38 | AD-56 |
| K Ln | ECO | 38 | AD-57 |
| K. Jay Ln | SJO | 13 | P-16 |
| Kale St | STB | 25 | X-30 |
| Kaley St | STB | 34 | AC-19 |
| Kaley St | STB | 34 | AD-19 |
| Kaley St | STB | 24 | Z-19 |
| Kaley St N | STB | 24 | Y-19 |
| Kaley St N | STB | 34 | Z-19 |
| Kaley St S | STB | 34 | AA-19 |
| Kaley St S | STB | 34 | AB-19 |
| Kalka Dr | MSH | 35 | AE-32 |
| Kalmia Ct | SJO | 33 | AA-11 |
| Kalorama St | STB | 24 | Y-24 |
| Kalorama St | STB | 24 | Y-25 |
| Kamms Ct | MSH | 35 | AC-31 |
| Kamp Kozy St | CSS | 7 | H-46 |
| Kankakee Rd | STB | 34 | Z-19 |
| Kankakee Tr | STB | 23 | Z-16 |
| Kansas Dr | GHS | 50 | AK-71 |
| Kapsa Dr | SJO | 33 | AA-11 |
| Karen Dr | EKT | 28 | U-56 |
| Karen St | ECO | 27 | Y-47 |
| Karington Ct | ECO | 39 | AB-64 |
| Kathmere Dr | SJO | 27 | Z-43 |
| Kathryn Ct | ECO | 39 | AE-61 |
| Kathryn Dr | ECO | 28 | Z-51 |
| Kathryn St | BRN | 5 | G-26 |
| Kathryn St | CSS | 5 | G-27 |
| Kathy Dr | SJO | 33 | AB-10 |
| Kathy Dr | SJO | 33 | AB-10 |
| Kauffman St | ECO | 38 | AD-50 |
| Kay Blvd | ECO | 39 | AG-62 |
| Kay Ln | SJO | 26 | S-39 |
| Kayla Ct | SJO | 27 | W-44 |
| Keasey St | STB | 34 | AB-24 |
| Keefer | ECO | 38 | AA-50 |
| Keely Dr | CSS | 17 | N-45 |
| Kehres St | ECO | 28 | W-51 |
| Kehres St | ECO | 28 | W-51 |
| Keller St | STB | 23 | X-15 |
| Keller St | STB | 24 | X-18 |
| Keller St | STB | 24 | X-20 |
| Keller St | STB | 25 | X-30 |
| Kelley St | SJO | 14 | Q-23 |
| Kelly Rd | SJO | 43 | AJ-11 |
| Kelly Rd | SJO | 45 | AJ-33 |
| Kelly Rd | SJO | 46 | AJ-36 |
| Kelsey Av | EKT | 39 | AC-60 |
| Keltner Rd | ECO | 39 | AB-61 |
| Kemble St | STB | 34 | AC-22 |
| Kendal | ECO | 39 | AE-63 |
| Kendall St | STB | 34 | AC-22 |
| Kenilworth Dr | EKT | 29 | V-61 |
| Kenilworth Dr | EKT | 29 | W-61 |
| Kenilworth Rd | SJO | 44 | AQ-23 |
| Kenilworth Rd | SJO | 44 | AR-23 |
| Kenilworth Rd | SJO | 14 | R-23 |
| Kenilworth Rd W | SJO | 24 | T-23 |
| Kenmore Av | EKT | 29 | X-61 |
| Kenmore Dr | CSS | 17 | M-47 |
| Kenmore Dr | SJO | 22 | V-8 |
| Kenmore St | STB | 24 | U-18 |
| Kenmore St N | STB | 24 | X-18 |
| Kenmore St N | STB | 24 | Y-18 |
| Kenmore St N | STB | 34 | Z-18 |
| Kenmore St S | STB | 34 | AA-18 |
| Kennedy Dr | STB | 35 | AE-27 |
| Kennedy Dr | ECO | 27 | V-47 |
| Kennedy Ln | EKT | 29 | W-62 |
| Kennedy St | CSS | 5 | D-31 |
| Kennesaw Ct | EKT | 29 | Z-62 |
| Kenneth Av | SJO | 25 | U-29 |
| Kenneth St | CSS | 17 | J-47 |
| Kenneth St | CSS | 17 | J-48 |
| Kensard Ct | MSH | 35 | AC-33 |
| Kensignton Ct | EKT | 29 | Y-58 |
| Kensington Av | SJO | 23 | Y-16 |
| Kensington Dr | NLS | 4 | E-21 |
| Kensington Pl | MSH | 36 | AD-37 |
| Kent Ct | SJO | 25 | S-30 |
| Kent Dr | SJO | 25 | S-30 |
| Kent Ln | STB | 25 | Y-30 |
| Kent St | RSL | 24 | V-23 |
| Kent St | EKT | 28 | X-53 |
| Kentfield Wy | GSH | 51 | AN-76 |
| Kentfield Wy | GSH | 51 | AN-76 |
| Kentfield Wy | GSH | 51 | AN-77 |
| Kentucky Derby Dr | SJO | 26 | X-40 |
| Kentucky St N | STB | 24 | Y-18 |
| Kentucky St N | STB | 24 | Y-18 |
| Kentucky St S | STB | 34 | AA-18 |
| Kenwood Av | EKT | 29 | Y-59 |
| Kenwood Av | STB | 24 | Z-20 |
| Kenwood Dr | SJO | 22 | W-9 |
| Kenwood Pl | GSH | 51 | AN-74 |
| Kenwood St | SJO | 33 | Z-11 |
| Kenyon Av | EKT | 29 | Y-59 |
| Kepess Ct | STB | 24 | V-18 |
| Kercher Rd E | GSH | 51 | AQ-75 |
| Kercher Rd E | GSH | 51 | AQ-76 |
| Kercher Rd W | GSH | 50 | AQ-72 |
| Keria Tr | SJO | 34 | AF-21 |
| Kerlin Dr | SJO | 26 | S-34 |
| Kern Rd | SJO | 43 | AH-16 |
| Kern Rd | SJO | 44 | AH-21 |
| Kern Rd | SJO | 43 | AJ-10 |
| Kern Rd | STB | 44 | AJ-25 |
| Kern Rd | SJO | 45 | AJ-31 |
| Kern Rd | SJO | 45 | AJ-33 |
| Kern Rd | SJO | 46 | AJ-36 |
| Kern Rd | SJO | 47 | AJ-45 |
| Kerr St | STB | 34 | AB-22 |
| Kerry Ct | STB | 35 | AF-27 |
| Kershner Ln | ECO | 29 | V-63 |
| Kershner Ln | EKT | 29 | W-63 |
| Kerslake Ct | STB | 35 | AB-28 |
| Kesco Dr | BTL | 31 | U-75 |
| Kesler Av | ECO | 38 | AC-54 |
| Kessington Rd | CSS | 9 | E-66 |
| Kessington Rd | CSS | 9 | F-66 |
| Kessington Rd | CSS | 9 | H-66 |
| Kessington Rd | CSS | 19 | L-66 |
| Kessler Blvd | STB | 24 | X-21 |
| Kessler Pl | STB | 24 | X-21 |
| Kestrel Hills Dr | CSS | 15 | P-30 |
| Kettering Dr | STB | 25 | X-29 |
| Kevin Ct | STB | 35 | AE-27 |
| Key Ct | SJO | 25 | S-30 |
| Keystone Dr | ECO | 51 | AP-77 |
| Keystone Dr | GSH | 51 | AP-78 |
| Kholhaas | EKT | 28 | Z-53 |
| Kidder Ct | ECO | 19 | Q-59 |
| Kilarney Ln | BRN | 4 | F-19 |
| Kilbourn St | EKT | 28 | Y-55 |
| Killarney Ct | SJO | 15 | Q-29 |
| Killdeer Ct | CSS | 15 | P-30 |
| Killian Av | ECO | 18 | Q-55 |
| Killington Wy Dr | SJO | 35 | AH-28 |
| Kim Ct | EKT | 29 | W-61 |
| Kimberly Ct | SJO | 33 | AD-9 |
| Kimberly Dr | ECO | 50 | AL-67 |
| Kime Av | ECO | 39 | AE-62 |
| Kindig Dr | STB | 35 | AG-26 |
| King Rd | NLS | 4 | G-21 |
| King St | EKT | 38 | AA-55 |
| King St | STB | 24 | X-21 |
| King's Ct | MSH | 35 | AD-32 |
| King's Ct N | MSH | 35 | AD-32 |
| Kinglet Ln | SJO | 25 | U-27 |
| Kings Crossing | SJO | 15 | Q-30 |
| Kings East Dr | BRN | 4 | G-20 |
| Kings Rd | BRN | 4 | G-20 |
| Kings West Dr | BRN | 4 | G-20 |
| Kingsfield Ct | SJO | 16 | Q-38 |
| Kingsland Ct | ECO | 29 | V-64 |
| Kingsmen Ct | SJO | 36 | Z-40 |
| Kingsmill Ct | STB | 35 | AG-25 |
| Kingston Ct | ECO | 39 | AA-64 |
| Kingston Ct | SJO | 45 | AK-26 |
| Kingsway Ct | SJO | 44 | AN-23 |
| Kintyre Dr | STB | 35 | AG-27 |
| Kintz Av | SJO | 25 | U-26 |
| Kinyon St | STB | 24 | X-21 |
| Kinzy St | EKT | 39 | AA-58 |
| Kiowa Ct | SJO | 25 | U-26 |
| Kirby Ct | STB | 35 | AE-25 |
| Kirby Dr | EKT | 29 | X-60 |
| Kirkland Rd | ECO | 20 | Q-74 |
| Kirkshire Dr | STB | 35 | AG-27 |
| Kirkwood Ct | EKT | 29 | W-63 |
| Kiser Ct | ECO | 29 | U-58 |
| Kish Rd | CSS | 5 | F-32 |
| Kitch Rd | SJO | 36 | AF-36 |
| Klein Ct | EKT | 28 | Y-55 |
| Klem Dr | SJO | 32 | AB-8 |
| Kline Rd | SJO | 46 | AK-37 |
| Kline Rd | CSS | 16 | P-38 |
| Kline St | SJO | 36 | AC-38 |
| Kline Tr | SJO | 42 | AK-6 |
| Kline Tr | SJO | 42 | AK-7 |
| Klinger St | STB | 34 | AE-24 |
| Klinger St | STB | 34 | AE-25 |
| Knight Ct | ECO | 38 | AC-52 |
| Knight Dr | BRN | 3 | F-13 |
| Knoblock St | STB | 23 | X-17 |
| Knoll Dr | ECO | 38 | AE-53 |
| Knoll Dr | ECO | 38 | AE-54 |
| Knollwood Dr | SJO | 24 | U-25 |
| Koko Ct | SJO | 14 | R-18 |
| Kollar Rd | ECO | 28 | Y-51 |
| Korn St | CSS | 5 | A-28 |
| Korn St | CSS | 5 | A-31 |
| Kosciuszko St | STB | 34 | AA-21 |
| Kousa Ct | GSH | 50 | AL-69 |
| Krau St | EKT | 28 | Z-55 |
| Kraus Rd | CSS | 17 | L-42 |
| Krause Rd | SJO | 27 | Y-45 |
| Krieghbaum Dr | ECO | 38 | AC-53 |
| Kripe Ct | MSH | 25 | W-31 |
| Kristi Ln | SJO | 27 | X-46 |
| Kristie Ct | SJO | 27 | W-45 |
| Kristine Dr | CSS | 5 | E-28 |
| Kroft Dr | SJO | 14 | Q-20 |
| Kruger Dr | BRN | 4 | A-19 |
| Kubitschek Dr | SJO | 27 | W-44 |
| Kulp Av | ECO | 39 | AD-61 |
| Kundered Rd | GSH | 50 | AH-68 |
| Kunstman Ct | STB | 24 | Z-23 |
| **L** | | | |
| La Porte Av | STB | 24 | Y-21 |
| La Rue | ECO | 38 | AA-52 |
| La Salle Av | BRN | 14 | M-25 |
| La Salle Av E | STB | 34 | Z-25 |
| La Salle Av E | MSH | 35 | Z-32 |
| La Salle Av E | MSH | 36 | Z-36 |
| La Salle Av W | STB | 24 | Z-22 |
| La Salle Av W | MSH | 35 | Z-31 |
| La Salle St | EKT | 28 | Z-57 |
| Labrador Point Dr | SJO | 27 | Y-45 |
| Lacey Ln | ECO | 30 | Y-72 |
| Lacey Ln E | ECO | 30 | Y-72 |
| Ladbrooke Ln | STB | 45 | AJ-27 |
| Lady Fern Ct | SJO | 25 | U-26 |
| Lafayette Blvd N | STB | 24 | Y-23 |
| Lafayette Blvd N | STB | 24 | Z-23 |
| Lafayette Blvd S | STB | 34 | AB-23 |
| Lafayette St | STB | 34 | AC-23 |
| Lafayette St | STB | 34 | AF-23 |
| Lafayette St | EKT | 28 | Z-56 |
| Lafayette St E | GSH | 51 | AN-74 |
| Lafayette St W | GSH | 51 | AN-74 |
| Lafollette St | CSS | 15 | N-28 |
| Lagoon Ct | STB | 24 | V-20 |
| Lagoon Rd | ECO | 30 | W-67 |
| Laguna Dr | ECO | 30 | W-68 |
| Laing Av | MSH | 36 | AB-37 |
| Lake | BRN | 2 | F-2 |
| Lake Ct | SJO | 26 | W-36 |
| Lake Dr | CSS | 20 | P-74 |
| Lake Dr | ECO | 19 | R-58 |
| Lake Forest Ct | SJO | 25 | S-32 |
| Lake Front Dr | CSS | 20 | L-74 |
| Lake George Dr S | MSH | 26 | X-34 |
| Lake Knoll Ct | SJO | 25 | S-33 |
| Lake Ln | SJO | 22 | Y-9 |
| Lake Park | SJO | 22 | X-9 |
| Lake Pointe Ct | SJO | 16 | R-34 |
| Lake Rd | SJO | 24 | W-25 |
| Lake Shore Dr | OCS | 37 | AA-44 |
| Lake Shore Dr | OCS | 37 | Z-44 |
| Lake St | SJO | 37 | AB-42 |
| Lake St | BCH | 3 | E-10 |
| Lake St | NLS | 4 | E-25 |
| Lake St | CSS | 5 | E-27 |
| Lake St | BCH | 3 | F-10 |
| Lake St | EDW | 17 | K-43 |
| Lake St S | STB | 34 | AA-18 |
| Lake Stream Ct | MSH | 26 | X-34 |
| Lake Tr | CSS | 21 | M-76 |
| Lake Tr | CSS | 21 | N-76 |
| Lakegeorge Dr N | MSH | 26 | X-34 |
| Lakeland Dr | ECO | 29 | R-58 |
| Lakeland Rd | ECO | 29 | S-58 |
| Lakeshore Blvd | MSH | 25 | W-30 |
| Lakeshore Dr | CSS | 5 | E-30 |
| Lakeshore Dr | CSS | 5 | E-32 |
| Lakeshore Dr | CSS | 10 | E-70 |
| Lakeshore Dr | ECO | 29 | S-65 |
| Lakeshore Dr N | SJO | 25 | S-32 |
| Lakeshore Dr S | SJO | 25 | S-32 |
| Lakeside Ct | MSH | 35 | AF-33 |
| Lakespur Dr | SJO | 34 | AH-25 |
| Lakeview Av | ECO | 18 | R-56 |
| Lakeview Dr | GSH | 50 | AJ-73 |
| Lakeview Dr | CSS | 10 | D-70 |
| Lakeview Dr | BRN | 2 | E-3 |
| Lakeview Dr | CSS | 8 | H-51 |
| Lakeview Dr | CSS | 18 | J-51 |
| Lakeview Dr | CSS | 17 | M-48 |
| Lakeview Dr | CSS | 17 | M-48 |
| Lakeview Dr | CSS | 21 | N-75 |
| Lakeview Dr | SJO | 16 | P-35 |
| Lakeview Dr | SJO | 27 | Q-36 |
| Lakeview Dr | SJO | 22 | Z-8 |
| Lakewood Dr | STB | 35 | AF-26 |
| Lakewood Dr | ECO | 18 | R-57 |
| Lakewood Dr | SJO | 35 | W-30 |
| Lakewood Dr | SJO | 22 | W-9 |
| Lakewood-Norwood Dr | SJO | 22 | V-9 |
| Lamar Ct | EKT | 38 | AA-55 |
| Lamar Ln | SJO | 27 | V-46 |
| Lamar St | STR | 35 | AF-28 |
| Lamar St | SJO | 25 | V-26 |

| Name | City | Pg | Grid |
| --- | --- | --- | --- |
| Luth Ln | NLS | 4 | G-23 |
| Luther Ct | STB | 34 | Z-25 |
| Lykins Ln | BRN | 4 | F-20 |
| Lyndale Dr | SJO | 22 | W-8 |
| Lyndzi Ln | ECO | 38 | AD-51 |
| Lynn Dr | ECO | 39 | AG-62 |
| Lynn Dr | CSS | 5 | E-30 |
| Lynn St | SJO | 22 | X-1 |
| Lynn St | SJO | 23 | X-15 |
| Lynn St | MSH | 36 | Z-34 |
| Lynn St W | SJO | 23 | X-16 |
| Lynn-Way Ct | ECO | 39 | AE-61 |
| Lynne Ln | EKT | 39 | AC-58 |
| Lynne Ln N | EKT | 39 | AB-58 |
| Lynne Ln S | EKT | 39 | AC-58 |
| Lynolds Dr | ECO | 31 | S-75 |
| Lynwood Av | SJO | 24 | U-20 |
| Lynwood Dr | GHS | 50 | AK-70 |
| Lyric Ln | ECO | 28 | S-51 |

**M**

| Name | City | Pg | Grid |
| --- | --- | --- | --- |
| MacArthur Av | STB | 25 | X-28 |
| MacDougall Ct E | STB | 35 | AF-27 |
| MacDougall Ct W | STB | 35 | AF-27 |
| MacGregor Rd E | STB | 35 | AF-27 |
| MacGregor Rd S | STB | 35 | AF-27 |
| MacGregor Rd W | STB | 35 | AF-27 |
| Madeline | BRN | 14 | M-22 |
| Madison County Cir | SJO | 17 | Q-42 |
| Madison Rd | SJO | 43 | AM-14 |
| Madison Rd | SJO | 44 | AM-19 |
| Madison Rd | SJO | 44 | AM-2 |
| Madison Rd | SJO | 45 | AM-29 |
| Madison Rd | SJO | 45 | AM-33 |
| Madison Rd | SJO | 46 | AM-35 |
| Madison Rd | SJO | 46 | AM-40 |
| Madison Rd | SJO | 47 | AM-45 |
| Madison Rd | ECO | 48 | AM-52 |
| Madison Rd | SJO | 42 | AM-8 |
| Madison St | MSH | 35 | AB-32 |
| Madison St | MSH | 35 | AB-33 |
| Madison St | NLS | 4 | G-21 |
| Madison St | BRN | 14 | N-22 |
| Madison St | EKT | 29 | Y-58 |
| Madison St | STB | 25 | Z-27 |
| Madison St | SJO | 36 | Z-40 |
| Madison St E | GSH | 51 | AM-74 |
| Madison St E | STB | 24 | Z-25 |
| Madison St E | STB | 25 | Z-26 |
| Madison St W | GSH | 50 | AM-73 |
| Madison St W | STB | 24 | Z-23 |
| Madison Tr | SJO | 45 | AM-33 |
| Madison Tr | SJO | 46 | AP-34 |
| Madron Lake Rd | BRN | 2 | A-3 |
| Madron Lake Rd | BRN | 2 | B-4 |
| Madron Lake Rd | BRN | 2 | D-4 |
| Magnetic Dr | SJO | 36 | AA-38 |
| Magnolia Av | EKT | 28 | X-55 |
| Magnolia Ct | GSH | 50 | AL-70 |
| Magnolia Rd | SJO | 34 | AE-18 |
| Magnolia St | STB | 34 | AC-21 |
| Magnum Dr | EKT | 29 | Z-63 |
| Magyar Ct | STB | 34 | AC-20 |
| Main Av | SJO | 24 | W-24 |
| Main St | MSH | 35 | AA-32 |
| Main St | MSH | 35 | AB-32 |
| Main St | STB | 34 | AD-23 |
| Main St | SJO | 35 | AF-32 |
| Main St | EDW | 17 | K-43 |
| Main St | SJO | 16 | Q-40 |
| Main St | MSH | 25 | W-32 |
| Main St | MSH | 25 | X-32 |
| Main St | STB | 24 | Z-23 |
| Main St E | NLS | 4 | G-25 |
| Main St N | BRN | 2 | A-8 |
| Main St N | GHS | 50 | AK-73 |
| Main St N | BRN | 2 | C-8 |
| Main St N | EKT | 28 | X-56 |
| Main St N | STB | 24 | Y-23 |
| Main St S | MSH | 35 | AD-32 |
| Main St S | ECO | 39 | AE-62 |
| Main St S | STB | 34 | AG-23 |
| Main St S | GSH | 50 | AM-74 |
| Main St S | GSH | 51 | AQ-74 |
| Main St W | NLS | 4 | F-22 |
| Main St W | EDW | 17 | K-43 |
| Malcalm St | CSS | 5 | G-79 |
| Malcolm Dr | EKT | 39 | AC-59 |
| Malcor St | SJO | 33 | AF-15 |
| Malibar Ct | ECO | 39 | AE-61 |
| Mallard Ct | ECO | 39 | AB-65 |
| Mallard Dr | BRN | 13 | J-16 |
| Mallard Dr | SJO | 22 | Z-9 |
| Mallard Ln | MSH | 25 | W-30 |
| Mallard Pointe Dr | SJO | 26 | S-37 |
| Mallow Ct | SJO | 15 | Q-27 |
| Malvern Wy | STB | 35 | AD-27 |
| Manchester Dr | STB | 25 | Y-29 |
| Manchester Dr | STB | 25 | Z-29 |
| Manchester Ln | GSH | 50 | AL-68 |
| Manchester Ln | EKT | 29 | V-60 |
| Manhatten Av | ECO | 17 | P-48 |
| Manion Rd | SJO | 14 | R-21 |
| Manitou Pl | STB | 24 | Y-23 |
| Mannix St | CSS | 5 | D-33 |
| Mannix St | CSS | 6 | D-34 |
| Manor Av | EKT | 29 | Y-60 |
| Manor Dr | MSH | 36 | AB-38 |
| Manor Dr | STB | 35 | AF-27 |
| Manor Dr | ECO | 29 | Z-63 |
| Manor Haus Ct | GSH | 51 | AP-76 |
| Manor Ln | ECO | 29 | V-62 |
| Manroe | CSS | 18 | M-54 |
| Mansfield Dr | SJO | 14 | R-19 |
| Maple | BRN | 2 | F-3 |
| Maple City Dr | GSH | 51 | AR-79 |
| Maple Ct | ECO | 38 | AE-53 |
| Maple Ct | GSH | 50 | AM-71 |
| Maple Ct | GSH | 51 | AP-76 |
| Maple Ct | BCH | 3 | F-10 |
| Maple Dr | CSS | 17 | M-46 |
| Maple Glen | CSS | 18 | P-55 |
| Maple Grove | ECO | 19 | R-59 |
| Maple Hill Ct N | STB | 24 | U-20 |
| Maple Lane Av | SJO | 25 | W-28 |
| Maple Leaf Tr | CSS | 16 | N-34 |
| Maple Leaf Tr | CSS | 15 | P-33 |
| Maple Rd | SJO | 34 | AE-18 |
| Maple Rd | SJO | 44 | AN-18 |
| Maple Rd | SJO | 44 | AQ-18 |
| Maple Rd | STB | 24 | T-18 |
| Maple Ridge Ln | SJO | 25 | T-30 |
| Maple Row | EKT | 28 | Y-55 |
| Maple St | STB | 34 | AA-21 |
| Maple St | MSH | 35 | AA-33 |
| Maple St | NLS | 4 | F-23 |
| Maple St | NLS | 4 | G-24 |
| Maple St | EDW | 17 | K-43 |
| Maple St | CSS | 17 | N-47 |
| Maple St | BTL | 31 | V-75 |
| Maple Valley Dr | ECO | 38 | AD-54 |
| Maplecrest Dr | GSH | 51 | AJ-75 |
| Maplehurst Av | MSH | 36 | Z-34 |
| Maplehurst Av | SJO | 26 | Z-34 |
| Maplehurst Run | SJO | 25 | T-29 |
| Maplehurst St | SJO | 24 | V-25 |
| Maplewood Av | MSH | 36 | AB-39 |
| Maplewood Av | STB | 23 | X-17 |
| Maplewood Av | STB | 23 | X-17 |
| Maplewood Dr | NLS | 4 | H-20 |
| Maplewood Dr | ECO | 19 | R-58 |
| Marble St | BCH | 3 | G-10 |
| Marblehead Dr | MSH | 36 | AD-36 |
| Marchelle St | SJO | 25 | S-30 |
| Margaret Av | MSH | 35 | AA-33 |
| Margaret Av | SJO | 26 | Y-41 |
| Margaret Av | MSH | 35 | Z-33 |
| Margaret Dr | SJO | 27 | Z-46 |
| Margaret St | BRN | 5 | H-26 |
| Marguerite Av | EKT | 29 | X-62 |
| Marguerite Wy | ECO | 49 | AK-62 |
| Maribou Pl | GSH | 40 | AH-69 |
| Mariellen Av | MSH | 36 | AB-37 |
| Marietta St | STB | 34 | AB-25 |
| Marigold Wy | STB | 24 | X-22 |
| Marilyn Av | GSH | 50 | AP-74 |
| Marilyn Av | GSH | 51 | AP-74 |
| Marina Dr | ECO | 29 | U-63 |
| Marine Av | EKT | 29 | Y-58 |
| Marine St | STB | 35 | AB-26 |
| Marine St | STB | 35 | AC-26 |
| Marine St | STB | 35 | AC-26 |
| Marion Av | SJO | 24 | S-25 |
| Marion St | NLS | 4 | H-24 |
| Marion St E | MSH | 35 | AA-32 |
| Marion St E | MSH | 35 | AA-33 |
| Marion St E | EKT | 28 | Z-57 |
| Marion St W | MSH | 35 | AA-30 |
| Marion St W | STB | 24 | Z-23 |
| Marion St W | EKT | 28 | Z-56 |
| Mark Allen Dr | ECO | 39 | AD-65 |
| Mark Ct | SJO | 26 | R-40 |
| Mark Dr | ECO | 30 | V-71 |
| Mark Dr | ECO | 39 | AA-64 |
| Marker Ln | SJO | 36 | AF-35 |
| Market | NLS | 4 | F-22 |
| Market St | SJO | 33 | AF-16 |
| Markle Av | EKT | 38 | AB-54 |
| Markle Av | EKT | 38 | AB-56 |
| Marks St | BRN | 14 | P-23 |
| Marks St | SJO | 24 | T-25 |
| Marks St | SJO | 24 | U-25 |
| Marlborough Dr | GSH | 51 | AR-75 |
| Marlowe Wy | SJO | 15 | P-31 |
| Marmont St | NLS | 4 | E-22 |
| Marquette Av | STB | 24 | Y-23 |
| Marquette Blvd | SJO | 23 | X-14 |
| Marquette Blvd | STB | 24 | X-19 |
| Marquette Dr | BRN | 14 | K-21 |
| Marratt Dr | MSH | 36 | AD-38 |
| Mars Dr | ECO | 38 | AA-51 |
| Mars Dr | CSS | 5 | D-32 |
| Mars Dr W | ECO | 38 | AA-51 |
| Mars Ln | SJO | 35 | AF-29 |
| Marshal St | STB | 35 | AA-28 |
| Marshall Av | STB | 35 | AA-30 |
| Marshall Av | EKT | 29 | X-62 |
| Marshall Blvd | EKT | 29 | Y-62 |
| Marshall Blvd | EKT | 29 | Y-62 |
| Marshall Dr | MSH | 36 | AC-36 |
| Marshall Dr N | SJO | 22 | V-7 |
| Marshall Sr S | SJO | 22 | V-7 |
| Marshlyn Dr | CSS | 5 | E-28 |
| Martin | EKT | 28 | Z-53 |
| Martin Av | ECO | 39 | AF-63 |
| Martin Ln | SJO | 25 | U-28 |
| Martin Manor Dr | GSH | 50 | AR-73 |
| Martin Manor Dr | GSH | 50 | AR-74 |
| Martin Rd | CSS | 17 | N-50 |
| Martindale | ECO | 39 | AC-61 |
| Martindale Rd | SJO | 43 | AN-10 |
| Martindale Rd | SJO | 43 | AN-13 |
| Martindale Rd | SJO | 44 | AN-21 |
| Martindale Rd | SJO | 47 | AN-45 |
| Martinsville Ct | SJO | 27 | W-43 |
| Marvin St | ECO | 29 | S-60 |
| Mary Beth Ct | SJO | 32 | AB-8 |
| Mary St | ECO | 39 | AE-63 |
| Mary St | CSS | 5 | D-31 |
| Marydale Dr | ECO | 39 | AG-64 |
| Marydon Ln | ECO | 37 | AC-47 |
| Maryland St | EKT | 38 | AA-57 |
| Mason St | CSS | 19 | J-62 |
| Mason St | CSS | 18 | K-57 |
| Mason St | CSS | 20 | K-67 |
| Mason St | BRN | 14 | N-23 |
| Mason St | EKT | 28 | Z-56 |
| Mason St N | MSH | 36 | AB-34 |
| Mason St S | MSH | 36 | AB-34 |
| Mason St S | MSH | 36 | AE-34 |
| Massachusetts Av | EKT | 28 | Z-54 |
| Mast Dr | ECO | 38 | AD-46 |
| Mather Av | EKT | 39 | AB-58 |
| Matthews Ln | STB | 35 | AH-26 |
| Maude St | ECO | 28 | V-53 |
| Maumee Ct | EKT | 38 | AB-57 |
| Maumee Dr | SJO | 17 | Q-43 |
| Max St | CSS | 17 | L-42 |
| May Apple Tr | SJO | 27 | Y-43 |
| May Apple Tr E | SJO | 27 | Y-44 |
| May Apple Tr W | SJO | 27 | Y-43 |
| May Rd | SJO | 24 | T-20 |
| May St | EKT | 39 | AA-58 |
| May St | CSS | 5 | M-39 |
| May St | CSS | 17 | M-44 |
| May St | CSS | 17 | M-47 |
| May St | CSS | 17 | M-49 |
| May St | CSS | 18 | M-52 |
| May St | SJO | 23 | X-15 |
| May St | SJO | 23 | X-16 |
| Mayfair Ct | SJO | 25 | T-29 |
| Mayfair Dr | SJO | 14 | Q-24 |
| Mayfair Pl | STB | 33 | AA-15 |
| Mayfield Dr | GHS | 50 | AK-69 |
| Mayflower Cir | STB | 33 | AB-14 |
| Mayflower Dr | NLS | 4 | H-20 |
| Mayflower Pl | GSH | 50 | AP-74 |
| Mayflower Rd | SJO | 33 | AD-15 |
| Mayflower Rd | SJO | 33 | AG-15 |
| Mayflower Rd | SJO | 43 | AH-15 |
| Mayflower Rd | SJO | 43 | AK-15 |
| Mayflower Rd | BRN | 3 | G-15 |
| Mayflower Rd | BRN | 13 | M-15 |
| Mayflower Rd | BRN | 13 | N-15 |
| Mayflower Rd | SJO | 23 | S-15 |
| Mayflower Rd | SJO | 33 | Z-15 |
| Mayflowerdr | STB | 33 | AB-15 |
| Maywood Ct | GSH | 51 | AN-77 |
| Maywood Pl | STB | 33 | AB-16 |
| McArthur Ct | SJO | 22 | V-7 |
| McCartney St | STB | 24 | X-21 |
| McClain Ln | CSS | 18 | J-55 |
| McCombs St N | RSL | 24 | U-23 |
| McCombs St S | RSL | 24 | V-23 |
| McCoy Dr | BCH | 3 | G-9 |
| McCumber St | BCH | 2 | F-9 |
| McDonald St | EKT | 29 | Z-59 |
| McDowell St | EKT | 29 | V-56 |
| McErlain St | SJO | 25 | W-27 |
| McErlain St | SJO | 25 | W-28 |
| McErlain St | SJO | 25 | W-29 |
| McGill St | STB | 24 | U-18 |
| McIntosh Ln | ECO | 50 | AQ-73 |
| McKee St | BRN | 14 | L-23 |
| McKelvy Av | ECO | 39 | AB-61 |
| McKinley Av | STB | 24 | Z-25 |
| McKinley Av | MSH | 25 | Z-30 |
| McKinley Av | SJO | 26 | Z-36 |
| McKinley Av | EKT | 28 | Z-57 |
| McKnight St | MSH | 36 | Z-35 |
| McNaughton Av | EKT | 28 | X-54 |
| McNaughton St | EKT | 28 | X-53 |
| McPherson St | STB | 34 | AA-22 |
| McPherson St | STB | 34 | AC-22 |
| McPherson St | EKT | 29 | X-58 |
| McQuade St | SJO | 33 | AB-10 |
| McWuade St | SJO | 22 | V-9 |
| Mead Rd | BRN | 3 | D-12 |
| Meade Rd | BRN | 14 | A-25 |
| Meade St | STB | 34 | AD-19 |
| Meade St N | STB | 24 | W-19 |
| Meade St N | STB | 24 | Z-19 |
| Meade St S | STB | 34 | AA-19 |
| Meade St S | STB | 34 | AD-19 |
| Meadow Bank Ln | ECO | 29 | W-66 |
| Meadow Crest Dr | SJO | 24 | S-17 |
| Meadow Dr | NLS | 4 | G-21 |
| Meadow Dr | CSS | 17 | P-44 |

| Name | City | Pg | Grid | Name | City | Pg | Grid | Name | City | Pg | Grid | Name | City | Pg | Grid |
|---|---|---|---|---|---|---|---|---|---|---|---|---|---|---|---|
| Neitzel Ct | STB | 34 | AB-24 | Northview Dr | STB | 24 | V-21 | Oakbrook Dr | STB | 24 | U-19 | Old Spanish Tr | SJO | 44 | AJ-21 |
| Nelson St | ECO | 38 | AC-55 | Northwood Ct | SJO | 33 | AD-10 | Oakcrest Dr | ECO | 27 | V-46 | Old Stable Ln | MSH | 35 | AB-31 |
| Nevada St | EKT | 28 | V-57 | Northwood Dr | SJO | 33 | AD-9 | Oakcrest Dr | STB | 25 | Z-30 | Old Sycamore Ct | SJO | 15 | R-31 |
| New Energy Dr | STB | 34 | AD-19 | Northwood Dr | ECO | 28 | W-53 | Oakdale Av | BRN | 14 | J-24 | Old Trace Ct | SJO | 26 | S-36 |
| New London Ct | STB | 25 | W-27 | Northwood Dr | STB | 25 | Y-27 | Oakdale Av | SJO | 24 | R-23 | Old Valley Loop | SJO | 25 | S-29 |
| New Rd | SJO | 43 | AP-14 | Norton Ct | MSH | 36 | AB-39 | Oakdale Av | SJO | 24 | S-23 | Old Valley Loop | SJO | 25 | T-30 |
| New Rd | SJO | 42 | AP-2 | Norton Dr | STB | 35 | AF-26 | Oakdale Av | SJO | 24 | S-24 | Old Walnut Ct | SJO | 14 | Q-19 |
| New Rd | SJO | 44 | AP-22 | Norton Rd | CSS | 11 | B-82 | Oakdale Dr | EKT | 38 | AB-56 | Old Walton Rd | BRN | 3 | E-12 |
| New Rd | SJO | 45 | AP-28 | Norton Rd | CSS | 11 | C-82 | Oakhill Ct | SJO | 15 | Q-31 | Olde Town Rd | ECO | 41 | AC-75 |
| New Rd | SJO | 45 | AP-33 | Nortwood Dr | MSH | 25 | Y-32 | Oakland Av | EKT | 38 | AB-55 | Oldham Ct | STB | 45 | AH-26 |
| New Rd | SJO | 46 | AP-40 | Norway Maple Ct N | STB | 24 | U-20 | Oakland Av | ECO | 38 | AE-55 | Oldmill Rd | SJO | 15 | R-21 |
| New Rd | SJO | 47 | AP-45 | Norwich Ct | STB | 45 | AH-26 | Oakland Av | GSH | 50 | AL-72 | Oldridge St | STB | 44 | AJ-24 |
| New Rd | SJO | 42 | AP-8 | Norwich Dr | SJO | 15 | R-30 | Oakland Av | SJO | 24 | T-23 | Olds Av | STB | 23 | Z-15 |
| New St | GSH | 50 | AL-73 | Norwood St | ECO | 38 | AB-53 | Oakland Av N | MSH | 36 | AA-40 | Olean Pl | EKT | 29 | X-63 |
| New York Cir | STB | 33 | AB-14 | Norwood St | CSS | 5 | D-31 | Oakland Av S | MSH | 36 | AB-40 | Olin | ECO | 27 | V-48 |
| New York Dr | STB | 33 | AB-15 | Notre Dame Av | SJO | 14 | Q-25 | Oakland Hill Dr | ECO | 38 | AD-55 | Olive Av | EKT | 28 | X-56 |
| New York St | GSH | 51 | AN-74 | Notre Dame Av N | SJO | 24 | X-25 | Oakland St | STB | 35 | AB-26 | Olive Rd | SJO | 33 | AC-12 |
| Newburg Ct | MSH | 25 | X-32 | Notre Dame Av N | STB | 24 | Z-25 | Oakland St | SJO | 14 | Q-22 | Olive Rd | SJO | 23 | V-12 |
| Newburg Dr | MSH | 25 | Y-32 | Notre Dame Av S | STB | 34 | AA-25 | Oakland St | SJO | 24 | S-23 | Olive Rd W | SJO | 33 | AC-12 |
| Newcome St | STB | 34 | AA-19 | Nottingham Ln | SJO | 14 | P-20 | Oakleaf Dr | CSS | 17 | M-48 | Olive St | STB | 34 | AB-20 |
| Newell Ct | EKT | 28 | Z-54 | Nottingham Ln | ECO | 39 | AG-64 | Oakleaf Pl | ECO | 28 | Y-51 | Olive St | OCS | 37 | AB-45 |
| Newell St | ECO | 28 | U-57 | Nottingham Ln | ECO | 29 | V-65 | Oakley Av N | MSH | 36 | AB-39 | Olive St | GHS | 51 | AK-75 |
| Newman St | ECO | 39 | AC-61 | Nottingham Shire Dr | SJO | 17 | Q-44 | Oakley Av S | MSH | 36 | AB-39 | Olive St N | STB | 24 | X-20 |
| Newport Ct | MSH | 25 | Y-32 | Nursery Ct | STB | 35 | AB-29 | Oakmont Central Dr | SJO | 24 | U-25 | Oliver St | STB | 34 | AC-22 |
| Newport Pointe Ct | SJO | 24 | S-25 | Nursery Dr | ECO | 39 | AA-63 | Oakmont East Dr | SJO | 24 | U-25 | Oliver St | STB | 34 | AC-22 |
| Newton Av | SJO | 44 | AR-21 | Nursey Av | SJO | 26 | Y-41 | Oakmont North Dr | SJO | 24 | U-25 | Olivia Cir | STB | 35 | AE-26 |
| Newton Dr | EKT | 29 | W-62 | Nutex Dr | STB | 23 | S-12 | Oakmont South Dr | SJO | 24 | U-25 | Olympic Dr | SJO | 22 | R-8 |
| Niagara St | STB | 35 | AF-28 | Nutmeg Ct | SJO | 34 | AH-25 | Oakmont West Dr | SJO | 24 | U-25 | Omer Av E | MSH | 35 | Z-32 |
| Nicar Rd | SJO | 45 | AQ-31 | | | | | Oakridge Av E | GHS | 50 | AK-73 | Ontario Dr | BRN | 3 | H-12 |
| Nicklaus Dr | GSH | 51 | AJ-75 | **O** | | | | Oakridge St W | GHS | 50 | AK-73 | Ontario Dr | BRN | 3 | H-13 |
| Nicole Dr N | SJO | 27 | S-43 | O'Brien St | STB | 24 | X-20 | Oaks Spring Dr | ECO | 27 | V-46 | Ontario Rd | BRN | 14 | N-25 |
| Nicole Dr S | SJO | 27 | S-43 | O'Brien St | STB | 24 | Y-20 | Oakside Av | SJO | 36 | AC-39 | Opal St | STB | 34 | AG-22 |
| Nicole Dr W | SJO | 27 | S-43 | O'Brien St | STB | 24 | Z-20 | Oakside Dr | SJO | 22 | W-9 | Orange Av | MSH | 36 | AB-39 |
| Nieb Ct | NLS | 4 | G-22 | O'Connor St | MSH | 35 | AB-32 | Oakside St E | STB | 34 | AD-24 | Orange Rd | SJO | 43 | AH-13 |
| Nieb St | NLS | 4 | G-21 | Oak Bridge Ct | SJO | 17 | Q-42 | Oakside St W | STB | 34 | AD-23 | Orange Rd | SJO | 43 | AM-13 |
| Niles Av | STB | 24 | Y-24 | Oak Brook Dr | ECO | 27 | U-46 | Oakton Dr | SJO | 25 | U-29 | Orange Rd | SJO | 43 | AQ-13 |
| Niles Av N | MSH | 36 | AB-34 | Oak Cir | ECO | 38 | AD-53 | Oaktree Ln | ECO | 20 | Q-68 | Orange Rd | BRN | 13 | M-13 |
| Niles Av N | STB | 34 | Z-24 | Oak Ct | GSH | 51 | AP-76 | Oakview Cir | SJO | 27 | Z-45 | Orange Rd | SJO | 13 | Q-13 |
| Niles Av S | STB | 34 | Z-24 | Oak Dale Dr | STB | 35 | AF-26 | Oakwood Av | EKT | 28 | T-57 | Orange Rd | SJO | 23 | S-12 |
| Niles-Buchanan Rd | BRN | 3 | F-14 | Oak Dr | CSS | 17 | M-47 | Oakwood Blvd | STB | 24 | W-21 | Orange Rd | SJO | 23 | Y-13 |
| Niles-Buchanan Rd | BRN | 3 | F-18 | Oak Dr | ECO | 27 | Y-46 | Oakwood Ct | ECO | 39 | AD-63 | Orange Rd | SJO | 23 | Z-13 |
| Nimtz Pkwy | STB | 23 | T-16 | Oak Forest Rd | BRN | 12 | N-7 | Oakwood Dr | GSH | 51 | AJ-68 | Orange St | EKT | 28 | W-57 |
| Nimtz Pkwy | STB | 23 | U-14 | Oak Grove Dr | ECO | 28 | Z-51 | Oakwood Ln | SJO | 17 | R-42 | Orange St | STB | 24 | Z-20 |
| Nimtz Pkwy | STB | 23 | U-17 | Oak Hill Blvd | SJO | 15 | R-31 | Oakwood Park Dr | STB | 24 | V-19 | Orchard Av | STB | 33 | AB-15 |
| Nittany Ct | SJO | 25 | S-38 | Oak Hollow Ln | SJO | 14 | R-19 | Oakwood Pl | ECO | 28 | Y-51 | Orchard Av | SJO | 33 | AB-42 |
| Noak Hill Dr | STB | 25 | X-27 | Oak Leaf Cove | STB | 24 | V-19 | Oakwood St | EKT | 28 | W-54 | Orchard Ct | MSH | 36 | AB-33 |
| Noble Ct | GSH | 50 | AL-73 | Oak Leaf Ct | SJO | 26 | X-36 | Oatfield Ct | SJO | 23 | R-12 | Orchard Dr | ECO | 50 | AQ-73 |
| Noble Ridge Dr | SJO | 34 | AH-21 | Oak Leaf Dr | SJO | 26 | W-36 | Oatfield Ln | GSH | 50 | AM-70 | Orchard Heights Dr | STB | 44 | AJ-24 |
| Noble St | EKT | 39 | AB-55 | Oak Leaf Ln | GSH | 51 | AP-76 | Ohio St | STB | 34 | AB-24 | Orchard Ln | ECO | 38 | AC-64 |
| Noelwood Dr | GSH | 51 | AR-75 | Oak Lined Dr | SJO | 17 | R-42 | Ohio St | MSH | 35 | AC-33 | Orchard Ln | BRN | 4 | H-19 |
| Nora St | ECO | 39 | AD-63 | Oak Ln | GSH | 51 | AN-77 | Ohio St | GSH | 51 | AN-75 | Orchard Ridge Ct | SJO | 25 | R-30 |
| Nora St | ECO | 39 | AD-63 | Oak Manor Dr | SJO | 27 | T-45 | Oil City Rd | CSS | 7 | C-50 | Orchard St | SJO | 14 | Q-24 |
| Norfolk Ct | MSH | 36 | AD-38 | Oak Manor Pl | ECO | 28 | Z-51 | Oil City Rd | CSS | 7 | F-50 | Orchard St | EKT | 29 | Y-58 |
| Norman | ECO | 50 | AQ-73 | Oak Park Ct | STB | 35 | AC-25 | Okema St | EKT | 38 | AA-54 | Orchid Av | GSH | 50 | AJ-67 |
| Norman St | STB | 34 | AF-23 | Oak Park Dr | STB | 25 | X-27 | Old 112 | CSS | 21 | J-78 | Orchid Rd | SJO | 33 | AA-13 |
| Normandy Dr | MSH | 25 | Z-32 | Oak Park Dr | STB | 25 | X-27 | Old 112 | CSS | 21 | J-79 | Orchid Rd | SJO | 33 | AB-13 |
| North | SJO | 17 | P-42 | Oak Rd | SJO | 33 | AA-14 | Old Bedford Tr | SJO | 26 | W-34 | Orchid Rd | SJO | 23 | Y-13 |
| North Dr | GSH | 51 | AM-70 | Oak Rd | SJO | 33 | AA-14 | Old Cleveland Rd | SJO | 23 | U-11 | Oregon Av | ECO | 37 | AA-49 |
| North Dr | ECO | 28 | V-56 | Oak Rd | SJO | 43 | AK-14 | Old Cleveland Rd | STB | 23 | U-16 | Oregon St N | OCS | 37 | AB-43 |
| North Shore Dr E | STB | 24 | Y-24 | Oak Rd | SJO | 43 | AP-14 | Old Creek Ct | SJO | 26 | Z-38 | Oriole Av | SJO | 32 | AA-9 |
| North Shore Dr W | STB | 24 | Y-22 | Oak Rd | SJO | 43 | AQ-14 | Old Dover Ln | SJO | 15 | Q-29 | Oriole Ct | STB | 44 | AJ-24 |
| North Shore Dr W | STB | 24 | Y-23 | Oak Rd | SJO | 23 | W-14 | Old English Ct | STB | 45 | AH-27 | Oriole Ct | ECO | 3 | AC-48 |
| North Side Blvd N | STB | 34 | AA-25 | Oak Ridge Dr | EKT | 38 | AD-56 | Old Farm Dr | EKT | 38 | AC-57 | Oriole St | CSS | 5 | C-32 |
| North St | SJO | 32 | AF-4 | Oak Ridge Dr | STB | 25 | Y-27 | Old Farm Rd | SJO | 16 | Q-35 | Orkney Dr | STB | 35 | AF-27 |
| North St | BRN | 14 | J-24 | Oak Run Dr | SJO | 25 | S-31 | Old Farm Rd | ECO | 27 | U-47 | Osage Dr | ECO | 39 | AB-65 |
| North St | EKT | 29 | Z-54 | Oak Springs Dr | CSS | 17 | J-49 | Old Hickory | SJO | 25 | T-29 | Osage Dr | SJO | 24 | U-25 |
| Northern Av | SJO | 25 | W-28 | Oak St | MSH | 35 | AA-33 | Old Jenifer Rd | SJO | 15 | Q-31 | Osage Lake Dr | MSH | 25 | V-32 |
| Northfield Dr | BRN | 14 | L-25 | Oak St | BCH | 3 | F-10 | Old Lantern Tr | SJO | 15 | Q-31 | Osborn Av | ECO | 27 | Y-48 |
| Northfield Dr | SJO | 16 | Q-35 | Oak St | NLS | 4 | F-23 | Old Mill Ct | SJO | 25 | S-25 | Osborn Ct | BRN | 15 | M-26 |
| Northfield Dr | ECO | 28 | S-55 | Oak St | NLS | 4 | F-25 | Old Mill Dr | ECO | 29 | W-65 | Osborne Rd | SJO | 44 | AQ-21 |
| Northfork Ln | ECO | 27 | W-46 | Oak St | BRN | 2 | F-3 | Old Mill Rd | SJO | 24 | S-21 | Osborne Rd | SJO | 45 | AQ-31 |
| Northill Ct | SJO | 15 | R-31 | Oak St | CSS | 7 | H-49 | Old Oak Ct | SJO | 17 | R-42 | Osborne Rd | SJO | 46 | AQ-34 |
| Northlea Dr | SJO | 33 | AA-12 | Oak St | CSS | 20 | L-74 | Old Oak Dr | SJO | 17 | R-42 | Osborne Rd | SJO | 46 | AQ-36 |
| Northlea Dr | STB | 24 | T-21 | Oak St | CSS | 17 | N-47 | Old Orchard Ln | ECO | 39 | AA-61 | Osborne Rd | SJO | 47 | AQ-45 |
| Northouth Ct | STB | 45 | AH-27 | Oak St | EKT | 28 | X-54 | Old Pine Ln | SJO | 26 | W-36 | Osborne Rd | SJO | 42 | AR-1 |
| Northridge Dr | SJO | 22 | R-9 | Oak St | STB | 24 | Z-22 | Old Port Cv | ECO | 30 | U-72 | Osborne Rd | SJO | 43 | AR-15 |
| Northridge Dr | SJO | 22 | S-9 | Oak St N | OCS | 37 | AB-44 | Old Post Ln | SJO | 25 | S-29 | Osborne Rd | SJO | 42 | AR-3 |
| Northridge Dr | SJO | 22 | S-9 | Oak View Dr | EKT | 28 | W-51 | Old Rd | CSS | 8 | H-51 | Osborne Rd | SJO | 42 | AR-6 |
| Northrop St | CSS | 9 | A-61 | Oakbrook Ct | SJO | 25 | S-31 | Old Sauk Tr | NLS | 4 | G-20 | Osceola Av | OCS | 37 | AB-45 |
| Northview Dr | EKT | 28 | S-56 | | | | | Old Settlers Trace | SJO | 32 | AC-8 | | | | |

| Name | City | Pg | Grid | Name | City | Pg | Grid | Name | City | Pg | Grid | Name | City | Pg | Grid |
|---|---|---|---|---|---|---|---|---|---|---|---|---|---|---|---|
| Pleasant View Rd | ECO | 39 | AF-61 | Praire Av S | MSH | 36 | AB-36 | Putnam Pl | STB | 24 | Y-18 | Red Bird Ct | SJO | 36 | AF-37 |
| Pleasant Wood Ct | ECO | 39 | AD-63 | Prairie Av | STB | 34 | AA-23 | Pyle Av | STB | 25 | X-28 | Red Blossom Dr | GSH | 50 | AN-71 |
| Pletcher Av | BRN | 14 | M-23 | Prairie Av | STB | 34 | AB-22 | | | | | Red Bud Ln | ECO | 37 | AB-47 |
| Pletcher St | EKT | 28 | Z-56 | Prairie Av | SJO | 34 | AD-18 | **Q** | | | | Red Bud Pl | ECO | 37 | AC-46 |
| Plover Ln | SJO | 25 | U-27 | Prairie Av | GSH | 50 | AM-71 | Quail Hollow Ct | SJO | 16 | Q-34 | Red Bud Tr | BRN | 3 | C-9 |
| Plum St | EKT | 28 | Y-55 | Prairie Ct | SJO | 16 | R-35 | Quail Pointe Dr | ECO | 27 | S-47 | Red Bud Tr | BRN | 3 | D-9 |
| Plym Park Dr | NLS | 4 | E-23 | Prairie Ct | EKT | 29 | Y-58 | Quail Ridge | SJO | 15 | Q-32 | Red Bud Tr | BRN | 3 | H-10 |
| Plym Park Rd | NLS | 4 | E-23 | Prairie St | EKT | 38 | AB-58 | Quail Tr | MSH | 25 | W-30 | Red Bud Tr | BRN | 13 | J-10 |
| Plym Rd | NLS | 4 | H-21 | Prairie St | CSS | 8 | H-55 | Quail Valley Dr | SJO | 25 | S-33 | Red Bud Tr N | BCH | 3 | E-11 |
| Plymouth Av E | GSH | 51 | AM-75 | Prairie St | SJO | 16 | Q-40 | Quailisland Dr | EKT | 28 | Y-52 | Red Bud Tr S | BRN | 13 | K-10 |
| Plymouth Av W | GSH | 50 | AN-72 | Prast Blvd | STB | 24 | Y-19 | Quality Dr | STB | 23 | S-12 | Red Bur Tr | BCH | 3 | F-10 |
| Plymouth Cir | STB | 33 | AB-15 | Prast Blvd | STB | 24 | Y-20 | Quebec St | ECO | 39 | AC-62 | Red Fox Ct | SJO | 34 | AG-20 |
| Pogwood Rd | SJO | 26 | Z-39 | Preakness Ln | SJO | 26 | X-40 | Queen St | GHS | 50 | AK-73 | Red Fox Dr | SJO | 16 | Q-36 |
| Pointe Blvd N | EKT | 28 | S-56 | Pregel Dr | MSH | 25 | Z-32 | Queen St | STB | 24 | X-21 | Red Fox Tr | SJO | 23 | U-10 |
| Pointe Dr | ECO | 29 | W-65 | Prescott Av | SJO | 14 | R-24 | Queen's Row | SJO | 25 | S-26 | Red Maple Ct | STB | 24 | U-18 |
| Pointe Dr | SJO | 17 | R-44 | Prescott Av | SJO | 24 | S-24 | Queensboro Av | MSH | 35 | AC-28 | Red Oak Dr | SJO | 17 | Q-42 |
| Pointe Dr W | SJO | 22 | V-7 | Prescott Dr | MSH | 36 | AD-37 | Queensboro St | STB | 35 | AG-28 | Red Oak Tr | CSS | 16 | L-37 |
| Pointers Wy | SJO | 26 | S-37 | Preston Dr | STB | 25 | Z-29 | Queensburo St | STB | 35 | AF-28 | Red Pine Dr | SJO | 17 | Q-45 |
| Pokagon St | NLS | 4 | E-23 | Preston St | CSS | 11 | A-79 | Quimby St | STB | 34 | AA-25 | Red Rasberry | SJO | 27 | T-45 |
| Pokagon St | NLS | 4 | E-23 | Prestonwood Ct | SJO | 16 | P-37 | Quince Rd | SJO | 32 | AA-8 | Redbud Ct | GSH | 51 | AP-76 |
| Pokagon St | SJO | 26 | X-37 | Preswick Ct | SJO | 27 | U-45 | Quince Rd | SJO | 32 | AF-8 | Redbud Ln | STB | 25 | Z-15 |
| Pokagon St | SJO | 26 | X-39 | Preswick Ln | SJO | 15 | R-32 | Quince Rd | SJO | 22 | U-8 | Redcoach Dr | MSH | 25 | X-31 |
| Pokagon St E | STB | 24 | X-24 | Priem Rd | ECO | 27 | Y-48 | Quincey St | SJO | 25 | T-31 | Reddick St | MSH | 35 | AC-29 |
| Pokagon St W | STB | 24 | X-23 | Primrose Av | EKT | 39 | AB-60 | Quincy Dr | MSH | 36 | AD-38 | Reddick St | MSH | 35 | AC-29 |
| Poland St | STB | 34 | AA-21 | Primrose Cir | ECO | 28 | Z-51 | Quincy St | EKT | 28 | X-57 | Redding Av | EKT | 28 | Z-57 |
| Poland St W | STB | 34 | AA-19 | Primrose Rd | SJO | 43 | AN-9 | Quite Ride Ct | SJO | 44 | AH-21 | Redfield Rd | CSS | 16 | N-36 |
| Poland St W | STB | 34 | AA-21 | Primrose Rd | SJO | 43 | AQ-9 | | | | | Redfield Rd | CSS | 16 | N-41 |
| Polaris Dr | SJO | 15 | P-28 | Primrose Rd | SJO | 22 | T-9 | | | | | Redfield Rd | CSS | 17 | N-46 |
| Polis St | BCH | 2 | F-9 | Primrose Tr | SJO | 12 | Q-8 | **R** | | | | Redfield Rd | CSS | 18 | N-55 |
| Pollitt Ct | MSH | 35 | AA-33 | Prince Albert Ct | SJO | 15 | Q-28 | R Workingham | SJO | 27 | Z-43 | Redfield St | CSS | 15 | N-32 |
| Polo Av | EKT | 39 | AD-61 | Princess Av | ECO | 29 | W-65 | Race St N | MSH | 35 | AB-32 | Redfieldrun | CSS | 16 | P-38 |
| Ponader Dr | SJO | 25 | V-28 | Princess City Dr | MSH | 35 | AA-31 | Race St S | MSH | 35 | AB-32 | Redspire Blvd | GSH | 50 | AL-69 |
| Ponader Dr | SJO | 25 | V-28 | Princess Dr | SJO | 35 | AE-32 | Raider Dr | ECO | 39 | AB-62 | Redstart Ln | SJO | 25 | U-27 |
| Pond St | SJO | 24 | R-23 | Princess Wy | SJO | 16 | Q-39 | Railroad St | SJO | 32 | AG-5 | Redstone Dr | SJO | 15 | Q-28 |
| Ponderosa Ct | SJO | 33 | AB-12 | Princeton Ct | SJO | 25 | T-31 | Railroad St | SJO | 43 | AK-15 | Redwing Dr | STB | 24 | V-18 |
| Ponderosa Dr | BTL | 31 | V-76 | Princeton Dr | MSH | 36 | AD-38 | Railroad Tr | SJO | 33 | AD-13 | Redwood Av | GSH | 50 | AH-67 |
| Ponderosa Rd | CSS | 8 | G-51 | Princeton St | EKT | 29 | Z-58 | Rain Drop Cir | SJO | 17 | R-46 | Redwood Ct | MSH | 25 | Y-31 |
| Ponderosa Rd | CSS | 8 | G-52 | Pringle Dr | GHS | 50 | AK-70 | Rainbow Bend Blvd | EKT | 28 | Z-53 | Redwood Rd | SJO | 42 | AL-7 |
| Ponsha St | SJO | 25 | W-28 | Prinz Ct | STB | 35 | AB-26 | Rainbow Dr | CSS | 10 | E-71 | Redwood Rd | SJO | 42 | AQ-7 |
| Ponsha St | SJO | 25 | W-28 | Priscilla Av | ECO | 37 | AC-48 | Rainbow Dr | STB | 24 | T-21 | Redwood Tr | SJO | 12 | R-7 |
| Poplar St | NLS | 4 | E-23 | Priscilla Ct | ECO | 37 | AC-49 | Rainbow Rd | CSS | 10 | F-70 | Reed Rd | BRN | 2 | C-8 |
| Poplar St | EKT | 28 | X-56 | Priscilla Dr | STB | 33 | AB-15 | Raintree Ct | ECO | 38 | AD-50 | Reedy Dr | ECO | 28 | T-63 |
| Poplar St | STB | 24 | Z-21 | Prism Valley Dr | MSH | 35 | AD-33 | Raintree Dr | ECO | 17 | R-47 | Reek Rd | SJO | 27 | Y-42 |
| Poplardr | GSH | 50 | AJ-67 | Pritchard Dr | BRN | 4 | B-21 | Raintree Dr | ECO | 29 | W-60 | Reese Dr | CSS | 5 | E-30 |
| Poppy Ct | MSH | 36 | AE-34 | Privet Ln | STB | 35 | AD-26 | Raintree Dr | SJO | 27 | Z-43 | Reeves Dr | SJO | 27 | Y-43 |
| Poppy Ct | MSH | 36 | AE-34 | Professional Dr | GSH | 50 | AN-71 | Raleigh Dr | SJO | 35 | AH-25 | Regency Park Dr | SJO | 15 | Q-31 |
| Poppy Rd | SJO | 33 | AB-10 | Professional Dr | GSH | 50 | AN-72 | Ralph Jones Ct | STB | 23 | T-17 | Regent Ct | STB | 45 | AH-26 |
| Poppy Rd | SJO | 33 | AC-10 | Progress Dr | STB | 23 | W-17 | Ralph Jones Dr | STB | 23 | T-17 | Regent St | ECO | 51 | AR-76 |
| Poppy Rd | SJO | 43 | AL-10 | Progress Dr | STB | 23 | W-17 | Ramblewood Ln | ECO | 39 | AA-63 | Regent St | NLS | 4 | F-23 |
| Poppy Rd | SJO | 13 | Q-10 | Prospect Av | GHS | 50 | AK-73 | Ramblewood Ln | SJO | 32 | AD-9 | Regent St | NLS | 4 | F-25 |
| Poppy Rd | SJO | 23 | U-10 | Prospect Dr | MSH | 36 | AA-34 | Rambling Rose Ln | MSH | 36 | AE-34 | Regina Wy | SJO | 13 | P-16 |
| Port Dr | SJO | 33 | AB-11 | Prospect Dr | SJO | 22 | W-8 | Ranch Rd | ECO | 39 | AE-63 | Regis Ct | SJO | 25 | R-33 |
| Portage Av | STB | 24 | V-20 | Prospect Pt | CSS | 5 | E-30 | Randall Av | CSS | 5 | F-27 | Reid Ct | ECO | 29 | V-65 |
| Portage Ct | STB | 24 | Y-22 | Prospect St | STB | 34 | AC-19 | Randolph St | STB | 35 | AC-26 | Reiner Ct | ECO | 39 | AG-61 |
| Portage Dr | SJO | 14 | R-18 | Prospect St | STB | 34 | AD-19 | Randolph St | STB | 35 | AC-27 | Reliance Rd | GSH | 40 | AH-67 |
| Portage Hwy | SJO | 24 | S-18 | Prospect St | EKT | 28 | Y-55 | Randolph St | GSH | 51 | AL-77 | Reliance Rd | GSH | 50 | AL-67 |
| Portage Ln | EKT | 39 | AC-59 | Protecta Dr | ECO | 30 | X-68 | Randolph St | EKT | 28 | X-53 | Rema Dr | CSS | 7 | H-50 |
| Portage Rd | BRN | 3 | H-16 | Providence Dr | MSH | 36 | AD-37 | Randolph St | EKT | 28 | X-55 | Remington Ct | ECO | 29 | W-65 |
| Portage Rd | BRN | 13 | L-17 | Provincial Ct | STB | 35 | AG-27 | Randy Dr | ECO | 39 | AD-65 | Remington Ln | GSH | 50 | AL-67 |
| Portage Rd | SJO | 13 | Q-17 | Provincial Dr | STB | 35 | AG-27 | Range Line Rd | BRN | 3 | D-13 | Ren St | EKT | 39 | AA-59 |
| Portage Rd | SJO | 14 | Q-17 | Pucker St | BRN | 4 | A-24 | Rasmussen Ct | STB | 34 | AA-24 | Renaissance Dr | NLS | 5 | C-26 |
| Portageway Dr | STB | 24 | U-19 | Pucker St | BRN | 4 | C-23 | Raven Hill | SJO | 33 | AC-10 | Renfrew Ct | STB | 35 | AG-28 |
| Porter Av | OCS | 37 | AB-46 | Pudding Ln | SJO | 45 | AK-26 | Ravenna Dr | SJO | 14 | Q-19 | Renfrew Dr | STB | 35 | AG-27 |
| Portland Av | ECO | 39 | AC-58 | Pulaski Hwy | BRN | 13 | J-11 | Ravine | SJO | 36 | Z-42 | Renwick Ct | SJO | 16 | R-34 |
| Portland Ln | STB | 25 | X-28 | Pulaski Hwy | BRN | 14 | J-24 | Ravine Dr | SJO | 25 | T-30 | Reo Av | STB | 33 | Z-15 |
| Portsmouth | EKT | 39 | AD-59 | Pulaski Hwy | BRN | 14 | J-25 | Ravine Rd | ECO | 50 | AQ-73 | Rerick Dr | STB | 25 | X-29 |
| Portsmouth Ct | MSH | 25 | Y-32 | Pulaski Hwy | BRN | 15 | J-26 | Rawstorne Ln | SJO | 26 | Z-42 | Reservoir Pl | GSH | 50 | AP-74 |
| Post Rd | ECO | 50 | AK-66 | Pulaski Hwy | BRN | 12 | K-4 | Ray Ct | ECO | 18 | R-56 | Reum St | CSS | 5 | H-27 |
| Post Rd | GHS | 50 | AK-68 | Pulaski St N | STB | 34 | AC-21 | Ray Dr | ECO | 18 | Q-56 | Revere Dr | GHS | 50 | AK-69 |
| Post Rd | BCH | 2 | G-7 | Pulaski St S | STB | 34 | AA-21 | Ray Dr | SJO | 26 | S-40 | Revere Pl | STB | 34 | AB-18 |
| Post Rd | BCH | 2 | G-8 | Pulaski St S | STB | 34 | AB-21 | Ray Ln | ECO | 29 | W-64 | Revere Rd | GSH | 50 | AL-68 |
| Post Rd | SJO | 16 | Q-35 | Pulling St | STB | 34 | AH-23 | Ray St | MSH | 36 | AB-39 | Revere Rd | GSH | 50 | AL-69 |
| Post Tavern Rd | SJO | 25 | S-29 | Punn Rd | SJO | 26 | W-40 | Raymond Av | CSS | 17 | M-47 | Rex Ct | BRN | 4 | B-24 |
| Post Tavern Rd | SJO | 25 | T-30 | Purdue Ct | SJO | 25 | S-32 | Reading Ct | SJO | 14 | R-21 | Rex Ct | ECO | 28 | S-51 |
| Pottawatamie Dr | ECO | 37 | AC-47 | Purdue Dr | SJO | 25 | S-32 | Reasor St | STB | 34 | AG-24 | Rex Dr | ECO | 29 | U-60 |
| Pottowattomi Dr | EKT | 28 | Y-56 | Purdy St | BRN | 4 | H-22 | Rebecca Dr | ECO | 39 | AG-64 | Rex St | STB | 24 | Y-22 |
| Powderhorn Cir | STB | 24 | U-20 | Purl St E | GSH | 51 | AM-74 | Rebecca Layne | BRN | 5 | G-26 | Rexford Ln | STB | 25 | X-29 |
| Power Dr | MSH | 36 | AB-38 | Purl St W | GSH | 50 | AM-73 | Rebecca Ln | ECO | 20 | R-68 | Reynolds Av | GSH | 51 | AM-75 |
| Powers St | NLS | 4 | E-25 | Pushane Ct | STB | 24 | Y-23 | Reckell | ECO | 29 | W-58 | Reynolds St | SJO | 33 | AA-10 |
| | | | | Puterbaugh Lake | CSS | 18 | M-54 | | | | | Reynolds St | BRN | 15 | N-26 |

| Name | City | Pg | Grid | Name | City | Pg | Grid | Name | City | Pg | Grid | Name | City | Pg | Grid | Name | City | Pg | Grid |
|---|---|---|---|---|---|---|---|---|---|---|---|---|---|---|---|---|---|---|---|
| Sailbay Ct | ECO | 19 | Q-60 | Sandy Pine Tr | SJO | 32 | AB-9 | Shadow Wood Ct | SJO | 17 | R-44 | Shore Dr N | CSS | 17 | J-49 | Shore Dr N | CSS | 17 | J-49 |
| Sain Dr | BRN | 14 | K-24 | Sandybrook Dr | SJO | 14 | R-18 | Shadow Wood Dr | SJO | 17 | R-44 | Shore Dr S | CSS | 17 | K-49 | | | | |
| St Andrews Cir | MSH | 25 | X-31 | Sandyridge Ln | SJO | 14 | R-18 | Shady Haven Pl | ECO | 29 | V-64 | Shore Dr S | EKT | 28 | Z-55 | | | | |
| St Andrews Pl | EKT | 38 | AD-56 | Sans Souci | SJO | 44 | AH-17 | Shady Hollow Ln | SJO | 14 | R-19 | Shore Ln E | ECO | 29 | X-64 | | | | |
| St Clair Av | EKT | 29 | Z-60 | Santa Anita Ct | ECO | 39 | AC-62 | Shady Ln | GSH | 50 | AJ-67 | Shore Ln E | ECO | 29 | X-64 | | | | |
| St Clair Ave | EKT | 29 | Y-60 | Santa Cruz Dr | ECO | 27 | X-49 | Shady Ln | CSS | 21 | N-76 | Shore Ln W | ECO | 29 | X-64 | | | | |
| St Johns Wy | STB | 24 | Y-18 | Santa Monica Dr | SJO | 26 | S-34 | Shady Ln | ECO | 18 | Q-56 | Shore Manor Ct | BTL | 30 | U-74 | | | | |
| St Joseph Av S | NLS | 4 | G-22 | Saphire Blvd | ECO | 39 | AA-62 | Shady Oak Dr | SJO | 27 | X-42 | Shore Manor Dr | BTL | 30 | U-74 | | | | |
| St Joseph Ct | MSH | 35 | AC-31 | Sara Ln | SJO | 35 | AG-32 | Shady Oaks Ct | MSH | 35 | AD-33 | Shore Manor Dr | ECO | 30 | V-70 | | | | |
| St Joseph St | OCS | 37 | AB-45 | Sarah St | MSH | 35 | AA-32 | Shady Shores Dr | CSS | 5 | E-31 | Shoreham Ct N | SJO | 24 | S-21 | | | | |
| St Joseph St | BTL | 30 | U-74 | Sarah St | SJO | 24 | S-23 | Shadyhaven Ln | ECO | 29 | V-64 | Shoreham Ct S | SJO | 24 | S-21 | | | | |
| St Joseph St | EKT | 28 | Z-56 | Saratoga Ct | SJO | 25 | S-31 | Shafer Tr | SJO | 16 | Q-37 | Shoreland Dr | BRN | 14 | N-21 | | | | |
| St Joseph St | EKT | 28 | Z-57 | Sarka Ln | NLS | 4 | G-21 | Shafer Tr | SJO | 16 | Q-37 | Shorewood Ct S | SJO | 33 | AC-10 | | | | |
| St Joseph St S | STB | 34 | AG-24 | Sassafras Ln | NLS | 4 | H-21 | Shaffer Av | ECO | 39 | AD-61 | Shorewood Dr E | SJO | 33 | AC-10 | | | | |
| St Lo Av | MSH | 25 | Z-32 | Sassafras St | ECO | 38 | AD-53 | Shaker Ln | SJO | 16 | R-41 | Short Dr | MSH | 36 | AA-34 | | | | |
| St Louis Blvd S | STB | 34 | AA-25 | Sassafrass St | CSS | 17 | J-49 | Shamrock Dr | SJO | 35 | AF-31 | Short Hair Dr | SJO | 27 | Y-44 | | | | |
| St Mathews Ct | SJO | 26 | U-35 | Saturn Cir | SJO | 35 | AF-30 | Shamrock Dr | GSH | 51 | AM-77 | Short Hair Dr | SJO | 27 | Z-44 | | | | |
| St Peter St S | STB | 34 | AA-25 | Saturn Dr | SJO | 35 | AF-29 | Shamrock Dr | BRN | 4 | F-19 | Short St | EKT | 39 | AA-58 | | | | |
| St. Andrews Cir | MSH | 25 | X-30 | Saturn Dr | SJO | 35 | AF-30 | Shamrock Hills Ct | SJO | 15 | Q-29 | Short St | SJO | 36 | AF-37 | | | | |
| St. Andrews Ct | SJO | 15 | Q-32 | Sawgrass Cove | EKT | 38 | AD-55 | Shamrock Hills Dr | SJO | 15 | Q-29 | Short St | BCH | 3 | F-10 | | | | |
| St. Ann's Ct | SJO | 22 | R-8 | Saybrook Dr E | GSH | 40 | AH-68 | Shamrock Hills Dr | SJO | 15 | R-29 | Showalter | SJO | 35 | AF-31 | | | | |
| St. James Ct | STB | 34 | Z-23 | Saybrook Dr W | GSH | 40 | AH-69 | Shandwick Ln | SJO | 15 | Q-30 | Showghn St | MSH | 25 | V-30 | | | | |
| St. Joe Rd | SJO | 24 | W-24 | Scarlet Maple Ln N | EKT | 29 | V-60 | Shannonbrook Ct | SJO | 15 | R-29 | Sibley St | STB | 24 | Z-20 | | | | |
| St. Joe River Rd | CSS | 21 | R-77 | Scarlet Maple Ln S | EKT | 29 | V-60 | Shanover Dr | MSH | 36 | AA-35 | Sichaun Dr | SJO | 27 | Y-44 | | | | |
| St. Joe St | ECO | 21 | R-77 | Scarlet Maple Rd | STB | 24 | U-19 | Share Bridge Dr | SJO | 17 | P-42 | Side Blvd N | STB | 24 | AB-25 | | | | |
| St. Joe St | ECO | 21 | R-78 | Scenic Dr | STB | 33 | AA-15 | Sharon Ct | ECO | 39 | AH-64 | Side Blvd N | STB | 35 | AB-29 | | | | |
| St. Joseph Av N | NLS | 4 | F-22 | Scenicview Dr | BRN | 4 | B-20 | Sharpe Bridge Ct | SJO | 17 | P-42 | Sidney Av | SJO | 23 | Y-16 | | | | |
| St. Joseph Mnr | EKT | 29 | X-60 | Scenicview Dr | BRN | 4 | B-21 | Shasta Dr | GSH | 51 | AM-76 | Siena Ct | SJO | 25 | S-33 | | | | |
| St. Joseph St | STB | 34 | AA-24 | Scent Tr | SJO | 23 | T-10 | Shavehead Lake St | CSS | 10 | D-72 | Sigerfoos Av | EKT | 38 | AB-56 | | | | |
| St. Joseph St | STB | 34 | AA-24 | Schellinger Sq | MSH | 35 | AB-30 | Shavehead Lake St | CSS | 11 | D-80 | Sigerfoos Av | ECO | 18 | R-57 | | | | |
| St. Joseph St | STB | 34 | AD-24 | Schirmer Pkwy | BCH | 3 | F-12 | Shaver Ct | ECO | 29 | U-58 | Sigerfoos Dr | ECO | 18 | Q-57 | | | | |
| St. Joseph St | STB | 34 | AE-24 | Schmidt Ct | MSH | 35 | AC-32 | Shawn Dr | ECO | 29 | U-59 | Sigler Av | ECO | 39 | AC-58 | | | | |
| St. Joseph St | STB | 34 | AF-24 | Scholum St | STB | 34 | AA-21 | Shawnee Ct | MSH | 25 | V-32 | Signal Hill Ct | SJO | 15 | R-33 | | | | |
| St. Joseph St | STB | 34 | AG-24 | School St | GHS | 50 | AK-74 | Sheffield Av | NLS | 4 | E-24 | Silsbee St | BRN | 14 | N-22 | | | | |
| St. Joseph St N | STB | 24 | Y-24 | Schumacher Dr | MSH | 25 | Y-31 | Sheffield Av | NLS | 4 | E-24 | Silver Ct | EKT | 28 | W-55 | | | | |
| St. Joseph St S | STB | 34 | AC-24 | Schumacher Dr | MSH | 25 | Z-31 | Sheffield Ct | STB | 35 | AH-26 | Silver Fox Tr | SJO | 22 | U-9 | | | | |
| St. Joseph St S | SJO | 44 | AF-24 | Schuster Dr | SJO | 34 | AF-19 | Sheffield Ln | ECO | 31 | S-75 | Silver Lake Ct | MSH | 36 | AA-36 | | | | |
| St. Joseph Valey Pkwy | SJO | 23 | Y-13 | Schwalm Dr | ECO | 38 | AE-52 | Shelburne Ct | ECO | 18 | Q-56 | Silver Leaf Ct | SJO | 25 | T-31 | | | | |
| St. Joseph Valley Pkwy | ECO | 39 | AB-65 | Scotch Pine Tr | SJO | 32 | AB-9 | Shellbark St | SJO | 24 | T-20 | Silver Ln | STB | 33 | AB-17 | | | | |
| St. Joseph Valley Pkwy | SJO | 33 | AC-16 | Scott Dr | CSS | 17 | J-49 | Shelton Ct | ECO | 29 | W-59 | Silver Maple Ct | STB | 24 | V-19 | | | | |
| St. Joseph Valley Pkwy | ECO | 39 | AC-64 | Scott St | STB | 34 | AG-23 | Shelton Dr | MSH | 36 | AD-39 | Silver Pheasant Dr | SJO | 27 | Y-43 | | | | |
| St. Joseph Valley Pkwy | ECO | 38 | AF-52 | Scott St | SJO | 44 | AH-22 | Shenandoah Dr | SJO | 25 | T-28 | Silver Spring Dr | SJO | 14 | R-18 | | | | |
| St. Joseph Valley Pkwy | SJO | 35 | AG-29 | Scott St | BRN | 14 | L-24 | Shephard Hill Ln | ECO | 39 | AG-60 | Silver Spur Ct | SJO | 16 | Q-40 | | | | |
| St. Joseph Valley Pkwy | SJO | 36 | AG-40 | Scott St | SJO | 24 | T-22 | Sherford Ct | SJO | 25 | S-33 | Silver Spur Ct | SJO | 16 | Q-40 | | | | |
| St. Louis Blvd N | STB | 24 | Y-25 | Scott St | EKT | 28 | Z-55 | Sheri Ln | ECO | 29 | W-64 | Silver St | ECO | 28 | W-56 | | | | |
| St. Louis Blvd N | STB | 24 | Z-25 | Scott St N | STB | 24 | Y-22 | Sheridan Av | NLS | 4 | E-25 | Silver Water Wy | ECO | 18 | R-55 | | | | |
| St. Mary's Rd | SJO | 24 | W-25 | Scott St N | STB | 34 | Z-22 | Sheridan Blvd | ECO | 27 | Y-47 | Silverbrook Av | NLS | 4 | G-23 | | | | |
| St. Patricks Ct | SJO | 15 | R-28 | Scott St S | STB | 34 | AA-22 | Sheridan Dr | GHS | 50 | AK-69 | Silverbrook Av | NLS | 4 | G-25 | | | | |
| St. Paul Pl | STB | 34 | Z-22 | Scott St S | STB | 34 | AC-22 | Sheridan Dr | CSS | 17 | M-45 | Silvercrest Dr | ECO | 39 | AC-64 | | | | |
| St. Peter St N | STB | 24 | Y-25 | Scottswood Cir | STB | 25 | Y-27 | Sheridan Pl | STB | 23 | Y-17 | Silverleaf Ct | MSH | 36 | AD-36 | | | | |
| St. Peter St N | STB | 34 | Z-25 | Scottswood Ct | ECO | 29 | V-64 | Sheridan Rd | ECO | 27 | Z-47 | Silverton Dr | GSH | 51 | AR-75 | | | | |
| St. Thomas St | SJO | 16 | Q-40 | Scottswood Dr | STB | 25 | Y-26 | Sheridan St | STB | 23 | Z-17 | Silverwood Ln S | GSH | 50 | AM-70 | | | | |
| St. Vincent St | STB | 24 | Y-25 | Scout Ln | MSH | 36 | AB-37 | Sheridan St N | STB | 23 | Y-17 | Silverwood Loop | SJO | 25 | S-29 | | | | |
| Sako Ct | ECO | 29 | Z-64 | Seaguilla | SJO | 26 | W-35 | Sheridan St S | STB | 33 | AA-17 | Silverwood Loop | SJO | 25 | T-30 | | | | |
| Salem Ct | EKT | 29 | W-63 | Sean Ct | SJO | 14 | Q-19 | Sheridan St S | STB | 33 | AB-17 | Simmons Dr | SJO | 25 | R-26 | | | | |
| Salem Dr | GSH | 50 | AR-74 | Searer Dr | SJO | 25 | T-29 | Sherman Av | STB | 24 | X-22 | Simon Ct | STB | 25 | Y-29 | | | | |
| Salem Dr | STB | 25 | Y-29 | Sears St | CSS | 10 | A-72 | Sherman Av | STB | 24 | Y-22 | Simonton St E | EKT | 28 | X-57 | | | | |
| Sample Rd | ECO | 37 | AE-47 | Season Ct | SJO | 27 | Y-43 | Sherman Rd | CSS | 17 | M-45 | Simonton St W | EKT | 28 | X-56 | | | | |
| Sample St | STB | 34 | AB-22 | Second St | ECO | 29 | S-64 | Sherman St | EKT | 28 | Y-56 | Simpson Av | EKT | 29 | Y-60 | | | | |
| Sample St W | STB | 34 | AB-17 | Section Rd | EDW | 17 | L-43 | Sherrill St | STB | 34 | AC-22 | Sioux Ln | SJO | 25 | U-26 | | | | |
| Sampson St | STB | 35 | AC-27 | Sedgefield Wy | GSH | 50 | AN-72 | Sherry Dr | SJO | 32 | AF-5 | Sioux Tr | NLS | 4 | G-20 | | | | |
| Sampson St | STB | 35 | AD-27 | Seebirt Pl | STB | 34 | Z-22 | Sherwood Dr | ECO | 39 | AG-64 | Siver Maple Ln N | EKT | 29 | V-60 | | | | |
| Sampson St | STB | 35 | AF-27 | Segway Ct | SJO | 34 | AH-21 | Sherwood Dr | SJO | 24 | T-24 | Siver Maple Ln S | EKT | 29 | V-60 | | | | |
| Samson Dr | BRN | 3 | F-13 | Selby Dr | ECO | 29 | X-65 | Sherwood Dr | SJO | 17 | Q-44 | Six Span Rd | ECO | 40 | AA-67 | | | | |
| San Jose Blvd | ECO | 27 | X-49 | Selkirk Dr | STB | 35 | AG-26 | Sherwood St | STB | 34 | AE-23 | Six Span Rd | ECO | 30 | X-67 | | | | |
| San Lu Rae Dr | ECO | 27 | X-49 | Sellers Ct | EKT | 29 | W-61 | Sherwood St | STB | 34 | AE-24 | Six Span Rd | ECO | 30 | X-67 | | | | |
| San Lucia Dr | ECO | 27 | X-49 | Sellon Av | SJO | 27 | X-42 | Shillelagh Ln | BRN | 4 | F-19 | Skybreeze Dr | SJO | 16 | R-35 | | | | |
| Sancome Av | STB | 24 | Y-21 | Selwin Ct | STB | 35 | AH-26 | Shirley | CSS | 15 | N-27 | Skye Ct | STB | 35 | AG-27 | | | | |
| Sandalwood Dr | ECO | 39 | AA-64 | Seminole Ln | SJO | 25 | U-26 | Shirley Av | STB | 44 | AJ-23 | Skylark Ct | SJO | 25 | U-28 | | | | |
| Sander Av | GSH | 51 | AM-75 | Senace St | MSH | 25 | V-33 | Shirley Dr | GHS | 50 | AK-67 | Skyline Ct | SJO | 35 | AF-29 | | | | |
| Sanders Av | EKT | 39 | AB-59 | Sendpointe Ct | SJO | 25 | S-33 | Shirley Ln | CSS | 7 | H-49 | Skyline Dr | SJO | 34 | AF-19 | | | | |
| Sandpiper Ct | SJO | 22 | Y-8 | Senecca Dr | GSH | 40 | AH-67 | Shirley Ln | CSS | 17 | J-49 | Skyline Dr | SJO | 35 | AF-29 | | | | |
| Sandwood Dr | STB | 24 | S-18 | Sequoia Dr | ECO | 39 | AB-65 | Shore Av | ECO | 38 | AA-52 | Skyline Dr | NLS | 4 | E-20 | | | | |
| Sandy Beach Dr E | CSS | 17 | N-47 | Serene Dr | SJO | 24 | U-25 | Shore Dr N | CSS | 8 | G-54 | Skyview Dr | GSH | 50 | AJ-72 | | | | |
| Sandy Beach Dr N | CSS | 17 | M-48 | Serville Ct | SJO | 14 | R-21 | Shore Dr N | CSS | 8 | H-52 | Slaby Blvd | STB | 33 | AA-15 | | | | |
| Sandy Beach Dr N | CSS | 17 | N-47 | Setter Dr | SJO | 27 | Y-43 | Shore Dr N | ECO | 18 | Q-58 | Sleepy Fox Tr | SJO | 23 | T-10 | | | | |
| Sandy Dr | GSH | 50 | AJ-74 | Settlers Cv Ct | SJO | 26 | S-40 | Shore Dr N | ECO | 19 | Q-60 | Slicks Ct | MSH | 35 | AB-31 | | | | |
| Sandy Lake Dr | SJO | 27 | S-43 | Settlers Tr | SJO | 37 | AG-44 | Shore Dr N | ECO | 18 | R-57 | Sly Fox Ct | SJO | 23 | T-10 | | | | |
| Sandy Ln | CSS | 5 | G-27 | Shadow Ct | SJO | 26 | S-40 | Shore Dr N | ECO | 27 | Z-47 | Sly Fox Ct | SJO | 22 | T-9 | | | | |
| Sandy Ln | ECO | 30 | W-67 | Shadow Ridge Dr | ECO | 50 | AP-72 | Shore Dr N | CSS | 8 | H-53 | Smalley Av | MSH | 36 | AB-38 | | | | |

| Name | City | Pg | Grid | Name | City | Pg | Grid | Name | City | Pg | Grid | Name | City | Pg | Grid |
|---|---|---|---|---|---|---|---|---|---|---|---|---|---|---|---|
| Sundown Rd | SJO | 23 | Y-13 | Sweetbriar Ct | MSH | 36 | AD-35 | Teconsek Dr | SJO | 17 | Q-43 | Timberline Trace E | SJO | 16 | R-41 |
| Sundown Rd | SJO | 33 | Z-13 | Sweetbrier St | CSS | 17 | N-44 | Tedrow Pl | SJO | 27 | W-44 | Timberline Trace N | SJO | 16 | R-40 |
| Sundrop Ct | SJO | 15 | Q-28 | Sweetspire Ct | ECO | 29 | V-65 | Tee Ct | SJO | 14 | R-18 | Timberline Trace S | SJO | 16 | R-41 |
| Sunfiel Loop | SJO | 25 | T-29 | Sweetwater Dr | ECO | 30 | W-68 | Temarac Rd | SJO | 12 | Q-2 | Timberline Trace W | SJO | 16 | R-40 |
| Sunfield Loop | SJO | 25 | T-30 | Sweetwater Wy | ECO | 18 | R-56 | Temple Ct | EKT | 28 | Z-57 | Timberwood Ct | ECO | 40 | AF-66 |
| Sunflower | ECO | 38 | AD-54 | Swygart St | STB | 34 | AC-21 | Tenbury | SJO | 16 | Q-36 | Timberwood Ct | MSH | 25 | Y-32 |
| Sunflower Dr | SJO | 27 | W-45 | Sycamore Ct | GSH | 51 | AP-76 | Tennessee St | ECO | 39 | AD-63 | Timothy Ct | ECO | 29 | U-63 |
| Sunntside Av | STB | 35 | AA-26 | Sycamore Ln | ECO | 27 | Y-47 | Teri St | STB | 34 | Y-47 | Tipton St | EKT | 29 | AA-59 |
| Sunnybrook Ct | RSL | 24 | U-23 | Sycamore Rd | SJO | 32 | AF-4 | Terlep Dr | EKT | 29 | Y-61 | Tipton St | EKT | 29 | Z-58 |
| Sunnycrest Dr | OCS | 37 | AA-44 | Sycamore Rd | SJO | 42 | AR-5 | Terminal Dr | STB | 23 | W-16 | Toledo Av | SJO | 27 | Y-44 |
| Sunnyfield Dr | EKT | 28 | W-54 | Sycamore Rd | SJO | 12 | R-4 | Terminal Rd | NLS | 5 | D-26 | Toledo Rd | ECO | 39 | AA-65 |
| Sunnyfield Pl | STB | 33 | AA-15 | Sycamore Rd | SJO | 26 | S-4 | Terminal St | CSS | 5 | C-28 | Tollview Dr | SJO | 25 | V-28 |
| Sunnymade Av | STB | 35 | AA-29 | Sycamore St | NLS | 4 | F-23 | Terminal St | CSS | 5 | C-30 | Tomahawk Ln | NLS | 4 | H-21 |
| Sunnymede Av | STB | 35 | AA-26 | Sycamore St | NLS | 4 | F-25 | Terrace Av | STB | 24 | Y-18 | Tomahawk Tr | STB | 24 | V-18 |
| Sunnyside Av | ECO | 39 | AD-62 | Sycamore St | STB | 34 | Z-24 | Terrace Dr N | CSS | 21 | K-75 | Tombstone Tr | SJO | 16 | Q-41 |
| Sunnyside Av | ECO | 39 | AD-63 | Sycamore St E | EKT | 28 | Y-56 | Terrace Ln | ECO | 38 | AD-55 | Tonti St | STB | 24 | Y-23 |
| Sunnyside Av | SJO | 42 | AK-6 | Sycamore St W | EKT | 28 | Y-56 | Terrace Ln | SJO | 25 | W-28 | Topaz St | STB | 34 | AG-22 |
| Sunnyside Av | SJO | 42 | AL-5 | Sylvan Ct | ECO | 30 | U-68 | Terre Coupe St | BCH | 2 | G-7 | Topinabee Rd | NLS | 4 | G-21 |
| Sunnyside Av N | STB | 35 | Z-26 | Sylvan Glen Dr | STB | 35 | Z-29 | Terri Brooke Cir | SJO | 17 | R-46 | Topsfield Rd | STB | 35 | AE-28 |
| Sunnyside Av S | STB | 35 | AA-26 | Sylvan Ln | STB | 33 | AB-15 | Terri Brooke Dr | SJO | 17 | R-46 | Topswood Ln | STB | 35 | AD-28 |
| Sunnyside Dr | EKT | 29 | X-60 | Sylvan Ln | EKT | 29 | V-61 | Terrie Shore Rd | CSS | 20 | N-74 | Torch Ct | SJO | 25 | S-28 |
| Sunnyslope Tr | SJO | 44 | AK-24 | Sylvan St | BCH | 3 | G-11 | Terry Ln | MSH | 36 | AB-39 | Totomee Ln | NLS | 4 | G-21 |
| Sunray Dr E | SJO | 27 | X-45 | Symonds Rd | BRN | 14 | K-23 | Terry Ln | MSH | 36 | AB-39 | Tower Rd | ECO | 37 | AB-48 |
| Sunrey Dr W | SJO | 27 | X-45 | | | | | Teton Ct | SJO | 14 | Q-20 | Towhee Ln | SJO | 25 | U-27 |
| Sunrise Ct | SJO | 43 | AK-13 | **T** | | | | Tharp Lake Rd | CSS | 9 | E-64 | Towle Av | MSH | 35 | AB-31 |
| Sunrise Dr | EKT | 38 | AB-55 | T Jefferson Dr | ECO | 31 | U-79 | Tharp Lake Rd | CSS | 9 | G-64 | Towline Rd | BCH | 2 | F-8 |
| Sunrise Ln | ECO | 39 | AE-61 | Tabor Hill Ct | SJO | 15 | R-33 | Tharp Lake Rd | CSS | 19 | M-63 | Towne Rd | ECO | 38 | AE-50 |
| Sunrise Rd | CSS | 18 | N-54 | Taddington Dr | SJO | 16 | Q-36 | Thatcher Rd | CSS | 8 | H-51 | Townsend Dr | SJO | 25 | U-27 |
| Sunrise Tr | SJO | 15 | Q-33 | Tade Ct | STB | 34 | AB-20 | Thatchwood Dr | GSH | 50 | AL-68 | Trader Ct W | STB | 24 | U-19 |
| Sunset Av | ECO | 29 | W-58 | Taelman Ct | SJO | 25 | S-30 | The Cir | EKT | 29 | X-59 | Traders Post Ln | SJO | 32 | AC-8 |
| Sunset Blvd | GSH | 50 | AL-71 | Taft St | NLS | 4 | G-25 | The Cir | EKT | 29 | X-59 | Trail North | SJO | 15 | Q-29 |
| Sunset Blvd | CSS | 21 | L-75 | Tailoaks Dr | ECO | 29 | S-61 | Thelma Ct | SJO | 26 | S-36 | Trail Ridge Dr | ECO | 27 | S-46 |
| Sunset Blvd | CSS | 20 | P-74 | Tailwind Ct | ECO | 37 | AC-49 | Thelma Dale | ECO | 19 | R-59 | Trailridge East | MSH | 36 | AE-33 |
| Sunset Ct | SJO | 27 | X-45 | Talbot St | STB | 25 | Y-26 | Theo St | MSH | 25 | W-31 | Trailridge North | MSH | 35 | AE-33 |
| Sunset Ln | CSS | 5 | C-32 | Tally Ho Dr E | SJO | 25 | S-28 | Theoda Ct | BCH | 3 | G-10 | Trailridge South | MSH | 35 | AE-33 |
| Sunset Ln | SJO | 24 | T-24 | Tally Ho Dr N | SJO | 25 | S-28 | Third St | NLS | 4 | D-23 | Trails Ct | SJO | 37 | AF-44 |
| Sunset Ln | ECO | 30 | W-66 | Tally-Ho Dr S | SJO | 25 | T-28 | Third St | ECO | 29 | T-64 | Trailwood Ct | SJO | 16 | R-41 |
| Sunset Ln | SJO | 27 | X-45 | Tam-O-Shanter | BRN | 14 | J-25 | Thirteenth St | NLS | 4 | G-24 | Tramore Ct | GSH | 51 | AQ-76 |
| Sunset Pl | STB | 33 | AA-17 | Tamarac Pl | STB | 35 | Z-28 | Thistle Ct | ECO | 29 | V-63 | Tramore Ct | SJO | 26 | R-34 |
| Sunset St | CSS | 18 | K-54 | Tamarack Dr | ECO | 19 | Q-60 | Thomas Ct | ECO | 28 | Z-52 | Tranquil Ct | SJO | 16 | R-35 |
| Sunset Strip | ECO | 28 | V-53 | Tamarack Rd | SJO | 32 | AF-2 | Thomas Dr | BRN | 4 | C-24 | Trappers Pass | SJO | 32 | AC-8 |
| Sunside Dr | BRN | 14 | K-23 | Tamarack Rd | CSS | 8 | G-51 | Thomas Ln | SJO | 33 | AA-10 | Travers Cir | MSH | 25 | Y-33 |
| Sunview Dr | SJO | 27 | X-45 | Tamarack Rd | SJO | 22 | S-2 | Thomas Ln | SJO | 41 | AD-76 | Travers Ct | EKT | 39 | AD-59 |
| Sunwood Dr | STB | 24 | T-21 | Tamarack Rd | SJO | 22 | U-2 | Thomas St | STB | 34 | AA-21 | Travers Ct | MSH | 25 | Y-32 |
| Sunwood Dr | ECO | 27 | V-47 | Tamarix St | SJO | 35 | AG-29 | Thomas St | EKT | 38 | AA-55 | Treasure Island Rd | CSS | 20 | M-74 |
| Sunwood Dr | ECO | 29 | V-66 | Tamer Ct | STB | 45 | AH-27 | Thompson Av | ECO | 18 | Q-57 | Treasure Island Rd | CSS | 21 | M-75 |
| Superior Blvd | EKT | 29 | Y-62 | Tamerlane Dr | STB | 45 | AH-27 | Thompson Rd | CSS | 5 | E-28 | Tremont Dr | MSH | 36 | AD-37 |
| Superior St | NLS | 4 | G-23 | Tammy Dr | SJO | 25 | S-31 | Thomson Rd | CSS | 5 | A-30 | Trent Wy | STB | 35 | AE-27 |
| Superior St | NLS | 4 | G-25 | Tanager Ln | SJO | 25 | U-28 | Thomson Rd | CSS | 5 | C-29 | Trentan Ct | MSH | 25 | X-33 |
| Superior St | EKT | 29 | Y-60 | Tangletree Dr | SJO | 17 | Q-43 | Thorn Rd | SJO | 42 | AN-1 | Trenton Ct | SJO | 25 | T-30 |
| Superior St E | OCS | 37 | AB-45 | Tanglewood Ct | MSH | 25 | X-31 | Thorn Rd | SJO | 42 | AQ-1 | Trenton Dr | STB | 23 | Z-16 |
| Superior St W | OCS | 37 | AB-44 | Tanglewood Dr | ECO | 40 | AF-66 | Thornacres Dr | BRN | 14 | M-21 | Trenton Ln | ECO | 30 | U-68 |
| Surface Av | SJO | 44 | AR-20 | Tanglewood Dr | GSH | 50 | AL-66 | Thornberry Ct | SJO | 34 | AF-20 | Trenton Ln | ECO | 30 | U-68 |
| Surges Rd | CSS | 15 | J-32 | Tanglewood Dr | SJO | 37 | Z-43 | Thorndale St | EKT | 38 | AB-57 | Trenton Pl | GSH | 50 | AN-71 |
| Surrey Ln | ECO | 39 | AG-64 | Tanglewood Ln | MSH | 25 | X-31 | Thorndale Dr | EKT | 38 | AB-57 | Trenton Wood Dr | SJO | 25 | S-45 |
| Surrey Ln | EKT | 29 | W-61 | Tara Dr | SJO | 23 | S-16 | Thorne Dr | ECO | 28 | T-53 | Treva St | ECO | 17 | P-48 |
| Surrey Ln | STB | 23 | Y-17 | Tara Ln | ECO | 29 | V-62 | Thornhill Dr | STB | 35 | AG-27 | Trillium Dr | SJO | 34 | AF-19 |
| Surrey Trace | SJO | 25 | S-29 | Tara Pl | ECO | 28 | W-50 | Thornridge Dr | EKT | 29 | W-63 | Trinity Ct | SJO | 25 | S-27 |
| Surrey Trace | SJO | 25 | T-30 | Tarrington Wy | SJO | 15 | P-30 | Thornsberry | ECO | 39 | AE-59 | Triple Crown Rd | MSH | 25 | AE-33 |
| Susan St | ECO | 27 | W-48 | Tarrington Wy | SJO | 15 | Q-29 | Thornton St | EKT | 28 | X-53 | Triple Dr | MSH | 25 | V-33 |
| Susquehanna Ct | ECO | 29 | W-66 | Tasher Av W | STB | 34 | AE-23 | Thrasher Ln | SJO | 25 | U-27 | Trout Creek Rd | BTL | 31 | T-76 |
| Susquehanna Rd | ECO | 30 | W-66 | Tasher St | STB | 34 | AE-24 | Thrush St | SJO | 25 | T-31 | Trout Rd | CSS | 20 | M-71 |
| Sussex Dr | STB | 23 | Y-17 | Taylor St | EKT | 39 | AA-59 | Thrush St | SJO | 24 | U-24 | Trowbridge Ln | SJO | 14 | R-21 |
| Sussex Ln | EKT | 29 | W-60 | Taylor St | EDW | 17 | K-43 | Thrush St | SJO | 24 | U-25 | Trowbridge Ln | SJO | 24 | S-21 |
| Sussex Point Dr | SJO | 16 | Q-36 | Taylor St N | STB | 34 | Z-23 | Thunderbird Ct | STB | 24 | V-18 | Troxel Av | EKT | 28 | Z-55 |
| Suszek Rd | CSS | 21 | K-80 | Taylor St S | STB | 34 | AA-23 | Tiara Tr | CSS | 6 | H-40 | Troxel Dr | SJO | 27 | W-44 |
| Sutherland Ln | STB | 35 | AF-26 | Taylor St S | STB | 34 | AC-23 | Tibbits St | EKT | 28 | Y-57 | Troy Av | EKT | 39 | AA-59 |
| Sutton Ct | GSH | 51 | AN-76 | Taylor St S | MSH | 35 | AC-31 | Tiffany Ct | GSH | 50 | AL-70 | Troy Ct | STB | 35 | AE-27 |
| Sutton Ln | ECO | 38 | AC-50 | Taylorst | GHS | 50 | AK-70 | Timber Cir | ECO | 39 | AA-63 | True St | SJO | 33 | AB-12 |
| Sutton Pl | STB | 45 | AH-26 | Tea Rose Ln | MSH | 36 | AE-34 | Timber Crest Dr | GSH | 51 | AR-75 | Tucker Dr | STB | 34 | AB-19 |
| Suwanee St | EKT | 28 | Z-54 | Teaberry Ct | ECO | 39 | AE-59 | Timber Ln | SJO | 26 | Y-40 | Tudor Ln | STB | 35 | AE-27 |
| Suzanne Dr | CSS | 7 | H-49 | Teal Ct | SJO | 26 | S-36 | Timber Ln | ECO | 27 | Y-48 | Tulain St | ECO | 27 | U-49 |
| Swallow Ct | SJO | 22 | Y-8 | Teal Rd | ECO | 20 | Q-73 | Timber Ln | STB | 35 | Z-30 | Tulip Ct | SJO | 16 | R-35 |
| Swanson Cir | STB | 25 | Z-28 | Teasdale Ct | SJO | 14 | R-21 | Timber Mill Ct | SJO | 25 | T-29 | Tulip Rd | SJO | 32 | AC-2 |
| Swanson Dr | SJO | 25 | U-28 | Teasdale Lake St | CSS | 10 | F-73 | Timber Rd | CSS | 10 | A-69 | Tulip Rd | STB | 22 | Y-2 |
| Swanson Mnr | EKT | 29 | X-61 | Teasdale Lake St | CSS | 11 | F-81 | Timber Tr | ECO | 40 | AE-74 | Tulip Tree Ln | ECO | 37 | AA-49 |
| Sweeney Av | SJO | 24 | V-25 | Tebay | SJO | 16 | Q-36 | Timber Tr | SJO | 26 | W-34 | Tulip Tree Ln | BRN | 3 | F-12 |
| Sweet Briar Dr | GSH | 50 | AH-69 | Technology Dr | STB | 23 | T-13 | Timberhurst Dr | ECO | 29 | T-58 | Tumbleweed Dr | GSH | 51 | AQ-77 |
| Sweet Clover Dr | GSH | 50 | AN-71 | Teconsek Dr | SJO | 17 | P-43 | Timberland Dr | SJO | 25 | U-31 | Tumbleweed Tr | SJO | 16 | Q-41 |
| Sweet Rd | CSS | 21 | J-77 | | | | | Timberlane Dr | SJO | 25 | U-30 | Turf Ct | SJO | 25 | T-28 |

| Name | City | Pg | Grid | Name | City | Pg | Grid | Name | City | Pg | Grid | Name | City | Pg | Grid |
|---|---|---|---|---|---|---|---|---|---|---|---|---|---|---|---|
| Weatherstone Ct | SJO | 25 | S-29 | Westmoor Pkwy | GHS | 50 | AK-71 | Ridge West | MSH | 35 | AF-33 | Winamac Lake Dr | MSH | 25 | V-33 |
| Weaver Ct | ECO | 38 | AA-50 | Westmoor St | STB | 24 | Y-19 | Wild Flower Ln | ECO | 29 | T-65 | Winchester Ct | GSH | 50 | AL-68 |
| Weaver Ln | GSH | 50 | AJ-70 | Westmoreland Ct | SJO | 22 | V-7 | Wild Flower Wy | STB | 24 | X-22 | Winchester Ct | NLS | 4 | E-21 |
| Weaver Rd | BRN | 3 | L-19 | Westover Dr | SJO | 24 | T-27 | Wild Game Dr | SJO | 27 | Y-44 | Winchester Ct | MSH | 25 | Y-32 |
| Weber Dr | SJO | 26 | Y-40 | Westpark | GSH | 50 | AL-69 | Wild Game Dr | SJO | 27 | Z-44 | Winchester Dr | ECO | 29 | W-65 |
| Weber Dr E | SJO | 26 | Y-41 | Westport Ct | SJO | 26 | S-34 | Wild Rose Ct | SJO | 34 | AF-19 | Winchester Tr | SJO | 16 | Q-41 |
| Weber Dr E | SJO | 26 | Z-41 | Westview Dr | BRN | 4 | C-20 | Wild Rose Ln | MSH | 36 | AE-34 | Winchester Trails N | GSH | 51 | AQ-77 |
| Weber Sq E | STB | 25 | Y-27 | Westview Ln | STB | 33 | AA-16 | Wild St | CSS | 5 | D-31 | Wind Rush Ct | SJO | 44 | AH-21 |
| Weber Sq W | STB | 25 | Y-27 | Westwind Dr | SJO | 22 | R-8 | Wilden Av E | GHS | 51 | AK-74 | Windemere Ct | SJO | 37 | Z-43 |
| Weber St | RSL | 24 | U-23 | Westwood Cir | MSH | 25 | Z-33 | Wilden Av W | GSH | 50 | AJ-69 | Windemore Ct | SJO | 25 | S-31 |
| Weber St | RSL | 24 | V-23 | Westwood Dr | SJO | 33 | AD-9 | Wilden Av W | GHS | 50 | AK-70 | Windfall Ct | STB | 23 | Z-15 |
| Webster | ECO | 38 | AC-53 | Westwood Dr | ECO | 28 | W-53 | Wilder Dr | STB | 25 | Y-29 | Windfield Ln | SJO | 15 | Q-33 |
| Webster St | MSH | 35 | AA-30 | Westwood Dr | ECO | 28 | W-54 | Wilderness Dr | ECO | 40 | AE-74 | Winding Brook Dr | SJO | 25 | W-33 |
| Webster St | STB | 34 | AB-21 | Westwood Dr | STB | 23 | Z-16 | Wildmere Dr | STB | 35 | Z-30 | Winding Brook Dr | SJO | 25 | X-33 |
| Webster St | STB | 34 | AC-21 | Westwood Forest Ct | SJO | 23 | S-10 | Wildon Ct | BRN | 3 | H-10 | Winding Waters Ln | ECO | 18 | R-55 |
| Webster St | STB | 34 | AC-21 | Westwood Forest Dr | SJO | 23 | S-10 | Wildwood Av N | EKT | 28 | Y-53 | Winding Waters Ln | EKT | 28 | S-56 |
| Wedgefield Ct | ECO | 39 | AB-64 | Westwood Rd | GSH | 51 | AP-74 | Wildwood Av S | EKT | 28 | Z-53 | Winding Waters Ln | EKT | 28 | T-56 |
| Wedgewood Ct N | ECO | 39 | AA-64 | Westwood St | GHS | 50 | AK-69 | Wildwood Ct | SJO | 37 | AD-43 | Windingwood Dr | STB | 25 | Z-29 |
| Wedgewood Ct S | ECO | 39 | AA-64 | Westwoodhills Dr | SJO | 23 | S-9 | Wildwood Ct | GSH | 51 | AP-75 | Windingwood Dr | STB | 25 | Z-30 |
| Wedgewood Dr | MSH | 36 | AD-35 | Westwynd Dr | ECO | 28 | Z-51 | Wildwood Dr | SJO | 37 | AD-43 | Windover Ln | SJO | 25 | T-29 |
| Wedgewood Dr | SJO | 14 | P-23 | Wetherington Ct | SJO | 15 | Q-30 | Wilkins Mill Ct | SJO | 17 | Q-42 | Windover Ln | SJO | 25 | T-30 |
| Wedgewood Dr | SJO | 14 | P-24 | Wexford Dr | SJO | 26 | R-33 | Wilkins Mill Dr | SJO | 17 | Q-42 | Windridge Ct | SJO | 15 | Q-33 |
| Wee Acres Dr | ECO | 31 | S-75 | Wexham Ct | STB | 35 | AE-28 | Wilkinson St | GSH | 50 | AL-71 | Windrow Dr | ECO | 29 | S-61 |
| Weiser Rd | BRN | 3 | H-17 | Weymouth | ECO | 39 | AA-65 | Wilkinson St | GSH | 50 | AL-73 | Windsomg Dr | ECO | 38 | AD-51 |
| Weiser Rd | BRN | 4 | H-18 | Weymouth Blvd | GSH | 51 | AQ-76 | Wilkinson St | EDW | 17 | K-43 | Windsor Av | SJO | 32 | AA-8 |
| Weistln | STB | 35 | AE-27 | Weymouth Blvd | GSH | 51 | AR-76 | Willard | EKT | 28 | Z-57 | Windsor Av | SJO | 32 | AD-8 |
| Welcome Ln | ECO | 30 | U-71 | Weymouth Dr | ECO | 39 | AA-64 | Willard Ct | EKT | 28 | Z-57 | Windsor Av | EKT | 28 | T-56 |
| Weller Av | SJO | 44 | AK-22 | Wheatfield Ct | SJO | 23 | R-12 | Willard Dr | SJO | 27 | Y-42 | Windsor Av | EKT | 28 | T-57 |
| Wellesley Ct | SJO | 24 | S-21 | Wheatfield Dr | SJO | 23 | S-12 | Willard Rd | ECO | 28 | V-53 | Windsor Cir | EKT | 29 | Y-58 |
| Wellington Ct | MSH | 25 | Y-32 | Wheatland Dr N | GSH | 50 | AL-71 | Willcrest Av | GSH | 51 | AM-77 | Windsor Ct | EKT | 28 | T-57 |
| Wellington Cv | SJO | 15 | R-32 | Wheatland Dr S | GSH | 50 | AL-71 | William Dr | GHS | 50 | AK-69 | Windsor Manor Ct | SJO | 15 | R-31 |
| Wellington Pkwy | SJO | 15 | R-31 | Wheatly Ct | STB | 35 | AG-25 | William Richardson Ct | STB | 23 | T-17 | Windsor Pl | STB | 23 | Z-16 |
| Wellington St | SJO | 24 | S-18 | Wheatly Dr | STB | 34 | AG-25 | William Richardson Dr | STB | 23 | T-17 | Windwick Ct | EKT | 29 | Z-62 |
| Wellington St N | STB | 24 | X-18 | Wheatridge Ct | SJO | 15 | Q-29 | William St N | STB | 34 | Z-23 | Windy Cove Ct | MSH | 36 | AA-41 |
| Wellington St N | STB | 34 | Z-18 | Wheatstone Dr | MSH | 36 | AE-34 | William St S | STB | 34 | AC-23 | Windy Ridge Ct | SJO | 22 | R-9 |
| Wellington St S | STB | 34 | AA-18 | Whipple Av | EKT | 29 | Z-63 | Williams Av | ECO | 39 | AB-63 | Windyridge Dr | SJO | 22 | S-9 |
| Wells Rd | BRN | 2 | G-1 | Whippoorwill Dr | SJO | 22 | Z-8 | Williams St | CSS | 5 | D-31 | Windyridge Ln | ECO | 30 | Y-71 |
| Wells St | NLS | 4 | E-21 | Whippowill Ln | ECO | 37 | AD-48 | Williams St | EKT | 29 | T-58 | Winfield Ct | SJO | 14 | Q-20 |
| Wells St S | MSH | 35 | AC-31 | Whispering Creek Ct | SJO | 34 | AH-21 | Williamsburg Ct | MSH | 25 | Y-32 | Wingsway Ct | SJO | 44 | AP-23 |
| Welworth St | SJO | 24 | V-25 | Whispering Hills Dr | SJO | 44 | AH-21 | Williamsburg Ct | STB | 23 | Z-16 | Winkler St | CSS | 15 | N-27 |
| Wembledon Ct | SJO | 14 | Q-25 | Whispering Hills Dr | SJO | 34 | AH-21 | Williamsburg Dr | SJO | 15 | Q-27 | Winn Pl | MSH | 35 | AE-33 |
| Wembley Dr | SJO | 25 | S-26 | Whispering Oak Dr | SJO | 26 | W-34 | Williamsville St | CSS | 9 | A-66 | Winn Rd | BRN | 3 | A-14 |
| Wembley Dr | SJO | 25 | S-26 | Whisperwynd Ct | ECO | 30 | Y-72 | Willis Av | STB | 25 | X-27 | Winn Rd | BRN | 3 | A-17 |
| Wendron Ct | SJO | 14 | Q-25 | Whisperwynd Ln | ECO | 30 | Y-72 | Willow | BRN | 14 | K-24 | Winn Rd | BRN | 4 | A-18 |
| Wenger Av N | MSH | 36 | AB-34 | Whitcomb Av | STB | 34 | AE-24 | Willow Bend | SJO | 16 | R-35 | Winn Rd E | BRN | 4 | A-19 |
| Wenger Av S | MSH | 36 | AB-34 | White Chapel Ct | SJO | 25 | T-29 | Willow Bend Dr | SJO | 25 | T-29 | Winslow Ct | STB | 45 | AH-26 |
| Wenger Av S | MSH | 36 | AE-34 | White Cloud Cir | SJO | 34 | AF-19 | Willow Bridge Ln | MSH | 36 | AA-36 | Winslow Dr | BTL | 30 | T-74 |
| Wenger St | STB | 34 | AB-24 | White Maple Ct | STB | 24 | U-20 | Willow Creek Ct | MSH | 36 | AA-36 | Winsted Dr | GSH | 51 | AN-76 |
| Wenger St | STB | 34 | AB-25 | White Oak Dr | STB | 25 | Y-27 | Willow Creek Dr | MSH | 36 | AA-36 | Winston Dr | STB | 25 | X-29 |
| Went Av | MSH | 26 | Z-33 | White Oak Ln | ECO | 27 | X-49 | Willow Creek Dr | SJO | 26 | X-37 | Winter Av N | GSH | 50 | AL-71 |
| Wentland St | SJO | 14 | Q-23 | White Oak St | CSS | 7 | E-43 | Willow Creek Rd | SJO | 26 | X-37 | Winter Glen Rd | SJO | 27 | S-45 |
| Werwinsk St | STB | 24 | Y-20 | White Pine Ct | MSH | 36 | AA-36 | Willow Dr E | RSL | 24 | U-23 | Winterav S | GSH | 50 | AM-71 |
| Werwinski St | STB | 24 | Y-20 | White Pine Dr | SJO | 33 | AB-12 | Willow Dr W | RSL | 24 | U-23 | Winterberry Dr | SJO | 25 | U-26 |
| Wesaw Rd | NLS | 4 | H-21 | White St | OCS | 37 | AA-45 | Willow Lake Dr | MSH | 36 | AA-36 | Wintergreen Ct | ECO | 29 | V-65 |
| Wescott Ln | ECO | 39 | AD-64 | White Water Creek Ct | MSH | 25 | W-32 | Willow Oak Ct | SJO | 23 | U-10 | Winthrop Dr | STB | 35 | AF-26 |
| West Av | GSH | 50 | AL-71 | Whitefeather Dr | STB | 23 | S-17 | Willow Run St | SJO | 24 | U-24 | Wise Cir S | STB | 34 | AE-24 |
| West Blvd N | EKT | 28 | Y-54 | Whitehall Dr | STB | 25 | Y-30 | Willow St | MSH | 35 | AA-33 | Wisteria St | SJO | 35 | AG-29 |
| West Blvd S | EKT | 28 | Z-54 | Whitehall Dr | STB | 25 | Y-30 | Willow St | BCH | 2 | F-9 | Withers St | CSS | 11 | A-79 |
| West Dr | MSH | 36 | AA-34 | Whiteman Ct | STB | 34 | AB-25 | Willow Wind Ct | ECO | 38 | AC-50 | Withers St | CSS | 11 | B-80 |
| West Park Lane East | SJO | 17 | P-42 | Whitesell Dr | SJO | 22 | W-8 | Willow Wy | GSH | 50 | AJ-67 | Witmer Av | EKT | 29 | Y-61 |
| West St | CSS | 18 | K-52 | Whiteshore Dr | MSH | 25 | W-30 | Willowbend Blvd | ECO | 30 | Y-71 | Wladen Ct E | STB | 34 | AG-24 |
| West St | BRN | 14 | N-25 | Whiteshore Dr | MSH | 25 | W-30 | Willowbrook Dr | STB | 25 | W-29 | Woldhaven St | STB | 34 | AE-25 |
| West St N | MSH | 35 | AB-31 | Whitestable Ln | SJO | 24 | S-21 | Willowdale Av | EKT | 28 | X-56 | Wolf Av E | EKT | 39 | AA-58 |
| West St S | MSH | 35 | AC-31 | Whitetail Dr | SJO | 26 | W-36 | Willowview Ct | EKT | 29 | Y-58 | Wolf Av W | EKT | 38 | AA-55 |
| West St S | MSH | 35 | AD-31 | Whitewater Ln | SJO | 14 | R-19 | Willowview Dr | ECO | 30 | V-67 | Wolf Rd | CSS | 5 | F-31 |
| West Weeping | | | | Whitfield Ct | MSH | 25 | Y-32 | Willowview Dr | ECO | 30 | W-68 | Wolf St | ECO | 37 | AA-48 |
|   Willow Run East | SJO | 17 | P-44 | Whiting Av | SJO | 24 | S-22 | Willshire Dr | SJO | 25 | W-29 | Wolkins Rd | BRN | 2 | A-6 |
| Westchester Ct | ECO | 27 | X-49 | Whitman | BCH | 3 | F-9 | Wilray Dr | ECO | 38 | AE-53 | Wolverton Dr | GSH | 51 | AQ-77 |
| Western Av | STB | 34 | AA-22 | Whitmer Ct | EKT | 28 | W-53 | Wilshire Blvd | ECO | 39 | AC-62 | Wood Chuck Ct | SJO | 17 | P-45 |
| Western Av | SJO | 32 | AA-8 | Whitner St | SJO | 44 | AL-21 | Wilson | BRN | 3 | G-12 | Wood Lake Rd | CSS | 11 | A-80 |
| Western Av W | STB | 34 | AA-20 | Whittington Cir | SJO | 27 | Y-42 | Wilson | BRN | 12 | K-1 | Wood Ln | MSH | 35 | AE-33 |
| Westfield Av | GSH | 50 | AL-72 | Whittler St | ECO | 38 | AD-53 | Wilson Av | GSH | 51 | AN-74 | Wood Song Dr | SJO | 22 | R-9 |
| Westfield Dr | BRN | 14 | M-25 | Wicklow Ct | SJO | 15 | R-33 | Wilson Av | SJO | 24 | T-24 | Wood Song Dr | SJO | 22 | S-9 |
| Westfield Pkwy | GSH | 50 | AL-69 | Widener Ln | STB | 34 | AF-24 | Wilson Av | STB | 35 | Z-28 | Wood St | EKT | 29 | Y-61 |
| Westfield Rd | SJO | 32 | AA-8 | Wightman | BRN | 14 | L-23 | Wilson Blvd | MSH | 35 | AB-30 | Woodale Av | SJO | 24 | S-23 |
| Westfind Av | SJO | 32 | AA-8 | Wigwam Ct | ECO | 30 | U-73 | Wilson Blvd N | MSH | 35 | AB-30 | Woodard Ct | ECO | 28 | V-53 |
| Westgate Dr | SJO | 25 | T-28 | Wilber St | STB | 24 | X-21 | Wilson Ct | ECO | 29 | W-59 | Woodard Ln | ECO | 28 | V-53 |
| Westlake Dr | ECO | 27 | W-48 | Wild Cherry Dr | SJO | 15 | R-31 | Wilson Ln | CSS | 5 | C-32 | Woodard St | CSS | 5 | G-28 |
| Westlane Av | ECO | 38 | AC-53 | Wild Cherry Ln | ECO | 37 | AA-49 | Wilson Manor S | SJO | 33 | AB-13 | Woodbine Ln | ECO | 39 | AA-63 |
| Westlea Dr | SJO | 33 | AA-12 | Wild Cherry | | | | Wimbleton Ct | SJO | 25 | S-26 | Woodbine Wy | STB | 23 | Y-17 |

| Name | City | Pg | Grid |
|---|---|---|---|
| Schmucker Middle School | SJO | 26 | Z-40 |
| South Western Michigan College | CSS | 5 | H-27 |
| St. Marys College | STB | 24 | W-23 |
| Swason High Lands ES | SJO | 25 | T-28 |
| Thomas A. Edison Middle School | STB | 25 | Y-29 |
| Thomas Jefferson ES | STB | 35 | AA-25 |
| Trinity Bible College and Seminary | EKT | 28 | W-55 |
| University Center | MSH | 25 | U-31 |
| University Commons | MSH | 25 | U-30 |
| University of Notre Dame | STB | 24 | W-25 |
| University Park Mall | MSH | 25 | U-31 |
| Warren Elementary School | SJO | 22 | Y-8 |
| Washington High School | STB | 33 | AA-16 |
| West Goshen Elem School | GSH | 50 | AL-72 |
| West Side School | NLS | 4 | G-22 |
| Wilson Elementary School | SJO | 33 | AA-14 |
| Wood Land Elementary School | EKT | 28 | X-51 |

## PARKS

| Name | City | Pg | Grid |
|---|---|---|---|
| 5th St Park N | GSH | 51 | AK-74 |
| 8th St Park N | GSH | 51 | AK-74 |
| Abshire Park | GSH | 51 | AM-76 |
| Allouez Park | NLS | 4 | H-22 |
| American Park | EKT | 29 | Y-58 |
| Backer Park | EKT | 29 | Z-60 |
| Ballband Park | MKT | 35 | AA-33 |
| Battel Park | MSH | 35 | AB-31 |
| Belleville Gardens Play Grounds | STB | 33 | AB-16 |
| Bendix Park | MSH | 36 | AC-36 |
| Bicentenial Park | EKT | 28 | Y-57 |
| Bingam Park | MSH | 36 | AA-34 |
| Boehm Park | STB | 25 | X-29 |
| Boland Park | STB | 24 | V-19 |
| Bonneyville Mill Park | ECO | 31 | V-82 |
| Booth Tarkington Park | STB | 25 | X-29 |
| Borley Park | MKT | 36 | AA-34 |
| Brownfield Park | STB | 24 | X-22 |
| Burdick Park | GSH | 50 | AN-74 |
| Central Park | MSH | 35 | AB-32 |
| Clevenger Park | NLS | 4 | G-23 |
| Coquillard Park | STB | 25 | Y-26 |
| E.B. Clark Nature Preserve | BCH | 3 | F-12 |
| East Race Waterway/Seitz Park | STB | 34 | Z-24 |
| East Goshen Park | GSH | 51 | AL-76 |
| East Harmon park | CSS | 10 | D-70 |
| Edison Park | STB | 25 | Y-28 |
| Elkhart Enviromental Center | EKT | 39 | AB-60 |
| Elliot Park | ECO | 28 | Z-50 |
| Fort St. Joseph Park | NLS | 4 | H-22 |
| Fred J. Hums Park | MSH | 36 | AC-38 |
| Fremont Park | STB | 24 | X-20 |
| Gans Park | EKT | 39 | AA-60 |
| George Wilson Park | MSH | 36 | AE-35 |
| Hamilton Park | STB | 35 | AG-26 |
| Harmony Park | SJO | 26 | X-39 |
| Harrison Park | STB | 34 | AA-18 |
| Helman Park | STB | 25 | Y-30 |
| Henry Frank Park | MSH | 25 | X-33 |
| Hillis Hans Park | MSH | 35 | AD-33 |
| Howard Parek | STB | 34 | AA-25 |
| Howard Twp Park | CSS | 5 | E-29 |
| Immigrant Park | MSH | 35 | AB-32 |
| Imus Park | MSH | 25 | Y-31 |
| Island Park | NLS | 4 | G-23 |
| Island Park | EKT | 28 | X-57 |

| Name | City | Pg | Grid |
|---|---|---|---|
| Kamm's Island | MSH | 35 | AB-31 |
| Kathryn park | BCH | 3 | F-10 |
| Keller Park | STB | 24 | W-22 |
| Kennedy Park | STB | 24 | Y-19 |
| La Salle Park Recreation Center | STB | 34 | Z-18 |
| Lafayette | GSH | 51 | AN-74 |
| Langle Park | EKT | 28 | Y-56 |
| Lasalle Park Recreation Ctr | STB | 24 | V-20 |
| Leeper Park | STB | 24 | Y-23 |
| Lincoln Park | MSH | 35 | AB-30 |
| Macnaughton Park | EKT | 28 | Z-54 |
| Madeline Bertrand Park | BRN | 14 | P-21 |
| Marshall Park | STB | 35 | AE-26 |
| Mary Gibbard Park | MSH | 35 | AC-29 |
| Merrifield Park | MKT | 36 | AA-34 |
| Miami "Monkey" Island Park | MKT | 36 | AA-35 |
| Mini Park | MKT | 35 | AA-33 |
| Muessel Grove Park | STB | 24 | X-21 |
| Nakomis Park | STB | 24 | Y-23 |
| Navarre Park | STB | 33 | AA-16 |
| New Park | GSH | 50 | AM-72 |
| Newman Recreation Center | STB | 34 | AA-25 |
| Normain Heights Park | MSH | 25 | Z-32 |
| Northside Blvd/ Viewwing Park | STB | 35 | AB-26 |
| O'Brien Park | STB | 34 | AF-24 |
| Oakridge Park | GSH | 50 | AK-73 |
| Odd Fellows Park | BRN | 14 | J-22 |
| Oliver Park | STB | 34 | AA-24 |
| Ox Bow County Park | ECO | 39 | AE-64 |
| Park | NLS | 4 | E-22 |
| Park | NLS | 4 | F-25 |
| Park | BRN | 14 | K-23 |
| Park | BRN | 13 | L-13 |
| Park | STB | 25 | W-28 |
| Parkovash Park | STB | 24 | X-23 |
| Payland Park | STB | 35 | AB-27 |
| Petro Park | MKT | 36 | AA-36 |
| Pierre Moran Park | EKT | 38 | AA-57 |
| Pinewood Park | EKT | 29 | W-62 |
| Pinhook Park | STB | 24 | V-20 |
| Plym Park | NLS | 4 | E-23 |
| Potato Creek State Recreation Area | SJO | 43 | AQ-10 |
| Potawatomi Park Pool and Zoo | STB | 35 | AA-27 |
| Prickett Marina Park | SJO | 36 | AA-39 |
| Pringle Park | GSH | 50 | AL-70 |
| Pulaski Park | STB | 34 | AA-22 |
| Randolph Street Mini Park | STB | 35 | AC-27 |
| Ravina Park | STB | 34 | AB-25 |
| Ravish Park | BCH | 13 | E-11 |
| Redbud Riverfront Park | BCH | 13 | E-11 |
| Redbud Riverfront Park | BCH | 13 | E-12 |
| Reith Park | GSH | 51 | AN-75 |
| Rice Park | EKT | 29 | Y-59 |
| Riverview Park | EKT | 29 | Y-61 |
| Rogers Park | GSH | 50 | AL-73 |
| Rose Park | MSH | 35 | AD-31 |
| Rum Village Park | STB | 34 | AD-21 |
| Rum Village Annex | STB | 34 | AD-20 |
| Rye Mini Park | STB | 24 | X-18 |
| St. Patricks County Park | SJO | 14 | Q-21 |
| Sampson Park | BRN | 3 | F-13 |
| Shanklin Park | GSH | 50 | AM-72 |
| Shetterly park | STB | 24 | Y-22 |
| Shoup Parsons Woods | GSH | 50 | AP-73 |
| Smith Park | BCH | 3 | G-11 |
| Sorin Park | STB | 25 | Z-30 |
| Spafford Woods Nature Preserve | BCH | 13 | E-12 |
| Stanley Coveleski Regional Stadium | STB | 34 | AA-23 |

| Name | City | Pg | Grid |
|---|---|---|---|
| Stickler Park | MSH | 36 | AA-40 |
| Stude Baker Park | STB | 34 | AC-25 |
| Studebaker Park | EKT | 29 | Z-59 |
| Three Rivers State Game Area | CSS | 11 | B-81 |
| Tolson Park | EKT | 38 | Z-57 |
| Twin Branch Energy Park | SJO | 36 | AA-38 |
| Twin Branch Park | MSH | 36 | AB-39 |
| Vassar Park | STB | 24 | Y-22 |
| Veterans Memorial Park | STB | 35 | AB-27 |
| Voorde Park | STB | 24 | X-18 |
| Walker Park | EKT | 29 | W-62 |
| Walker Field | STB | 34 | AC-21 |
| Ward Baker Park | MSH | 36 | AC-34 |
| Weaver Park | BRN | 2 | C-2 |
| West Goshen Park | GSH | 50 | AM-71 |
| West Harmon Park | CSS | 10 | D-69 |
| Wheelock Park | STB | 24 | U-22 |
| Willowdale Park | EKT | 28 | W-56 |
| Woodlawn Nature Center | EKT | 28 | V-57 |
| Woolawn Park | STB | 24 | W-21 |
| Youth Park | EKT | 29 | Z-59 |

## CEMETERIES

| Name | City | Pg | Grid |
|---|---|---|---|
| Barron Lake Cemetery | CSS | 5 | D-31 |
| Bethel Cemetery | CSS | 9 | D-61 |
| Bowman Cemetery | STB | 35 | AC-26 |
| Calvary Cemetery | NLS | 4 | G-21 |
| Carlton Cemetery | ECO | 28 | S-51 |
| Cathcart Cemetery | BTL | 31 | U-75 |
| Cedar Grove Cemetery | STB | 24 | X-25 |
| Cemetery | ECO | 40 | AD-73 |
| Cemetery | SJO | 42 | AJ-4 |
| Cemetery | CSS | 6 | C-38 |
| Cemetery | BRN | 3 | D-17 |
| Cemetery | CSS | 9 | D-62 |
| Cemetery | BRN | 2 | H-5 |
| Cemetery | BRN | 14 | J-22 |
| Cemetery | EDW | 17 | J-44 |
| Cemetery | CSS | 18 | M-53 |
| Cemetery | ECO | 29 | T-59 |
| Cemetery | ECO | 30 | U-69 |
| Cemetery | STB | 24 | W-22 |
| Cemetery | SJO | 23 | X-15 |
| Chain Lake Cemetery | CSS | 10 | B-67 |
| Chapel Hill Memorial Gardens Cemetery | SJO | 27 | Z-44 |
| City Cemetery | MSH | 35 | AA-31 |
| City Cemetery | STB | 24 | Z-21 |
| Community Cemetery | STB | 24 | W-24 |
| Cornell Cemetery | ECO | 41 | AF-81 |
| Crawford Cemetery | CSS | 7 | E-48 |
| Cripe Cemetery | ECO | 51 | AM-79 |
| Dick Cemetery | CSS | 5 | C-28 |
| Dierdorff Cemetery | GSH | 51 | AP-74 |
| Elkhart Prairie Cemetery | ECO | 51 | AQ-77 |
| Eutzler Cemetery | SJO | 16 | AE-36 |
| Fairview Cemetery | MSH | 35 | AA-31 |
| Ferrisville Cemetery | SJO | 45 | AH-32 |
| Five Points Cemetery | CSS | 17 | N-59 |
| Godshalf Acre Cemetery | CSS | 18 | P-52 |
| Grace Lawn Cemetery | EKT | 29 | Z-59 |
| Harris Prairie Cemetery | SJO | 16 | Q-36 |
| Hebrew Cemetery | MSH | 35 | AA-30 |
| Hess Cemetery | ECO | 50 | AP-72 |
| Highland Cemetery | SJO | 24 | V-19 |
| Hoke Cemetery | ECO | 49 | AQ-60 |
| Howe Cemetery | BRN | 13 | K-11 |
| Hungarian Sacred Heart Cemetery | SJO | 33 | AA-11 |
| Inbody Cemetery | ECO | 50 | AQ-67 |
| Long Cemetery | CSS | 11 | G-78 |

| Name | City | Pg | Grid |
|---|---|---|---|
| Merritt Cemetery | CSS | 10 | B-71 |
| Miller Cemetery | ECO | 49 | AQ-59 |
| Morris Cemetery | ECO | 41 | AH-76 |
| Mount Calvary Cemetery | SJO | 44 | AN-22 |
| Mt. Zion Cemetery | CSS | 9 | D-66 |
| Neff Cemetery | ECO | 41 | AC-81 |
| Noffsinger Cemetery | ECO | 37 | AE-48 |
| Oak Ridge Cemetery | BCH | 2 | F-8 |
| Oak Ridge Cemetery | ECO | 31 | U-77 |
| Oakgrove Cemetery | CSS | 21 | J-78 |
| Oakridge Cemetery | GSH | 50 | AK-72 |
| Olive Cemetery | ECO | 48 | AJ-51 |
| Pine Creek Cemetery | ECO | 40 | AB-70 |
| Pleasant Valley | SJO | 27 | Z-44 |
| Plum Grove Cemetery | CSS | 20 | L-69 |
| Porter Cemetery | SJO | 43 | AQ-11 |
| Praire Street Cemetery | EKT | 39 | AB-58 |
| Proctor Cemetery | ECO | 30 | U-71 |
| Reams Norton Cemetery | CSS | 8 | A-53 |
| Rest Haven Cemetery | SJO | 47 | AP-42 |
| Rice Cemetery | EKT | 29 | Y-60 |
| Rinehart Cemetery | CSS | 20 | L-71 |
| Riverview Cemetery | SJO | 24 | V-20 |
| Rodgers Cemetery | CSS | 6 | H-39 |
| Rowe Cem | ECO | 39 | AA-63 |
| St. Johns Cemetery | ECO | 49 | AM-65 |
| St. Johns Cemetery | SJO | 45 | AN-32 |
| St. Joseph Cemetery | SJO | 33 | AA-12 |
| St. Josephs Cemetery | BRN | 14 | M-22 |
| Shaffer Cemetery | CSS | 9 | G-58 |
| Shavehead Cemetery | CSS | 11 | E-75 |
| Shutts Cemetery | ECO | 47 | AQ-49 |
| Silver Brook Cemetery | NLS | 4 | G-24 |
| Smith Chapel Cemetery | CSS | 16 | N-36 |
| South Lawn Cemetery | SJO | 44 | AJ-23 |
| Studebake Cemetery | GSH | 50 | AJ-70 |
| Stutsman Cemetery | ECO | 49 | AK-65 |
| Sugar Grove Cemetery | ECO | 40 | AD-67 |
| Sumption Prairie Cemetery | SJO | 43 | AH-14 |
| Trout Creek Cemetery | ECO | 21 | Q-76 |
| Truitt cemetery | CSS | 15 | M-33 |
| Union Cemetery | SJO | 45 | AQ-26 |
| Van Buskirk Cemetery | SJO | 45 | AK-28 |
| Violett Cemetery | GSH | 50 | AR-73 |
| Wenger Cemetery | ECO | 49 | AL-60 |
| West Goshen Cemetery | GSH | 50 | AM-71 |
| Yellow Creek Cemetery | ECO | 49 | AQ-60 |

## GOLF COURSES

| Name | City | Pg | Grid |
|---|---|---|---|
| Bent Oak Golf Course | EKT | 38 | AD-56 |
| Black Squirrel Golf Course | GSH | 50 | AM-71 |
| Blackthorn Golf Course | STB | 23 | U-14 |
| Brookwood Golf Course | BRN | 3 | F-12 |
| Chistina Creek Country Club | ECO | 28 | W-56 |
| Eberhart Municipal Golf Course | MSH | 36 | AA-35 |
| Elbel Park Golf Course | SJO | 12 | R-8 |
| Elcona Country Club | ECO | 40 | AA-71 |
| Elks Country Club | ECO | 28 | V-56 |
| Erskine Municipal Golf Course | STB | 34 | AF-25 |
| Four Lakes Golf & Country Club | CSS | 18 | L-53 |
| Garver Lake Golf Course | CSS | 17 | L-47 |
| Juday Creek Golf Course | SJO | 26 | U-35 |

**NOTES:**

_____
_____
_____
_____
_____
_____
_____
_____
_____
_____
_____
_____
_____
_____
_____
_____
_____
_____
_____
_____
_____
_____
_____
_____
_____
_____
_____
_____
_____